PRAISE FOR

NAKED IN DANGEROUS PLACES

"Great explorers possess bravery, a cast-iron stomach, and insatiable curiosity about what lies around the next bend. Cash Peters has none of these attributes. But he is very, very funny, and his misadventures in exotic locales make for the best travel writing I have read in years."

—Peter Allison, author of *Whatever You Do, Don't Run*

"Like most travelers, but too few travel writers, Cash Peters understands that nightmares are twice as entertaining as dreams—especially when they come true. Peters's iconoclastic charm unaccountably fails to seduce South Seas cannibals and Hollywood producers, but proves a winner in this sharp-witted recap of two years in the company of such exotic and dangerous creatures. Someone should make a TV show out of it."

—Chuck Thompson, author of *Smile When You're Lying*

"It takes a clever new hook to grab and maintain my attention when it comes to travel writing. *Naked in Dangerous Places* is fascinating, funny, and endearing."

—Doug Lansky, editor of *There's No Toilet Paper . . . on the Road Less Traveled*

NAKED
IN
DANGEROUS PLACES

Also by Cash Peters

Gullible's Travels:
The Adventures of a Bad Taste Tourist

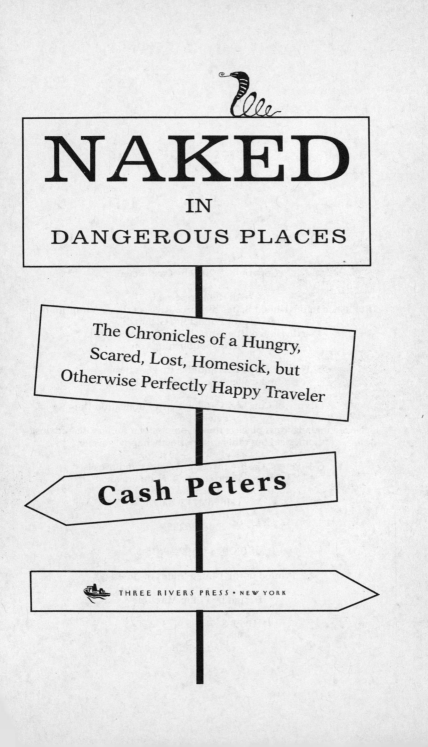

NAKED IN DANGEROUS PLACES

The Chronicles of a Hungry, Scared, Lost, Homesick, but Otherwise Perfectly Happy Traveler

Cash Peters

THREE RIVERS PRESS • NEW YORK

Published in the United States by Three Rivers Press, an imprint of the Crown Publishing Group,
a division of Random House, Inc., New York.
www.crownpublishing.com

Three Rivers Press and the Tugboat design are registered trademarks of Random House, Inc.

Library of Congress Cataloging-in-Publication Data
Peters, Cash.
Naked in dangerous places : the chronicles of a hungry, scared, lost, homesick, but otherwise perfectly happy traveler /
Cash Peters. — 1st ed.
1. Peters, Cash—Travel. 2. Voyages and travels.
3. Television program. 4. Manners and customs. 5. Local history. I. Title.
G465.P4772 2009
910.4092—dc22
2008025285

ISBN 978-0-307-39635-8

Printed in the United States of America

Design by Philip Mazzone

10 9 8 7 6 5 4 3 2 1

First Edition

For Ruth

Contents

Contents

Acknowledgments

First, let me thank the lovely people at Discovery for allowing this story to be told. That was pretty darned decent of them and I appreciate it. Unfortunately, it couldn't be the whole story. If I told you the *whole* story, this wouldn't be a book, it would be a twelve-volume set and you'd never get it home on the bus. In order to squeeze in as much as I could, therefore, I tweaked the timeline a little, occasionally condensed recurring situations into one, and made a fraction of the characters composites of several real people I encountered during the making of the series. I didn't want to do this, and the individuals in question probably won't thank me for it, but remember, it was either burden you with a dozen unwieldy, expensive volumes you might never read, or the single, rather cute one you're holding right now. That said, none of this distorts the narrative too much. What follows is how things went down, pretty much.

Additional dollops of gratitude go out to my amazing agent, Betsy Amster; my lawyer, Dina Appleton; Brandi Bowles for championing the book at Crown; Adam Korn for his insightful edit; Heather Proulx for *her* insightful edit and voracious enthusiasm; Ronald H. Brower for his help with the Eskimo language stuff; the Lonely Planet guides and Wikipedia for doing what they do; plus Bill Margol, Len Richmond, David Austin, Terry Danuser, Ryan Ely, Lulu Baskins-Leva, Christine Richards, Sylvana Robinson, Sheril McCormack; the brilliant C. Dalaklis for his guidance (which I so foolishly ignored); the production people at the office; and the gifted and long-suffering crews who came out on the road with me—in particular Michael Gatt for his wit and the steady education in kindness. But, above all, to Stanley for still being there when I finally returned home.

NAKED

IN

DANGEROUS PLACES

Updraft

1

Shocking News

"This is it. We're going down."

A painful grinding sound from one of the engines heralds a sharp drop in altitude. And painful grinding sounds of any kind on a plane are never good, right? I've seen documentaries. First comes the grinding, then you smell smoke. And from there it's all pretty straightforward: you crash.

With a violent shudder we tip suddenly to the left.

Yup, here it comes.

Bags somersault to the floor. Tasha, our field producer, is thrown forward, almost banging her head on the seat in front. My Gatorade is jolted from my fingers and skitters away, disappearing into the cockpit.

"Mayday, Mayday!"

That's me panicking, by the way, not the pilot. A trained professional, he's busy surveying the ground through a small triangular panel of Plexiglas to his left, no doubt trying to figure out how long it'll be before we hit something.

Immediately he sits up straight again.

Uh-oh! Not much farther now, then.

As I'm hanging on, mortified, five rods of brilliant sunlight burst through the starboard windows and sweep the tiny cabin from front to back like deep-sea divers searching a sunken wreck for bodies, something that could actually become a reality very shortly if we don't level our descent. Although, of course, you learn not to express such things out loud. For a start, it might annoy Eric, our field production coordinator. And you never want to do that. It was he who booked us on this bucking clockwork junk heap in the first place, following a minor altercation at check-in back in Australia over the staggering amount of equipment and other luggage we'd wanted to wheel aboard the aircraft, the combined weight of which was so preposterously excessive that, according to the waspish airline clerk, it would have "negated every one of the laws of aerodynamics." (She probably had a good point. I have no idea how many laws there are, but let's say for the sake of argument fifteen. I mean, who in their right mind would choose to break *all fifteen laws* of aerodynamics? It's crazy.)

"Okay. Here's an idea," Eric argued, running a thin hand through his salt-and-pepper hair. "What if we redistribute the equipment between the various cases? How about that?"

"Er . . . you *could,* I suppose. But . . . wouldn't . . ." Her brow corrugated into a frown. ". . . the total weight . . . be exactly the same?"

"In a way."

"Then no! No, you can't."

I saw his round shoulders quiver with suppressed rage. Oh dear.

Sensing a small mutiny in the making, one of many this trip, I exchanged an "uh-oh" glance with Tasha, and distanced myself by flopping down on a suitcase, cracking open

The Da Vinci Code,[1] and letting the rest of them get on with it.

Letting other people get on with things is very much my way. I'm terribly hands-off as far as problems are concerned.

"Look, darlin'," Eric growled, hooking himself over the desk, "here's the deal, okay? We're trying to make a television show . . ." Ooh, clever. Playing the glamour card. ". . . so what would it take to get us o—?"

But the poor woman had heard enough. "Sir, please stand to one side. You—everybody in this group—stand to one side and let the other passengers through. Next."

With great relief, the young couple behind us shuffled forward in line, tickets at the ready . . .

"What if—"

. . . only to stop again with a groan. Eric wasn't budging.

"Next!"

". . . we bought more seats for the bags?"

"Sir, the flight's full. If you like, we can put the excess on tomorrow's flight. That m—"

"Nope," he cut her off, then sighed heavily. "No, don't worry, it's fine. We'll go elsewhere." Turning his back: "You're not the only major airline that goes to Vanuatu, you know."

This brought a smile to her face.

"Well, actually, sir . . ."

---

[1] I know, it's wrong. I shouldn't have, and I'm sorry. But, having leapfrogged over the entire Harry Potter brouhaha without so much as blinking, I realized that if I didn't help fan at least one cultural wildfire soon, I'd be locked out of every dinner-party conversation from now 'til eternity.

The phone call that started it all came out of the blue.

"Hi, is that Cash?" a male voice said. Cordial, controlled. *"How's it going?"*

"Great. Why . . . who are you?"

"I'm the new vice president of development at ———" and he named a certain TV network, one I was not entirely familiar with. But who cares? He was a TV executive! A TV executive calling me—that is to say a complete nobody, a non-TV person—at home. *". . . and I'm a big fan of your work. Big fan . . . love your radio stuff . . ."* His words drifted in and out like AM static. *". . . I listen to you sometimes when I'm . . . great stuff. . . . Anyway, look, you might be interested in talking with us . . . maybe we could meet up, and . . ."*

Meet up? Ohmygodohmygodohmygod!!!!

I leaped up onto my washing machine and sat there, legs crossed to prevent myself doing cartwheels across the kitchen, possibly tearing a ligament.

"Thanks," I said, not really taking anything in. "Er . . . I mean, sure. Yeah."

"How about Wednesday? I'll be in L.A. for a programming conference, so I'm thinking, how about we get together over a coffee?"

Coffee?

I didn't bother checking my calendar. To do that I'd have had to buy one. But I knew that, in Hollywood, it's important that you play hard to get. The other person must hear you struggling to rearrange your schedule, otherwise they won't respect you. Everything's politics. A game.

"I'm only in town for a couple days. As I said, Wednesday's best for me."

I have to say, this couldn't have come at a better time. He'd caught me at a highly pivotal stage of my broadcasting career, in the sense that I didn't have one. In fact, the technical term for what I'd experienced so far in broadcasting, I believe, is "a slump." A twenty-three-year slump as a travel journalist on public radio, first in England, then later, after that flopped badly, in America, where my career had continued to flatline in spectacular fashion, going nowhere, doing nothing, and impressing absolutely no one. Well, except for this guy apparently, the deputy-vice-whatever-he'd-said-he-was of a remote cable network I'd never watched. It was a miracle.

"What day do you have in mind?"

"I just told you—Wednesday!!"

Er . . . Wednesday . . . Wednesday . . . hm, let me see.

"Act breezy," I told myself. Nonchalant, like you don't care. Never gush in negotiations. The less you appear to want what the other person is offering, the more of what he's offering he'll want to offer you.

After a lengthy pause to suggest I was flicking through a list of engagements a mile long, debating if there was *even one* I could drop to squeeze him in, I concluded that—oh look!—there was. What luck!

"That's okay. I'm sure I can switch things around," I said eventually, closing my imaginary calendar. "Yup. Wednesday it is."

"Excellent. I'll call you later with a time and place."

"Sure. One thing, though: how will we rec—"

"Looking forward to seeing you."

"—ognize each other?"

The Twin Otter is listing badly. We're battling fifty-mile-an-hour headwinds from the southeast. With each monstrous gust, the wings flap, as if the charter plane, suspecting all may be lost, is pondering flying for real. Each time it does, the cases containing our delicate camera equipment convulse erratically, emitting the kind of noise a box of tools makes when you drop it from a second-story window.

Below us, far below, but approaching faster than any reputable flying manual would advise, I'm sure, a Band-Aid of trimmed green swings into view among the trees. An airstrip! This is it—we're here.

Mark, our cameraman, twists around, and, steadying himself against his seat across the aisle, turns the camera on me, eager to capture the about-to-be-buried-alive look on my face.

"I'd rather you didn't," I tell him. "I'm not feeling too good."

The brutal rotations of the plane have left me dizzy, weightless. My breakfast is working its way back up my throat.

For a moment Mark looks concerned. But only for a moment. Then he sticks his eye to the viewfinder and shoots me anyway, his smile on full beam.

Bastard. I've never met anyone so determined in all my life.

Oh wait, yes I have. One person.

And he died.

It was a sound engineer at the radio station I used to work for in London years ago: Adrian. Wonderfully gregarious guy: blonde, craggy, debonair in an English-nobility kind of way, yet also, by some weird quirk of genetics, one of those type A daredevils—like certain reality TV cameramen I could name—who are convinced they're utterly indestructible. Not only that, but they're driven to test out this crackpot hypothesis again and again and again, until, inevitably, something bad happens.

After radio, Adrian made a radical life change. He became a professional skydiver, notching up ten thousand successful drops and in the process making quite a name for himself. Until one day not too long ago, he was up in the sky experimenting with a new type of parachute, one that doesn't open before you hit the ground, apparently, when he plunged to his death in a tangled frenzy of wires and nylon sheeting. Terrible, *terrible* tragedy. And an awful loss. In a world seemingly crammed with gray, timid people leading lives of humdrum conformity simply because they're afraid to take risks and live out their fullest potential, heroes like Adrian, those who stipulate the terms of their own expendability, should, I feel, be treasured (though never, *ever* emulated) and looked up to, if only to teach us as a culture that we're looking up to the wrong people and may want to rethink our priorities a little.

I worry about Mark sometimes for similar reasons. He's a wonderfully talented man: totally solid, dependable, you couldn't wish for better. But . . . well, the word "limitation" appears to be as alien to him as "adventure" is to me. That stocky frame of his, which is more athletic than it looks, belies a tremendous strength of character that I quite envy. He's able to smile through most difficulties and see light at the end of a tunnel even as it's caving in on him. That's what makes him such a great cameraman, and so perfect for our show, because he's willing to go right out on a limb and get what he wants in situations where less impulsive people—me, for instance—might hold back.

Right now, despite the brutal rocking of the plane, he's perched on the edge of his seat, belt unbuckled, camera steadied against his shoulder, relishing each violent bump and jolt and every last smoky cough of the propellers on our rapid descent.

"Eric! You're in shot," he yells.

"Sorry." The producer yanks in his elbows, and everyone else does the same.

Circling the clouds in uneven condor swoops, the plane bobs through a thermal current into a crossword of air-pockets, ten feet down, twenty across, up seven, down nine, causing Tasha to almost bang her head on the seat a second time . . .

"Holy . . ."

. . . as we try to align ourselves with the runway.

". . . sheeeeeeeeeeeeeeyit!"

Braced, with teeth clenched, I glance at the cockpit for some sign, anything will do, that we're not about to die. The pilot, in a crisp white shirt to suggest competence, with impressive yellow epaulettes like the ones real pilots might wear, is sitting with his head erect, back stiff, gripping his half-moon steering wheel with the intensity of a six-year-old on his first go-kart ride. Or maybe he's praying—hard to see from this angle.

Undeterred, Mark wedges the camera in against the seat and continues. This could be his one and only chance to shoot our landing.

I do my bit as host, squinting through the porthole at the sun-speckled ocean below, and our destination: Tanna Island, a mysterious paw print of brooding jungle fringed with misty beaches and rippling banks of submerged coral that fan out from the shoreline like frilled cuffs, visible only to birds, air travelers, and, I guess, if things don't go their way, skydivers in free fall. To my left, two raised cat's tails of drifting smoke carve up the horizon, one from the distant smoldering volcano, which I know from my guidebook to be Mount Yasur, the other belching from deep within the hardwood forest, cause unknown.

If you imagine this archipelago to be shaped like a catapult, then Tanna is halfway down the handle, and contains some of the last few virginal tracts of land on the planet. For the next week, this Stone Age wilderness will be our hellhole away from home, and the closer we get to it, the more trepidation I feel. I think perhaps Sir Arthur Conan Doyle was right. Maybe dinosaurs do still walk the earth. If that's true and they're going to be anywhere, it's down below us. I can feel it.

Dinosaurs, or something far, far worse.

No one really has a clue where Vanuatu is. In that respect it's a bit like the human spleen. But basically, we're talking about a cluster of eighty-three cyclone-battered islands in the South Pacific between Fiji and the Solomon Islands.

Until tourism happened here—and it took a long time to happen, for reasons that will become obvious—the only people who'd ever been able to say with any certainty that this remote Polynesian country existed at all was a ragbag assortment of mariners and missionaries who stopped by to say hello during the seventeenth and eighteenth centuries.

Many scavenger nations—among them the Spanish, the Dutch, the French; oh, and the biggest troublemakers of them all, I'm sorry to say: the British—came barreling through the Tropics at some point, colonizing every lump of land they could find. Perhaps the most notable visitor of all was Captain James Cook in 1774. Bright guy. Though very full of himself, from what I hear. Also a bit of a prancing dandy if you believe the rumors. Spent a lot of his life sailing cavalierly back and forth across the globe chasing down someplace called *Terra Australis Incognito,* a legendary land that people raved about and said was really worth finding, but without ever finding it. In portraits, he's often seen in tights and a wig, poring over a map like an expert. But don't be fooled; he had absolutely no idea where he was going.

According to records, many early visitors, including Cook, when they first stepped off their ship onto Vanuatu's mist-enshrouded, palm-fringed beaches pounded by ten-foot waves, were held spellbound by the primitive, uninhabited magnificence of everything—its untouched savanna overrun with wild horses, the brooding hinterland embroidered with groves of coconut and banana, waterfalls tumbling into clear pools shaded by lush banyan trees and neck-high vegetation—and driven to conclude that they'd found Paradise.

What records don't show, however, is if, once these visitors had settled in, their enthusiasm faltered any, or they had second thoughts. Especially when:

a. It became clear that the islands weren't uninhabited at all and were in fact littered with indigenous tribes, known collectively as the ni-Vanuatu—or ni-Van—most of whom were distinctly hostile to intruders; and

b. They were subsequently set upon by the ni-Van, thrashed with sticks and clubs, run through with spears, dragged by their hair into the hills, and finally—just when they thought it was over and the natives were roughing them up merely as a precursor to releasing them back to their ship with a stern warning never to return—boiled alive and eaten, a common fate in those days for anyone who stopped off in Vanuatu to say hello.

Though *not* Captain James Cook, you'll be pleased to hear.

Sensing a certain antagonism from the welcoming committee—"They by no means seem reconciled to the liberty we took in landing upon their coast," he wrote in his journal at the time[2]—he made his escape, giving the place a sparkling new name as he left.

Explorers used to do that a lot. Upon arriving in a new country, and overriding all wishes of the locals, they'd sweep aside centuries of tradition and instantly rename it, the way you might a litter of puppies. "This one I shall call Whitsuntide," Cook would say as he wafted by, "and this one over here Desolation, and that one Cape Circumcision." He was a menace. And, true to form, the day he saw Vanuatu, he cried, "From now on this shall be called the New Hebrides—because it reminds me of Scotland, which I discovered while I was looking for Brazil." Then he pranced off back to his ship, HMS *Disoriented,* and sailed out to sea once again to renew his quest for Antarctica.[3]

Having plunged out of the sky like a torn kite, we're down at last.

Spontaneous applause trickles through the cabin and the pilot grins broadly.

Following a short taxi along a surprisingly smooth, freshly mown runway, the propellers' last few guttural sputters give way to total silence, interrupted only by the occasional buzz of an insect or a bird's staccato trill.

It's like someone suddenly switched off your hearing aid.

---

2 If you don't believe me, read *The Journals of Captain Cook,* edited by Philip Edwards, or *Farther Than Any Man,* by Martin Dugard, or my own book, *Captain Clueless,* out next summer.

3 Which went pretty much as it always did. He took another of his famous wrong turns and ran aground in Hawaii, where he was ambushed and stabbed to death. Whether this setback forced him to cancel future expeditions is not documented.

Once we're fully at rest, the pilot runs around to drag out the bags, aided by Mark and his soundman, Todd, a well-built guy of Polish descent with a balding head, big heart, and downtrodden smile, who claims he's the least important of the crew, there to make up the numbers. "Oh, I'm just tagging along with Mark," he'll mutter, disingenuously, bottom lip pushed into a pout. "I'm not important." But that's not so. Without him there's no sound, and without sound on a show like this the pictures are mostly worthless. That aside, Todd is simply a gem of a man. Funny, solid, and reliable. He brings to the production, I feel, whatever Baloo brought to *The Jungle Book,* only without the annoying songs and the ant-eating, and everyone loves him for it.

As I struggle out of the plane, the heat hits me like a falling couch. It's not even lunchtime, but the thermometer's already into triple digits.

"Hey—stay there!" Mark calls out to me. Muscular legs in baggy khaki shorts run to a spot several feet away, from where he can shoot me struggling out of the plane door. "Everyone clear the frame. Eric—you need to move back, please. Okay, Cash—go inside the plane and come out again. Quiet, everyone."

Obediently, they fall silent. They have to. I'm supposed to be alone.

That's the premise of the series we're making. A stranger, dumped in a strange country with no money, no food, no facilities, and nobody to help him find them, has to survive for three or four days on his own. Which all looks very wonderful on paper, but is proving harder to execute in practice than we thought.

For a start, if I were really on my own out here, the show would never get made. Who would tell me where to go and what to do? Who would film me going there and doing it? Who would record the sound? Who would make sure that everyone I talked to along the way signed a legal release form to allow what they say to be featured on TV and to prevent them from changing their mind later? And who would boss the others around until they couldn't stand him any more? That's what we have a director, cameraman, sound technician, field producer, and coordinating field producer for. And the audience is savvy enough to know that. They're aware of the conceit/deceit of reality TV. That it's a group effort and I can't possibly be alone. Yet, in the name of maintaining the illusion and being entertained, they and we pretend I am.

Once the long shot is complete, Mark wants one more rerun for close-ups.

"And remember to act surprised," he calls out.

"I will."

Returning inside the aircraft, I re-emerge from the door, surveying the terrain as though I didn't spot it the first two times, looking perplexed, listening, sniffing.

The air here in Vanuatu is strange. That's the first thing you notice. It's unlike anything we're used to in Los Angeles. Can't decide what's so different about it at first. Then, I have it: it contains oxygen. From *trees*, too, not a cylinder! Can you believe that? As a city kid who grew up in Manchester, England, and is now based in Hollywood, this is a first for me. I suspect my lungs are going to have a problem adapting.

Several feet to my right, out of shot, Tasha's feeling the same way. Taking a moment to absorb the alien wooded landscape around the airport, she soaks up the almost eerie tranquility and breathes in deep lungfuls of healthy air, then combats the evils of both by firing up her iPod and lighting a cigarette.

Behind me, the propellers chug back to life. We're going up again! Just me and Camera Mark this time (and possibly the pilot if he has a few minutes), for a rerun of the landing sequence. That way we can pick up shots we missed on the way in, of my face staring out of the window in horror, with the island in the background. As it is, on this occasion the flight is a whole lot smoother and convinces me that I was probably wrong when I referred to the plane as a clockwork junk heap; it's not as unsafe as I'd first thought. That, or I've become better at not crapping my pants in panic.

Once we're down on the ground, the Twin Otter begins taxiing back the way it came. The pilot's been given orders to circle twice overhead to ensure we get a shot of him flying off. This he dutifully does, before banking away to the west. Moments later, swallowed by clouds, the plane's steady hornet-swarm drone recedes into the distance, its place taken by silence once again. And that's when it really hits us. Even daredevil Mark, I'm thinking. That, land or crash on Tanna, the result is the same: you're stuck.

There's no way off this volcanic, bug- and possibly dinosaur-infested prehistoric island. Not until tomorrow at the very earliest. Or, if we complete our mission—which is by no means certain—in six days' time, when the plane will return to pick us up.

Or whatever's left of us.

2

Star Jones Misses Her Big Chance

The Hyatt Regency Century Plaza Hotel is a concrete-and-glass boomerang occupying what used to be the old 20th Century Fox back lot in Beverly Hills. The day I was there, its cavernous marble lobby—part reception and part café-bar—was filled with tables and comfy couches and waiters rushing between them, bringing trays of coffee to hyperactive media types, who at first sight appeared to be talking to each other like normal people, but who, because addressing the person you're sitting with is considered soooo passé in L.A., had headsets in their ears and were talking to someone else entirely.

Because of some kind of convention going on upstairs, the place was busy, busy, busy.

"Hey—Cash?" A man in a dark suit bore down on me. "Great to meet you at last. Thanks for coming." He flashed a smile. "So how's it going?"

"It's going great."[1]

And I swear, as these words left my lips, he went: "Aaaaaaaah!"—just like that—the way dying aunts do with their last breath, at the same time cupping his ear, as if he'd caught a distant fairy bell ringing.

"What's the matter?"

"That voice," he sighed. "How many times have I heard it on the car radio? It's great to see the face behind it. You have such a fantastic cadence."

I do?

The short, friendly executive, pumping energetically at my hand the way he might to raise water from a well, didn't fit the Hollywood stereotype at all. In fact, his intelligent eyes and characterful good looks were at odds with the ranks of bland, homogenized go-getters lounging around in the lobby café that day. Although I will say one thing for him: he was strikingly compact. That was my first thought when he walked over: "How beautifully proportioned you are." Like a prototype for something the Japanese are thinking of making, but which they have yet to find a use for. A *real* man, sure, only scaled down for convenience and ease of storage.

"With your suit off, you probably resemble a very excitable thumb," I mused to myself as he steered me out through a set of glass doors onto a hot terrace.

We found a table with an umbrella, to protect us from the blazing Southern California sun, and settled ourselves in.

---

1 Huge mistake, this. When someone in Hollywood asks you how you are, you *never tell them.* Only a total novice would mistake an idle inquiry for real concern. Best thing: say nothing. The other person will not notice. Nobody in the entertainment business has any interest in how you are, only what you can do for them.

"Anyways"—right down to business—"if you don't mind my asking: what do you think of our network? Ever seen it?"

No, was the truth. Not until that first day he'd called me up. After which, curious obviously, I'd rushed to my TV and flicked up through the channels, past CNN, past QVC, even past the silly little home decorating networks where, every time you switch on, some butch woman in a tool belt is ridiculing newlyweds for their lack of grouting skills; way up, past the gay channel, past Oprah's channel, past a channel devoted entirely to boring people to tears, which I won't name, though I'm aware it could be any one of a dozen (why is it that so many networks these days seem to have the Stepford Wives as their target demographic?), until finally I hit a cluster of travel and leisure networks that I had no idea came as part of my basic cable package, one of which was midway through an hour-long special that I think is fairly typical of shows at this end of the dial: *The World's Top 10 Pony Trekking Vacations.* And oh boy, I'll tell you this for nothing: I was horrified. *Horrified!!* And disappointed. And chagrined, if that's even a word.

"Er . . . well, I may possibly have caught it once . . ." I fumbled around, trying to think of a polite way of describing the show I'd watched, ". . . and, I'll be honest with you, it was . . . ," crappity crap crap crap, ". . . not my cup of tea at all."

"Exactly!!"

He surprised me by almost bouncing out of his seat with excitement.

"Research has shown," he continued in short breaths, "that people only watch shows like that for eleven minutes at a time. D'you know why that is?"

Since I was in full self-sabotage mode by now and he seemed genuinely interested in my opinion, I took a daring position. "Because they're awful?"

His eyes dimmed slightly. "Er . . . well, I wouldn't put it quite like that. I mean, I know where you're going with this, and the problem . . ."

"The *problem,*" I cut in, emboldened, "is that too many travel and leisure programs on TV—and I mean generally—are just talking wallpaper. That's why I don't watch them. And when I do, it's only for eleven minutes. Much of the time they sugar-coat the truth with a bunch of bland PR blurbs and pass it off as information. I mean, where are the real, gritty travel experiences? The third-rate rental cars with used condoms under the seat. The inedible food that glues your jaws together. The hotels claiming to have ocean views, and they do, but only if you climb up on the roof with binoculars. That's real travel. That's what it's like for regular people. Oh, and FYI," I tacked on by way of a final flourish, "I find most TV travel hosts to be bland, characterless, patronizing, over-smiley mannequins."

"Exactly!" he said, even more excited. "Which is why I called you."

"I'm sorry?"

"The shows you're referring to, they're old-school. On our network, we intend to populate our schedules with fascinating, authentic shows and cool hosts. Cool hosts who are *passionate* about travel." He trained his eyes on me without blinking. "And you, Cash, would be perfect. You're personable, funny . . . and . . . er . . ."

Er . . . ?

When no other adjectives came to mind he stopped and stared. And I stared too.

Quite honestly, I was trying not to show how enthusiastic I was, but, oh my God, I so wanted to be on TV in the worst way. I'd even go as far as to say I *needed* to be on TV. Really. With my radio career in the doldrums, where else was I going to go?

It's just that . . .

Well, I didn't want to do a travel show.

I'd been a travel journalist for over twenty years and it had never worked out. I'd simply ended up lonely, depressed, jaded, and, often, less informed about a place at the end of a trip than before I'd set off. That's precisely why I'd stopped—because I was no longer *passionate* about travel. What I needed was a new challenge. Something interesting and different, but—and I can't stress this enough—*in no way travel-related*.

"So what do you say?" His eyes were trained on me.

"No thanks. That's very kind of you, but I'm going to pass."

Is what I wanted to say. But he was so very excited the whole time, and you don't like to hurt an excited guy's feelings. So instead I mumbled a plausible excuse. Something about currently fielding other offers and not being sure which one to take.[2]

"Well, at least think about it," The Thumb said, wilting. (Nobody turns down the chance of having his own TV show. Ever! It's unheard of.) "Hey, why not come up with a list of

---

2 Which wasn't a total lie. There *were* offers. The first was a cooking show called *Recipe for Disaster,* suggested by a TV producer in Nashville. His idea was for a half-hour program in which I would break into a different celebrity's home each week while they were out and rustle up a three-course meal before they got back. Then we'd eat, presumably while we were waiting for the cops to arrive. The second show idea was from the same guy. In response to my telling him a flat-out no to his first suggestion, he'd come up with a variation: this time the celebrity would be forewarned that I was going to break in, and so might not be quite as freaked out when they came home and found a TV crew turning their kitchen upside down. Which wasn't bad, I guess. Yet, though this promised to cut down substantially on the jail time, I still wasn't interested.

things you might like to do, and e-mail them to me anyway? Let's start there."

"Great."

And that was it. The thrust of our meeting.

Despite not being interested, but having been utterly bamboozled by the man's earnestness—he'd blown the smoke so far up my ass that it was clouding my brain—that same afternoon I sat in a local coffee shop for twenty minutes and rustled up a bunch of ideas that would make good television. And how did I know they would? Well, because they were straight rip-offs of shows already on the air, that's how. Shows that, as far as I could tell, seemed to be doing rather well.

My favorite idea of all was a broad copy of the CBS hit reality game show *Survivor,* only I called it *All Washed Up* and changed things around a little: made it more personal, got rid of the game element. And, just to be on the safe side, the survival element as well, turning it into more of an entertainment show. I had this notion that the host could be dumped, literally, out of a boat, and washed up with no money on a series of faraway islands, forcing him to coexist with the indigenous culture, brave the elements, and live on his wits, which he would do very successfully due to his ample reserves of strength, determination, and tenacity.

Wow, how brazen of me, you're thinking, ripping off someone else's idea like that. But wait. The only reason I felt okay about doing this was because:

a. I never imagined in my craziest nightmares that any network would go for it. Most cable channels are run on a shoestring. No way would they be able to afford something as epic and ambitious in scale as *All Washed Up;* but on the other hand . . .

b. If the show did, against the odds, get made, I was convinced that The Thumb would come to his senses and bring in a real TV host to present it. Someone with experience. Celebrity lawyer Star Jones, for instance. Viewers would love to see her dumped on a faraway island and left there, I'm sure. Or that guy who used to be in *The Partridge Family*, the angry one who seems hell-bent on hurting himself. He'd do. A professional, basically. A man's man. Someone who'd be unafraid to rough it a little, and wouldn't mind, if the job called for it, getting eaten by wild animals. After all, who in their right mind would want to risk big money on a show as elaborate as *All Washed Up*, then have it feature a complete unknown who lacked every quality necessary to carry the idea off—including, but not confined to, personal strength, determination, and tenacity? It didn't make sense.

Although, having said that, you know what did make *perfect* sense? Being removed as host but seeing the show get made anyway. In other words, selling the idea to a network with deep pockets for a boatload of money and then, if it turned out to be a smash hit, coining in the residuals for the rest of my life. Brilliant!

With that in mind, I confidently e-mailed my list to The Thumb, then sat back and waited.

And waited.

In the lengthy gap that followed, I confess that the initial rush of enthusiasm (masquerading as cool detachment) I'd been feeling started to wane a little. Obviously, he hadn't liked what I'd sent. Or, worse, he'd liked it, but saw no point wasting money remaking programs that were currently showing on other networks, or wasting valuable time telling me so.

But then, just as I was on the verge of giving up and moving on, the phone rang.

"Hey, is that Cash?" It was The Thumb—bursting with enthusiasm, as ever. *"I've been talking to people around here and we like the* All Washed Up *idea very much. Really, man, we think it's gonna be great and you'd be the perfect host. LET'S DO IT."*

What? Me? Go traveling again? Oh . . . er . . .

Simultaneously elated and depressed, I thought, "Fabulous!" and also, "Hell, no!" both at the same time. This was certainly not the career breakthrough I was hoping for.

"Are you okay?" he said. *"You don't sound thrilled."*

"No. No, it's fine. I'm fine. Really."

Yippee! Oh crap!

I've lived in Hollywood for eleven years, in one of the leafier, more upscale neighborhoods close to Griffith Park, an area that seems to attract a wide range of media types, including studio executives and celebrities. Ours is a seductively peaceful enclave, where the only real sound you hear all day is ecstatic birdsong, the hum of distant traffic, and, just occasionally, when you least expect it, the thunderous roar of SUVs filled with paparazzi as they take off up the street, letting us know that one of our celebrity neighbors has just left his house and is on his way to the supermarket.

By sheer good fortune, my partner and I also live next door to an important Hollywood TV executive. You won't know him—he's Vice President of Overseas Sales (Pacific Rim) for one of the major studios. But if you ever travel to Bangkok and see an episode of *According to Jim* and hate it, then, chances are Matty had something to do with it. He and his glamorous wife are immensely smart people. Worldly, practical, no-nonsense. Not like us on our side of the fence, whose disorganized, schemeless lives they watch play out from their upstairs window with dismay, if not outright disdain. Basically, they're the Kravitzes to our Darren and Samantha. But because he's in showbiz, Matty's a good guy to know, especially if you want free *According to Jim* DVDs. So when crunch time came for agreeing to do the show, naturally I went over to gauge his reaction.

The verdict was swift and cruel: "You're going to die," he said.

And this was before I'd even sat down.

"How long will the series take to make?" Pouring himself a glass of wine.

"By the time we're done," I said, "up to a year."

"*A year?*" He shook his head. "And what's your job on the show? What are they asking you to do?"

"Well, of course I'll be traveling, and hosting it, writing the script . . ."

"That's too much."

". . . logging the tapes, coproducing it, doing the voice-over . . ."

"Oh God."

". . . coediting it, supervising the sound mix, and representing the network at various junkets to promote it. The whole thing's my show, so a lot of jobs fall to me."

Off the back of a long sigh, the Vice President of Overseas Sales (Pacific Rim) took another sip of merlot, easing back into the couch while he weighed up all the options. Then, conclusively and with the kind of conviction that got him where he is today, he declared: "Yup—you're going to die."

"Oh, great. Thanks."

"I'm serious. You can't be traveling around the world each week like that without destroying your body, your health, your relationship, and your social life. It's too much pressure on one person. Nobody wears that many hats in TV and survives. And if you're allergic to foreign food . . ."

Which I am. Some. Mostly stuff with preservatives and additives in. Plus shrimp, crab, lobster—the bottom-feeders. Also, I touch gluten or dairy products at my peril. And as for oil—if I eat oil of any kind in any way, my body begins to break down. It's like I'm being consumed alive from the inside by a virus. Which is why I go to enormous lengths never to touch it. Easy to do when I'm at home, of course, and in control of my environment, but out on the road visiting distant lands, particularly in the Middle East or the Mediterranean, where oil's practically all they eat, that was going to be a whole lot trickier.

"Nothing is worth killing yourself for," he continued. "For God's sake, you're a radio journalist." Which is his shorthand for saying, *You don't do anything*. "This will be like going from zero to one hundred in ten seconds. You're taking on way too much. If you work this schedule for a year," he concluded, "you'll end up on coke, or in the hospital, or both. Nobody works that hard."

"Maybe I'll be the first."

"No." He was adamant. "No, no, no." Looking me straight in the eye, he said with great gravity, "Trust me, Cash, this is going to kill you."

3

A Kiss from a Ghost

"Everybody in?"

Bundling ourselves aboard a white shuttle van, we bounce, suspension creaking like old bedsprings, out of the airport and onto the main road, with a second vehicle trailing close behind carrying all our camera gear.

Maybe I shouldn't be, but I'm feeling nervous. About the show generally, but also about the lack of amenities on the island.

Time has not only stood still in parts of Tanna, I hear, but it actually seems to be going backwards, with the result that there's a great big gaping hole where convenience ought to be. Everyday facilities you and I take for granted in our world are almost completely absent from theirs. Simple, fun things. Like electricity, for instance. Or fresh running water. Or technology. There are no laptops here, no TV, no cell phones, no Cheerios, no fresh water, no towels, no magazines, no Hot Pockets; come to think of it, they have no pockets, period. Because they have no trousers. That's what I'm hearing. And that's precisely why season nine of *Survivor* was set here.

In 2004, eighteen type A contestants were flown in and dumped on Efaté, the country's main island. The chief inducement being, of course, money: one million dollars in the pot. Which must have seemed like a helluva prize going in, but whose value diminished rapidly, I'm sure, as the full horror of what they'd signed up for unfolded. Paradise, it turns out, is not all it's cracked up to be—something the contestants quickly found out as they ran cheerfully ashore on Day One, straight into the yawning jaws of Mother Nature, who for the next thirty-nine days mauled them alive. I watched every episode. I saw the whole thing play out. The bug-ravaged flesh, the menacing filth, the starvation—ugh! How I wish I could scrape those images from my retinas. Even Robinson Crusoe would have perished.

According to the guidebooks, some parts of Tanna Island are shockingly primitive, and covered in the kind of impenetrable, steamy jungle frequently described as "godforsaken" by old-time novelists, even down to the smoldering volcano I mentioned earlier. They are so bleak, so far from civilization, that they're the very last place on earth you'd ever want to be stranded, even for a TV show.

Viewed from the air coming in, the terrain is coarse and forbidding. A verdant fist shaken angrily at visitors to scare them off. By the time we reach the ground, though, all that has changed. The jungle turns out to consist of gorgeous lush woodland filled with sinewy streams and butterfly-peppered glades and warm sunshine, like you might find in rural New England. All of which makes our twenty-minute drive to the hotel the most delightful treat, as we roar along a winding artery of dusty black asphalt that hugs the coastline, flanked by dense undergrowth through which a tangle of improvised pathways twists out of sight into intriguing leafy darkness.

Whenever we draw to a stop, which is often—once to let a family of pigs cross the road, another time because our driver spots a friend of his pushing a cart filled with strange hairy vegetables and wants to say hi—a loose crowd congregates and, for a short while, the van takes on the role of a waterless aquarium, as inquisitive faces press up against the glass, checking us out with impenetrable brown eyes.

I must say, these people don't look a bit like they do in encyclopedias—glum, hostile, naked. That's the next big surprise. Instead they're happy, welcoming, relaxed, reserved, and quite stylishly dressed in some cases. Their daywear tends toward surf-shop casual: baggy Hawaiian this, loose-fitting summer that. One kid even sports a Jackie Chan T-shirt. How, I wonder, can folks who are preyed upon daily by velociraptors possibly move with unhurried grace and have such transparently kind faces?

Farther along, in a clearing, I spot some gangly teenagers in yellow soccer shirts kicking a ball about while their parents—mostly the fathers—sit close by, propping themselves up against a tree in the shade. At the same time, not too far away, weary-looking women in floral Mother Hubbards are hard at work, staggering along the road in the sun, spines stiff as mop-handles lest their bodies buckle under the weight of the heavy bundles balanced on their heads.

"What language do they speak here?" Tasha asks our driver. She's itching to talk to someone.

"Bislama," comes the reply.

"Oh! So how do I say hello?"

Actually, I know the answer to that. There are phrases in the back of my guidebook. According to this, if you want to say "Hello" to a Tanna person, you say, *"Alo."*

"You say, '*Alo,*'" the driver agrees, then goes on to provide us with a string of other words and phrases we might find useful during our stay.

"If you want to say, 'Good morning,'" he shouts, driving forward and staring back at us at the same time, an alarming technique, "then in Bislama you say, *'Gud morning!'*"

Oh, really?

"'Telephone' is *telefon*. 'Market' is *maket*. 'Excuse me' is *skusmi*. And 'thank you,'" he adds, "translates as *'tank yu.'*"

Okay. Got that. Anything else?

One more: "A simple 'yes' and 'no' can be communicated easily and efficiently by using the Bislamic words *'yes'* and *'no.'*"

Hm.

I've always had a gift for tongues and dialects, but this one came particularly easily. Honestly, the *nerve* of these people, claiming to speak a foreign language when they don't.

Suitably encouraged, Tasha decides to give it a go.

"Alo!" She puts her face to the van window and calls to a small boy hovering bashfully by a hibiscus bush. He laughs and runs away.

Hm. Maybe she didn't pronounce it correctly.

For the remainder of the drive the crew zones out. Five heads bob lazily against torn leather seats, showing only vague interest in a vista of untamed jungle scenery that people *not* here to shoot a travel show would most likely consider captivating and be taking photos of like mad. This lot, however, they're diehards. Though still relatively young, most of them have seen and done it all many times over.

Eventually, Eric and the two Marks close their eyes and nod off, the tinny scratching of their respective iPods competing with the erratic growl of the van's worn-out gears as we continue on toward the hotel.

Personally, since I wish to retain my hearing into old age, I don't own an iPod. So instead, too anxious to doze, I lose myself in a thick folder of research materials.

According to this, the people in Vanuatu speak around 110 different languages in total. That's roughly one each.

In the early days, because there were many villages spread across the island, the inhabitants had only limited contact with one another. So, rather than remain mute for centuries, which I guess was an option, each community went ahead and developed its own language. As a result, a total of nine hundred separate tongues developed in Melanesia.[1] Then, as Vanuatu metamorphosed from a grab bag of isolated tribes into a unified nation, the tongues were consolidated, merging with English and French to become Bislama, a term that derives from the French word *"beche-de-mer"*—literally, sea cucumber. But of course! I mean, what else would you call your national language? "Sea cucumber" was a natural choice.

Before very long, the van turns in through an anonymous gate and rumbles down a narrow track leading to the hotel.

"Alo," I call to one of the porters as I disembark.

"Alo," he calls back, shooting me a relieved smile, as if to say, "Thank *God* someone took the time!"

"Alo," I call to the man at the reception desk.

---

1 Melanesia is the collective name given to islands located in West Central Oceania, including Fiji, New Caledonia, the Solomon Islands, etc. It's bounded by Micronesia to the north, Polynesia to the south, and to the east by . . . well, let's just call it Amnesia, because quite honestly I don't remember the name of it.

"Alo," he beams, sounding Australian. After a brief flurry of the usual paperwork, he hands me the key to my bungalow.

"A bungalow? Oooh, how great. *Tank yu*."

My linguistic dexterity earns an enthusiastic grin, generating the same rush of triumph in me that Doctor Dolittle must have felt when addressing his first terrapin.

Check-in complete, I'm just debating which of the crew I should enlist to carry my bags when a teenage porter scurries over and grabs them.

"Alo," I say.

"Alo. Me carry, sir," he insists, grabbing handles.

Sir.

Hm, being British, I rather like that. We had an empire once. I'm not sure what happened to it; doubtless we squandered it away on women and booze. Still, like it or not, that unique sense of unearned authority as well as an inbred right to lord it over the little people remains in my blood to this day, I can't help it.

"Why, *tank yu,*" I say to the porter.

And without help—though to be fair, none was offered—he staggers off, dragging the luggage along a wiggly wooded pathway that takes us through wild gardens of plumeria and radiant orchids.

The production office has done us proud. On other occasions, either out of necessity or to save money, we've been holed up in scruffy wayside motels that were, in my opinion, one step up from wrapping yourself in cardboard and sleeping under a viaduct. But this time—perhaps because motels and viaducts have yet to reach Tanna—we've been booked into a glorious five-star resort nestling right on the edge of the ocean and, at high tide, very possibly in it.

The bungalows are basic, but comfortable. I only have one complaint about mine: the roof doesn't fit. Some might say I'm quibbling to bring this up—"Typical Westerner, so spoilt. Can't sleep unless his bloody roof's nailed down"—but I'm sorry, that's how I am. In most hotels these days it's become quite the thing for the ceiling of your room to be attached to the walls. So much so that I no longer ring up in advance to check. But not here. Here, there's an alarming four-inch gap between the top of the walls and the beginning of the thatched eaves, a gap that, unless I'm mistaken, leads directly to the outside, the *same* outside where millions and millions of bugs are.

Oh, and, not to be a whiner, but the bungalow door ends woefully short of the floor. An open invitation to any insect or rodent, and possibly midgets as well if they crouch, that wants to just walk right in.

I figure I can fix the door by wedging a rolled-up bath towel underneath it. But the gap around the ceiling—well, that I have no answer to. *Unless* it's a clever device for ventilating the place, and . . .

A-haa, I see!!!

"How," I ask the porter before he leaves, "do I make the roof go down?"

He regards me a little weirdly at first, then brightens up when I start conveying roof-lowering movements to him through the medium of mime. "Yes," he nods.

"I knew it. Is there a lever . . ."

"Yes," he replies.

". . . or a switch?"

"Yes."

"No—which one? Which is it? Lever or switch?"

He's looking puzzled now.

I turn to the room and spread my arms. "Can—you—show—me—where—the—roof—control—is? Where in the room?"

"Yes," he says.

"Fabulous, thanks."

And I wait.

We both do.

For quite a while, actually.

Until eventually I snap, "You've forgotten where it is, haven't you?"

He nods again. "Yes."

Then, slightly panicked, he gives a small bow and shoots out the door without his tip.

Well!

More than a little annoyed, I set about searching for the controls myself, because I know I'll never sleep if I'm exposed to the outdoors in this way. Optimistically, I even flick what appears to be a light switch. But in keeping with a roof that doesn't fit, they also have lights that don't work.

As I'm cursing my bad luck, Tasha arrives at the door carrying a clipboard and wearing her backpack, a fine sheen of perspiration across her brow.

Actually, at a certain angle, and with the afternoon sun glancing off her face like it is now, she bears a striking physical resemblance to a young Sharon Stone, her beauty enhanced further by a winsome street-urchin quality that most actresses would die for, that tends to attract male attention wherever we go, drawn by the large brown eyes, big smile, and funky, short, blonde-streaked hair that sticks out in wisps and tufts at all angles, as if it was cut in the dark. With a potato peeler. By Andrea Bocelli.

As she absorbs the interior of my bungalow, her lips hitch into an "Ugh!" shape, and I know she's thinking exactly what I'm thinking: found the lever that lowers the roof yet?

Preempting her, I shake my head. "I was just looking for it when you arrived."

"Looking for what? What are you talking about?"

Oh. Okay. Then she wasn't thinking what I was thinking. Sorry.

"My room is full of bugs. I'm so pissed," she shudders. "They're everywhere. God, how could the office send us here during bug season?"

"Maybe they didn't know. *Every* season's probably bug season in Vanuatu."

"Yeah, well, it sucks, and I'm going to tell them."

"But how? How will you tell them? There's no *pablik telefon*."

"No what?"

"Oh, I'm sorry." Realizing she doesn't speak Bislama, I translate.

"I spoke with the owners of the hotel just now. The island has radio phones. Also, they have a satellite phone we can use. Like the one in *Jurassic Park*. It's not ideal, but I can at least call the office tonight, confirm that we got here okay, and th—" as she's talking, a fly lands on her bottom lip and rests there. "Ugh! Ugh! Yeuw!" She flaps it away with both hands. "YEUW!!! I can't bear it."

For a moment or two we lapse into depressed silence, jointly surveying the stick furniture in the room, the rough stone floor, and the raised roof, which looks like it was made from glued-together Weetabix. Then she collects herself and explains what she came for.

"Tomorrow," she says, "we begin shooting for real. We're aiming for an 8 A.M. call time. So be at the van in your show clothes by 7:50, okay? Right now, the boys and I are heading out to scout locations."

"You're leaving me alone?"

I hate it when they do that—go off without me. Each time it happens, I notice they all bond just a little more, and I feel left out just a little more, widening the gulf between us.

"Well, you can't come, *obviously,*" she insists. "You're not allowed to see it. Don't worry—we won't be long. In the meantime, rest, chill, whatever, okay? I'll see you at dinner."

With a cute little wave, she charges off toward reception at her usual brisk clip, thumbs hooked inside the straps of her backpack, mind already on to the next thing.

Shortly after, I hear van doors slam and an engine burst into life. Then, after a brief grapple with seat belts and some general disorganization, the hand brake is let off, tires scrunch across gravel, and everyone-but-me disappears back to the main road and away for their little afternoon excursion.

The main building of the hotel is a large, airy log cabin–type structure straight out of the *Architectural Digest: Places You Think You'd Like to Live but Would Probably Regret Later On* edition. En route to the deck, I find the same middle-aged man standing in reception . . .

"Alo."

"Alo," he says again.

. . . and begin quizzing him about the fake light switches in my room.

A lively conversation follows. Well, lively from my side at least. He just stares at me like I'm a moron. "They're not fake light switches, sir. They're real light switches."

"But they don't work."

"Yes, they do."

"Mine don't."

"Yes they *do.*"

"Then, sir," I reply, "I invite you to come to my bungalow and try flicking them."

"I don't need to come and flick them, *sir.* I know they work. Because . . ."

"Well, I'm sor—"

". . . *because* we switch the generator off each day until 6:30 P.M."

Ah. I see.

What I didn't know—How could I? Nobody told me—was that Tanna, despite its overall tendency toward the primitive, is, paradoxically, one of the most eco-advanced places on earth. The people strive in all kinds of ways to conserve their environment, including using energy resources sparingly, which, while enlightened and highly admirable, is nonetheless—and not to sound selfish or anything—a damned nuisance when you want to take a shower and can't heat your water.

"Oh, and another thing. If you could please send someone to lower the ceiling in my bungalow before nightfall I'd be most grateful. Your porter told me there was a lever somewhere . . ."

The guy's eyebrows shoot up. "He said that?"

". . . but I'm damned if I can find it. And I don't want bugs crawling in. Or midgets."

"Midgets?"

But mainly bugs.

Rather than engage in further argument, I thank him for his attention and, ignoring his continued quizzical expression, stroll off in search of the sundeck.

Despite the hotel being a mere few feet from the water's edge, where you'd think there'd be a breeze, there isn't. The air in the main bar-lounge is unbearably hot and sticky, another harbinger, I suppose, of what lies ahead. Seriously, you could steam broccoli in here. And of course, that makes the place a magnet to flies. Bluebottles especially. Big chubby ones carve a zigzag path between tables, coming in to land like ghastly winged tumors in my hair and on my bare arms to get at my sweat.

Settling down in an angular slatted chair on the deck, I order a margarita from the bar, to be followed over the next couple of hours by three more, then break open *The Da Vinci Code* and thereafter divide my time equally between plowing through a dozen cliff-hangers in as many chapters, and, when that gets old, watching the sun slide dramatically into the ocean in a tantrum of citrus hues, before finally throwing itself over the horizon like a hysterical soprano. In its wake a dense, hostile darkness descends, the likes of which I've never encountered before.

Once the light fades in Vanuatu, you're as good as blind. It's coal-shaft black out there. Ghoulishly, back-of-your-closet black. Convulsing flames in small kerosene lamps distributed among tables in the restaurant do their best to provide occasional golden pockets of reassurance, but it's not enough to make the slightest dent on the monolithic emptiness of the world beyond this one.

At my feet, a lazy surf gurgles and eddies into rocky inlets barely visible through the gauze of night. After that, several yards out and just below the surface, lies a ring of coral one hundred meters deep. Then nothing. You don't touch land again for another four thousand miles—*four thousand!*—not until you hit the Great Barrier Reef.

That fact alone has me totally creeped out.

For the first time, I'm beginning to appreciate how difficult it must have been being an explorer three centuries ago.

The only reason Captain Cook found Tanna at all, I hear, was because Mount Yasur happened to be erupting on the eastern side of the island that particular night, tossing orange fireballs into the sky like distress flares. Otherwise I'm sure he'd have missed it entirely, the way he so often did, sailing merrily by in his ship *The Resolution,* and running aground on the Great Barrier Reef months ahead of schedule.

With the onset of night, I feel a slight chill skitter across the back of my neck. A fleeting, barely perceptible breath, like the icy touch of winter.

A kiss from Cook's ghost perhaps?

A warning? Telling me I've committed to something I shouldn't have.

"You idiot, signing that goddamned contract! You know you didn't want to. Now look—look at the mess you're in."

Suddenly, the world I'm used to and feel comfortable in—of leafy suburbs, celebrity neighbors, of food stores open around the clock, movie theaters, Starbucks on every corner, my beautiful home, my relationship—feels like it's in a different galaxy.

Once, when I was a little kid in England, I lost my parents in a department store. They walked off in one direction and I got sidetracked and ran off in another. Before I realized I couldn't see them anymore, it was already too late; they'd gone and I was lost.

Every child has moments like that. Most, by the time they get to be adults, have assimilated them and moved on. For some reason, I never did. That sense of abject abandonment, the helplessness, the distress I felt sitting in the rug department crying my eyes out that day, has stayed with me all these years: the dread of going unmissed, the fear that nobody knows I'm here, nobody cares, and nobody's coming back for me. And that same thumbprint of anxiety returns to haunt me once again now, as I look out from the deck of the hotel at . . . well, nothing.

Soon after, the restaurant begins to fill up with a trickle of guests arriving for drinks or dinner. Still no sign of the crew, though. Then, at 8:35 P.M., just as I'm starting to grow concerned, I catch a familiar rustle of shorts moving at speed behind me and Tasha gallops in, looking grubby and anything but her usual spirited self. Eric, an equally unsmiling string bean, strands of gray flopping about his pale face, follows close behind. Both sport brown smudges and skid marks across their cheeks and clothes. Their shoes are caked in mud.

"So?" I ask, a little fruitily (it's four margaritas later—Sir is hammered!), "Do we have a show?"

Clearly in shock, Eric makes an effort to talk. "Dude," he sneers, throwing down his papers on the table, "I . . . I mean . . ."

"What is it? What's happened?"

He shakes his head. "Good luck, is all I can say. Good luck making something of this place."

The two of them swap loaded glances.

"*Obviously,* we can't go into detail," Tasha says. "It would spoil the surprise."

"But what she's trying to say is that parts of this place are horrible . . . and other parts are really, *really* horrible."

Oh, come on! It's a Pacific island. How bad can it be?

"Dude, you have no idea. Ask Todd and the two Marks. They thought the same thing. Wait 'til tomorrow, you'll see."

"Ugh!" Tasha shivers again. "You should see how they—" In danger of saying too much, she clams up. Mustn't give the game away. "Anyways, I'm gonna take a shower, boys, and get this crap off me. Dinner at 9:15?"

Shocked sober by their news, I remain glued to my seat for the next thirty minutes or more, staring out at the bleak Atlantic waves (wherever they are), alarmed. No, *more* than alarmed—frightened, actually, at what I've let myself in for, not only here on this one show, but in the rest of the season. More islands, more out-of-the-way places, more bugs, more mud, more 100-degree days . . .

It's Day One.

Not even Day One.

The day before Day One.

We haven't filmed a single shot yet, apart from the landing sequence, but already I'm tempted to lock myself in my bungalow and never come out.

4

The Land That Trousers Forgot

Daylight in Vanuatu is greeted with the same heightened sense of relief I imagine rich people must feel after a night of rioting, as they emerge from the basement to find that their Mercedes didn't get torched after all.

All I know is, when I open my eyes first thing and discover that the blanket of grim, vampiric darkness has lifted, replaced by a foamy sunlight trickling onto my bed, I am so thrilled not to have been eaten alive by bugs (although, with the ceiling stuck in a raised position like this, God knows they tried) that I spring to my feet singing.

After a quick shower, I float toward the dining room on a cloud of profound gratitude for the simplest of earthly pleasures—sunshine, hot water, and a breakfast of scrambled eggs, with toast and jam, followed by a big bowl of grated raw cabbage, which I assume to be a local delicacy and complimentary, because I certainly didn't ask for it.

By the time I arrive at the van, the driver and some

porters are busy cramming the last of the equipment we'll need into the rear. Despite yesterday's horrors, the crew, including Eric, seem to be in remarkably high spirits and raring to go.

"Did you see Tasha in the restaurant?" he asks.

Before I can reply, here she comes, breezing up the path toward us—"Morning, boys!"—cigarette in hand, taking sips from an espresso cup, a little flustered after dealing with the office in L.A. via the satellite phone, but otherwise happy enough.

One of Tasha's main duties is to concoct a progress report each day, to reassure our two executive producers and the guys at the network that the shoot is on schedule, everyone's behaving themselves, and—most important—we're finding time to make an actual TV show while we're on the road, not squandering the budget on fine wines, spa treatments, and high-end souvenirs, which, by the way, if we weren't being scrutinized so tightly, I, for one, most certainly would.

"Okay, guys!" Mark, our young, upbeat director, claps his hands to move everyone out. His face, half-hidden behind a drape of mousy bangs that don't quite meet in the middle, is bleached white. Poor guy, he's sick again. Been plagued by stomach problems since the Australia shoot last week, although he assures me he's feeling a little better today, which is a relief. You don't want to be falling ill in a place as remote as Tanna Island, that's for sure.

"Let's go, people," Eric shouts. The cheap sunblock he's just slathered on his forehead twinkles in the frosting of premature gray at his temples. "We're late."

Things are really cooking in the neighborhood today. The narrow byways of Tanna are teeming with people, mostly young women in bright summer skirts migrating along the roadside with languorous strides. Some are accompanied by kids, whom they steer onto the hard shoulder at the last moment to avoid oncoming traffic. And when I say oncoming traffic, I mean us. I don't think I've seen another motorized vehicle the entire journey. Most people can't afford a car, and, strictly speaking, don't need one anyway—it's a small island; where are they going to go?—so they walk.

Lurching into the bush, we plow along curling canyons of tall grass, passing more women along the way, tiny babies swinging from their shoulders in loose cotton papooses. Some carry woven palm-leaf baskets laden with okra, bananas, and mangoes. Others just stand there and watch us go by, one arm slung casually over a cow's neck.

Incidentally, we've been here almost twenty-four hours already and I've yet to see a man do this: shoulder anything, carry anything, or sling his arm over a cow's anything. Every time you lay eyes on a guy on Tanna he's either loafing around laughing with his pals, sitting on the ground in a watchful stupor, or dawdling among the trees, swinging a zig-zaggy tree branch he's turned into an improvised weed whacker, which he clearly thinks gives the impression that he's busy mowing, when it's obvious to everyone that it's just a useless stick and the women are doing all the bloody work.

In time, the heavily wooded trail narrows to the point of being impassable and we have no option but to continue on foot, each of us lugging a piece of Camera Mark's equipment: the tripod, a battery pack, a light, a bag with filters and lenses in it.

Eager to be a team player, I do my bit. I carry his Pepsi.

"Wait here, Cash," Director Mark orders after a few yards. "I don't want you to see what's up ahead." That's how they maintain the element of surprise.

Waving everyone on, he leads them through a clump

of bushes until they disappear, abandoning me in the woods alone.

The setup for one of these shows is complicated. It takes ages to block out camera angles and to frame things—where the sun is, where I will walk, where the crew will stand so as not to be in shot, basically fielding all possibilities before we get around to shooting anything. That's the problem with spontaneity; it takes so much planning.

Usually, while all of this is going on, I'm left by myself.

I don't complain. I'm aware it has to be this way. It's the hook of the show, not knowing where I'm being taken. But that still doesn't make the alone times any easier to deal with. We've shot just three episodes so far, but already there's an odd "us and him" situation developing. If this continues I can see us eventually splitting into two groups: the *in* group and the *out* group. The *out* group being me. It's a shame, but as host of the show I'm not strictly a member of the crew, so I tend to be excluded from all meetings, discussions, excursions, planning lunches, and so on. As a result, all too often I'm left limping along behind the herd like a lone, bewildered wildebeest—or a bewilderbeest, even—forgotten, ignored, and doubtless flagged by predators as an easy kill.

It's not a lost cause yet, but quite clearly, in the name of self-preservation, I have to do *some*thing to heal this rift.

As I continue to loiter among the trees in the hot sun, brushing flies from my face, trying to come up with an ingenious idea for yokoing my way into their beatles, I spot Tasha walking by a gap in the foliage up ahead.

"Hey, what's going on back there?" I call out to her, being extra friendly.

"You'll see. Not long now." And she disappears again.

"Oh," I whimper. "Okay."

My clothes are starting to itch. The crew's lucky, they can

wear what they like during the shoots; I can't. And unfortunately, to the daffy lady hired to buy my wardrobe in L.A., the words "steamy jungle setting" must have conjured up images of *A Passage to India* and of me flitting about the set in light cocktail attire, the sort of thing one might wear to a polo match, for instance. Or in court when I'm suing her. Because I'm standing here in ninety-four-degree heat in a thick shirt, heavy beige pants, and white sneakers, roasting.

Eric reappears to give me instructions, which he does with the mild disdain of a Best Buy assistant who's been asked one too many questions about photocopy paper and is about to snap. "Alright, here's what's going on. It's the opening of the show. You've wandered out of the airport and you stumble into this place."

"How?" I ask.

"What d'you mean, how?"

"I've just landed. The airport's fifteen miles away. How could I have stumbled fifteen miles in two minutes? It's not—"

"Pah! We'll shoot a walking montage later. Nobody will ever know."

"They won't?"

"Nope."

"Oh."

"When Mark shouts 'Action,' you walk out of here"—indicates bush—"and along here"—indicates pathway—"and into there"—indicates large clearing beyond. "Then you'll find . . . er . . . well, you'll see . . . just talk to . . . whoever . . . Okay?"

"Okay."

"Oh, and wipe your forehead. You're sweating."

No shit.

Thirty seconds later, Mark's piercing whistle ricochets among the trees.

"Action, Cash!"

Not knowing what to expect, I follow the path around the bushes and step into a dreamy, dappled glade overhung by magnificent banyan trees, their branches a matrix of spindly fingers locked together into a protective atrium above my head, in the shade of which stands a huddle of topless women wearing ankle-length grass skirts. *Alo!* At Director Mark's request, they have their arms folded over their boobs. It's either that or we pixelate them later, to spare the blushes of puritanical Christian watchdog groups in the American Midwest who have set themselves up as the sentinels of good taste, not only for themselves, but for the rest of us as well, and for whom tits, I'm told, are taboo.

"Anyone here speak English?" I ask breezily.

"'Es."

A young man, conveniently placed on the edge of the glade, steps into my eyeline. Athletic, he has a beautiful round face carved into a goofy gap-toothed grin. His name is Tom, he reveals, soft-spoken to the point of being inaudible.

"Hi, Tom. My name's Cash. You speak English?"

"'Es, I speak English," he says.

Of course you do, I thought to myself. It's television!

Did I mention that, unlike the women, Tom's *completely* naked?

Actually, that's not quite true. He's wearing just the one item: a provocative, permanently erect sheath made from coconut leaves tied in place with a string around his waist like a thong and decorated down below with a dangling sporran of hay. This is a *nambas*. I don't want to go into details, but let's just say that it does for the penis what buns do for hotdogs. It's also considered a powerful male fertility symbol. *Nambas* come in all different dimensions. Tom's, I'd say, is about the size of a small car-jack handle.

"You come and meet the chiff," Tom says.

"Chiff?"

"The village chiff. You meet him."

"Oh, the *chief*! How great, yes, I'd love to. Thanks."

Like a kitten mesmerized by a metronome, I walk into the village, trying not to look down at his horny verticalness, while completely aware that I am doing so roughly every three and a half seconds.

All around, suspicious eyes peer out at me from huts as I stumble by. Frightened kids take a step back into the safety of their mothers' arms. Men, all of them naked too but for their *nambas,* stop what they're doing (which is nothing, of course) and watch.

The first building we come to is a dusty shack known as a *nakamal,* or tribal meeting house, on the porch of which someone has mysteriously left a sack of screwdrivers.

"Cash, this is our chiff."

"What is? Oh—*this*!"

Wizened and wrinkly, with a foaming froth of sepia-gray hair on his head and two smaller froths at his jowls, it's the oldest person I've ever seen in my life! Little more than a loose arrangement of bones tied together at the neck, he has a craggy tobacco-yellowed smile and an arced spine crushed by the years into an unyielding parabola. Because of this, he crouches. Out of respect, I crouch too. Around here they call the chief Bigman. *Yeremanu*. A word meaning "what he says goes." *Everyone* defers to him, and therefore so must I. Chiefs are thought to possess great magic powers, so you don't want to get on the wrong side of one—say, by mistaking him for a bag of tools, for instance.

"Hello there, I'm Cash. How lovely to meet you," I beam, reluctant to shake his hand lest it turn to dust. "This is an honor for me."

Off to one side, Tom translates.

"How old is he, the chief?"

"One hundred seven years old."

"One hundred seven??"

"'Es."

While my facial expression may say I'm impressed, privately I'm thinking, jeez, what a bitter *curse* longevity is. I never, ever want to live as long as this, or to look like him if I do. If I am not dead by the age of ninety I want to be stuffed in a box and cremated anyway. To hell with the formalities. Then, after a small celebration for grieving friends, my ashes—and I've made an express provision for this in my will—are to be taken to Yorkshire in the north of England and flung in my sister-in-law's face. She knows why.

After an awkward moment of introspection, the conversation with the chiff draws to a close. "Anyway, nice to have met you." I smile.

And the smile is returned warmly. Lovely man.

"How come the chief lives to one hundred seven?"

"Because we eat food and we live long," Tom says, walking away.

"The secret to longevity is in the food?"

"'Es. Come, I show you the garden."

Visiting Yakel Village is like stopping off at Bedrock and saying hello to the Flintstones, except that Yakel is ten times more primitive. There are no cars—not even ones with holes in the bottom that you move with your feet. The houses are ramshackle huts like thatched tents made of braided sticks, cane, coconut leaves, and mud. And your waste disposal isn't a hog sitting under the sink with its mouth open. Though that's only because they don't have sinks.

Five families live here altogether, according to Tom. Roughly 140 people per family. Each man in the tribe has up to nine children, and, believe me, it shows. There are little kids everywhere, and they're free-range, running about as they please, climbing trees, idly sitting on the ground picking nits out of their mother's hair, or, in some cases, brandishing giant machetes as long as my arm, with which they expertly slice the skin off wild grapefruit, while coyly examining me from the corner of their eye, showing curiosity without wanting to appear to. Where there aren't children there are chickens, piglets, and stray dogs. The dogs are just rib cages with legs, snuffling for scraps between the huts, and, when they find none—because if there were scraps, the kids, chickens, or piglets would surely have snapped them up by now—they flop down exhausted in a dusty corner, looking like there's only a fifty-fifty chance they'll ever get back up again.

We emerge from the cover of trees onto a sward of parched grass.

"Come—see this." Tom directs me to one of the larger huts. "This is our kitchen."

Inside, it's dark. A dying fire coughs sparks that only by some miracle don't set the straw roof alight. Grapefruit and cabbages and a few vegetables I can't name are stacked up on makeshift stick shelves, alongside crude pots and pans.

"You have one kitchen for the whole village?"

"No, for one family," he says. "Every family has its own kitchen."

"Oh, okay. And who does the cooking?"

For a moment Tom looks totally affronted by the question. Isn't it *obvious*?

"Women!" he retorts brusquely. "The women do it." And to underscore the point, in case I'm in any doubt at all, he adds, "*Not* the men."

"Well, of course, *not* the men," I respond, adding a curt, "Perish the thought." Though it's possible my sarcasm is lost on him, because he just shrugs and walks out.

"Hey—dude, over here!"

Director Mark shouting to Camera Mark. He's found a large pig for us to film. The poor creature is cooped up in a tiny circular cell made of shaved wooden posts that allows it to perform the occasional three-point turn, but not much else.

Tanna society is rooted in subsistence farming. The people survive by traditional means: hunting, fishing, rearing animals, growing their own fruit and vegetables. There's a strong social hierarchy, or *hunggwe,* here, and a man's standing in that hierarchy is determined in the main by how many pigs he owns. The greater the number of pigs in his yard, and the fancier their tusks, the richer he is considered to be.

"How long does the pig have left to live?" I ask, watching the poor creature slam into the pen with its head, then its ass, then its head again.

"If you want to make the pig big and fat," Tom says, "three or four yizz."

My God! *Three or four years* wedged in a space that size—it's barbaric.

"And how long has it been now?"

"Three yizz."

Ah. So the nightmare's almost over.

"In our village," Tom continues, misreading my anxious hand-wringing as an invitation to please tell me more, "we buy the wife with the pigs."

"So," I say, already pursuing a new train of thought, "what happens if you become sick and . . ." Half a pace later I stop dead. What did he just say? "You buy your wife and she comes with a pig?"

"No—you buy *with* the pigs," he corrects.

"Ohhhhhhhhh, you buy your wife *using* pigs!"

Seems the women in this culture are not only made to do all the back-breaking heavy-duty work that men won't touch, but they're also traded on the open market like chattels. The average wife costs between six and ten pigs, I'm told. Worst of all, and the biggest irony yet: among the many chores the women in Yakel have to complete each day is . . . guess what! Yes, they have to tend to the pigs. *The very pigs* they're going to be traded for later on.

No wonder the life expectancy of females in one of these *kastom* villages is relatively short. Whereas a man may live to 107, many women die prematurely. And when they do, I have no doubt they consider it a blessed relief.

It's devilishly hot out here. The midmorning sun licks my back, leaving a trail of sweat down my spine and causing my spiffy Banana Republic cocktail slacks to stiffen like cardboard before gluing themselves to my legs. At every turn, kids and their mothers stop and stare, amazed to see a white guy stroll through their remote village followed by a TV crew. And look, he's wearing trousers! In this heat. How crazy is that?

Believe me, indigenous people, I hear you.

The path down to the garden is a deep groove worn through the forest by countless feet over countless centuries. It slopes gently in some places but is almost perpendicular in many others, and pitted with holes, roots, and a million other opportunities to injure yourself.

"Tom and Cash—stay there. Don't move."

Camera Mark, doubtless relishing the challenge of possibly tripping and breaking his neck, races ahead, chunky legs covering the terrain in small leaps, dragging the rest of the crew behind him, slithering wildly over loose stones, skidding into foliage, and becoming entangled in vines. Twenty feet away, he braces himself against a sapling.

"Okay, and . . . action. Go, Cash. Walk toward me."

Tom is barefoot. Yet he springs across the rock-strewn terrain many times faster than I do, and with only a fraction of the histrionics, even offering to take my hand at one point and lead me over a gulley by means of a fallen tree trunk.

"You're so remote out here in the jungle. Do you not find yourself," I ask him as we go, "wanting things from the outside world?" Would he not like a television, for example?

Sensible question. I mean, he can see how much fun we're having making the show. Who wouldn't want to set their TiVo to watch this debacle every week?

After a moment's thought he shakes his head. "No."

"So you've *never* seen television?"

"No. We have no TV, no radio either."

"That's unbelievable. So what do you sit and stare at each evening?"

"Stare?" he asks, not even amused. "We don't stare. We don't like TV. We like the life." And without offering specifics, he walks on.

To the naked eye, the Yakel garden is a lush and shambolic but quite unspoiled wilderness on the banks of a chuckling stream. Sadly, I'm not a botanist (And I'd be grateful if you'd stop telling people I am. *Tank yu.*), so quite honestly I have no idea what the trees here might be: Mulberry? Banana? A pandanus or two? Not a clue. It's certainly beautiful, though. Serene, sunny, extremely green, and . . . a mess.

Every day, the men of the tribe come down here, take out their machetes, and harvest fruits, vegetables and . . . something else. Something very special. A root I've never heard of before today, called *Piper methysticum.* Popularly known as kava.

Kava is Polynesian chloroform, part of the black pepper family, a distant cousin of the coca plant, and the angry ex-wife of marijuana. Apparently, it's either chewed or mixed with water, then drunk to combat stress and anxiety, treat cramps, or chase away migraines. Or you can just get stoned on it—your choice.

Captain Cook himself was high on kava during his visit to these islands in Historical Times.[1] Even Pope John Paul

---

[1] The Past is divided into eight distinct periods, so that people sitting history exams can remember them better.

i. **Modern Times.** Covers the period generally known as "nowadays." Began about ten years ago and is still going on.

ii. **Yesteryear.** A sunny, carefree era, remembered only by lonely grandmothers and tiresomely chatty uncles, and which happened just long enough ago that it prevents you arguing with them, when gas was a penny a gallon, songs had tunes you could hum, acid reflux was still called indigestion, cigarettes were considered nutritious, and wars were fought for good reason.

iii. **Days Gone By.** An ill-defined time shortly before the birth of everyone alive today, spoken of with great fondness and recorded at length in books, but otherwise with no proof that it existed at all. For instance, Marconi is said to have invented the telephone in Days Gone By. Yeah, right.

iv. **Historical Times.** 1300 to 1870 A.D. Americans fought the Civil War. Shakespeare copied Francis Bacon's plays and sold them as his own. The fifteen laws of aerodynamics were written down. Captain Cook sailed the world, randomly renaming things, and was killed in Hawaii (renamed the Island of Sudden Stabbings). And *Vanuatu was discovered.*

v. **The Days of Yore.** 1000 to 1300 A.D. (Later merged with the Dark Ages to avoid confusion.)

vi. **Ancient Historical Times.** 5000 B.C. to 1000 A.D. Incorporates Biblical Times and the era of great ancient civilizations: Greeks, Ephesians,

II, who built a reputation on issuing broad statements of Christian policy so retrogressive in nature that they made sense only if you were totally wasted, was given kava when he came to the South Pacific years ago. Also, anyone who's ever stopped by Fiji on vacation has probably tried the commercial variety that's sold in bottles. But that's Fiji. Here in Yakel they don't have a commercial variety, it seems. Theirs is hard core, the real thing, no decaf. Pulped up into a liquid and drunk, it allegedly opens up a mystical bridge to the supernatural, putting you in touch with the spirits. According to tradition, kava is consumed only by the men of the tribe. It's their way of relaxing after . . . well, after a long day of relaxing.

"Here," Tom announces, diving into the undergrowth and pouncing on a clump of heart-shaped leaves, which he quickly tears aside. "This is kava."

After another little search, he picks up a tree branch off the ground, whittles it to a point, and hands to me.

"What do I do with this?"

Do?

Corinthians, Colossians, Romans, and a bunch of other people St. Paul wrote to. During this time, Buddha invented doing nothing and called it meditation, Vesuvius erupted, Atlantis sank, and aliens visited our planet and gave us Stonehenge, marijuana, pyramids, Scientology, fire, algebra, and wheels.

vii. **Time Immemorial.** A catch-all for the five thousand years before history really got started, when nobody can account for what happened, but certain things—things that were showing promise and would come into their own later on—are thought to have had their origins. Man, for instance. And fish. Otherwise, lots of waiting around.

viii. **Prehistoric Times.** Started with the Big Bang and lasted for hundreds of millions of years. Made famous by its colossal ice ages and the Jurassic Era, *when dinosaurs ruled the earth.* Grrrr.

For a few moments, the words just kind of hang in the air like damp washing.

Then the penny drops.

Oh no! No, no, no. Are you crazy? I don't dig, I'm sorry.

But this is TV. And I'm afraid on TV there's a rule: The host must participate in all activities whether he wants to or not. So, egged on by Eric and both Marks, I crouch and with great reluctance start hacking away at the soil.

Kava—same as most Stephen Sondheim musicals—doesn't yield its fruits without a struggle. First you must find it—and, as I said, in a garden as haphazard as this it could be anywhere—then you must disinter it, but *carefully,* because the roots, where the narcotic compounds lie, are fragile and snap easily.

"Dig down!" Tom urges after watching me get nowhere for a while.

"I *am* digging down," I snap back, scratching feverishly at the ground with my stick. "Look at me! There's nothing here."

It's no use. Whatever soil I manage to extract from the hole just rolls right back in again. It's like having an expensive mortgage. I'm spending all my time paying off the interest, making no inroads into the principal. This is my *Sunday in the Park with George.*

"Use the stick."

"*I'm using the stick, Tom!* But nothing's happening."

To make matters worse, the cheap sunblock I slapped on my forehead earlier in the day is starting to mingle with my sweat. Together they form salty rivulets that dribble into my eyes, stinging and blinding me. And Tom is no help. He just stands there, berating me with his eyes, the way he might if I were, for instance, one of his wives.

"Dig down with the stick," he urges again.

"TOM—I *AM* DIGGING DOWN WITH THE BLOODY

STICK! Look at me, I'm digging down." Even as I'm proving my point by dragging it hard across the ground, the damn thing snaps. Sonofabitch!

"What happened?"

"What d'you think happened? I broke my stick!"

"Wait—I find you another."

"No, no, it's okay, I'm good," I leap in. "You know what?" And I let out a long sigh. "Maybe I'm more suited to doing women's work."

"No," he says very firmly. "Men dig kava only. Not women."

Thirty seconds later, with sweat cascading off my chin, I quit again. "Come on, Tom, can't we skip kava for today? Let's go without. Let's have bananas instead."

Well, that does it! You'd think I'd just made a casual offer to castrate him with his own machete, because instantly the most peculiar silence envelops us.

Go without kava? These people *never* go without their kava. It's the mainstay of their life; their savior, their mistress, their reward each night for making it through another miserable twenty-four hours in this humid, monstrous pit of hell.

Through a halo of circling flies, I see him glowering. Until, in the end, perhaps realizing that, left to the likes of me, nothing will ever get done—which is a pretty fair assessment—he crouches down by the hole and pitches in, shovelling dry earth aggressively with his bare hands, until . . .

Success!

"Hey look, we've done it!"

. . . we uncover a set of bagpipes.

Yay!

Three gentle tugs, and out pops a bulbous vegetable with a dozen frayed woolly tendrils dangling from the bottom like dreadlocks. All of a sudden, the mood in the garden lightens.

The addict has his fix; he's happy again. And, after repairing the damage we've done, kicking the loose soil back into the hole and patting it down, we set off on the long steep trek home, with Tom dangling the dirty, disgusting object at his side proudly, like a severed head.

"So how about a telephone?" I begin again. "Wouldn't you want a telephone?"

"No."

"A car?"

"No."

"How about electricity?" I try to explain electricity, and how it's all the rage where I live. "Come on, you've got to want that. Refrigeration, air conditioning, lights. Who doesn't want lights?"

But he's resolute. "No."

"A microwave oven, a toaster . . . ?"

"No, no."

"Do you even know what they are, Tom?"

No. But even if he did, something tells me he wouldn't want them.

"We like the life," he repeats. "We like our culture. Our *kastom.*"

Kastom refers to customs (forgive me if I translate these difficult words for you): the many diverse traditions the tribe adopted centuries ago and which it insists on sticking to even today, despite overwhelming evidence that there may possibly be a better way.

Tanna was first settled in about 400 B.C., during Ancient Historical Times, by Melanesians from neighboring islands. These early pagan tribes were a superstitious bunch. They believed that mankind was evolved from volcanic rocks—which was a bit of a hard sell, I'm guessing, even then. The world, they claimed, was created by a rock spirit called Wuhngin who lived inside a mountain. Wuhngin decreed that it was the woman's job to do the household chores, from cooking to gardening, while the men, he insisted, should focus all their efforts on sitting and not much else. Well, suffice it to say, the menfolk *worshiped* Wuhngin.

Skipping forward now a couple of thousand years to Historical Times . . .

During the sixteenth and seventeenth centuries, wave after wave of missionaries set sail from Europe, especially Portugal and Spain, to indoctrinate the people of the South Pacific with Christianity. The place became a virtual revolving door for every Tom, Dick, and Pedro with a Bible and a torch to read it by, determined to save "the savages" and their souls by doing away with their ancient version of reality—a rich heritage of pagan folklore, dances, beliefs, ceremonies, as well as a bunch of other stuff they were absolutely sure God wouldn't approve of, the way Christians so often are—and replacing it with their own.

"Listen up, indigenous people, for I give you the Book of Matthew, Chapter 1," the missionaries would stand on the beach and say in pidgin English, only to find to their astonishment—"*¡Ay, Dios mio!*"—that they were met, not by the naive, grinning, warmhearted Polynesians they'd seen in all the brochures, but rather by a bunch of violent men and women who resented complete strangers waltzing in and trashing their culture.

"*¡Ay, mierda!! Nos están tirando cocos!*" ["Shit! They're throwing coconuts at us!"] the Spaniards cried as a rain of missiles showered down upon their heads. "*¡Huye! ¡Huye! ¡Ay! Todos al bote. ¡Ay, ay!*" ["Flee! Ouch! Everyone back to the boat. Ouch!"]

And quite honestly, if teams of very determined missionaries over many centuries couldn't change these people and their customs, no way is a U.S. TV crew going to.

"We like the life," Tom says again.

As if to answer my further unspoken questions, he adds: *no,* the tribe doesn't seek progress; *no,* the tribe doesn't feel it's missing out by not having modern amenities; and *no,* the tribe doesn't regret being out of step with the world beyond these shores. And that's their final word on the matter. At least until this policy comes up for review, in, say, another ten million years or so.

Back in the village again, it's lunchtime. In the spirit of the show, that means I have to eat what the tribe eats, which is something called *laplap,* Tanna's national dish. It's a lasagna/pudding cooked in a fire pit and fashioned from layers of cabbage, bananas, coconut milk, and a little more soil than I'm used to, all bound up in a parcel of coconut leaves. A big parcel it is, too. About the size of a tractor seat. It takes six women and a child to maintain the fire and pile on the rocks that weigh it down, then to take the rocks off again and lift the *laplap* free of the smoldering ashes onto a tree stump, where it's hacked into individual slabs using bush knives and transferred to a plate. And when I say plate, I mean leaf.

"It's good," Tom says, chomping on his *laplap.* "You try."

Staring at the thick wad of steaming green slime in my hand, I'm seriously inclined to give it a miss. But Mark and Eric are looking on and there's a camera trained on me. So, taking a deep breath, I close my eyes and sink my teeth deep into it.

Hm. He's right, actually, it's not bad. Bit dry, bit gritty, but okay. For all the world like chewing a tractor seat, in fact.

The crew, for its part, is spared the complex soily goodness that is *laplap.* For them, the hotel restaurant has packed two heavy-duty plastic coolers with sandwiches, fresh fruits, potato chips, and chocolate bars. These, plus bottled waters and sodas, are unloaded off the back of the van in a clearing, allowing everyone to take a well-deserved break. Except for Director Mark, who's not feeling well, his already gaunt face suddenly geisha pale. Cursed with a rogue digestive tract, he always seems to be sick with something. Right now he maintains he's not really sick at all; he just needs to take a dump somewhere, and then he'll be fine.

"Go over there," Camera Mark tells him. "Crap in the woods. Nobody will see."

It is, after all, what everyone else does around here.

The patient is horrified. "Dude, are you *serious*? Look at this place. It's unsanitary. Nah—I'll wait 'til we get back to the hotel."

And, clutching his stomach, he turns his back on the food and retreats to the van, where he sits half in, half out for the next twenty minutes, staring forlornly at the ground.

A big feature of each episode in the series is that I must find a generous stranger to give me a bed for the night. The challenge is to get them to offer it. Once they agree to that on principle, my job is done; I'm not required to actually sleep there. After all, this is entertainment, it's not a survival show; the audience isn't going to care whether I stay 'til morning or leave after ten minutes. All that matters is that someone makes the offer.

In this instance, the "bed" Tom has set up for me is a dirty strip of coconut matting on the ground in the corner of a hut. A dark hut at that. A dark hut filled with spiders, and crawling with licorice-colored beetles and ticks and fleas and God knows what else.

"It'll be okay, I'm sure," Eric says, not sounding sure at all. At the same time he scans the hut with his flashlight and finds, clinging to a beam right above where I'd be sleeping, a large six-legged green *some*thing with huge red bulging eyes.

"What the hell is that?"

Nobody's able to say. Some kind of land-based lobster, possibly?

Even Tom draws a blank. Whatever it is, it's yet one more reason why I won't be sleeping here for any length of time. And also why we must stop nuclear testing in the Pacific. That thing was probably a squirrel once.

Aside from the irradiated-wildlife issue, the pillow Tom has given me has been improvised out of half a log sawn from a tree.

Half a log!!

Well, I'm sorry. I don't do logs. I don't do bugs. I don't do mutated squirrels. And I don't do coconut matting covered in spiders. If the crew thinks they're leaving me here for twelve hours while they return to a five-star beach resort and sleep under mosquito netting between freshly starched cotton sheets tonight, they have another thing coming. And for once Eric agrees. So the decision is made that, since staying the night here might endanger my life, and since not killing the host is a priority on this show—otherwise there won't be any future ones—we'll just grab a few shots of me snoozing on the ground in my spiffy shirt and casual trousers, and that will be it.

The final scene we need before we leave Yakel is the kava ceremony . . .

"Where you'll get to drink kava, Cash."

"Oh no I won't."

I'm adamant about that. No drugs for Sir. If necessary I'll pretend.

. . . which we've been told takes place at sundown. That gives us an hour to kill. Rather than waste it, Todd and both

Marks take off on a circuit of the village to shoot B-roll, leaving me and Tasha to tidy away the lunch things.

B-roll is an important part of making a travel program. You see it a lot on TV. It's filler, basically—pretty, scenic shots of mountains, rivers, banyans, skeletal dogs, pigs, children, flowers, plus, whenever possible, a few shots of the host looking hunky (this is the bit I like!) as he strides purposefully across a beach, or scales precipitous cliffs, or marches with confidence down hillsides without falling (after several attempts), waving to total strangers who have no idea why he's waving, peering into people's homes uninvited, or just picking stuff up off the ground and staring at it intently in a way that suggests he's interested, when really he's not at all.

Once the boys have gone and we're alone, Tom bums a cigarette off Tasha, then he and I sit together quietly on a log, watching wild pigs chase dogs through shafts of sunlight, and dogs chase squealing children back the other way.

"You smoke, Cash?" Tom asks, taking a long drag of his cigarette.

"No. I don't."

And that, one would think, would be the end of that conversation. We can move on to more interesting topics: "How about iPods? Wouldn't you want an iPod?"

But my response apparently has hit him like a crossbow dart between the eyes. "*You don't smoke?* Really?"

You should see the guy's face. The incredulity.

"No, Tom, I don't smoke."

"But why you not?" he asks, audibly expelling a long blue plume into the air as a tempting example of how manly he looks and how majestic a true warrior can seem when immersed in a toxic cloud of gas. It seems that, here in Yakel, smoking goes hand in hand with "living the life," even as it's steadily shortening it.

"Oh, I dunno . . . because it's bad for you, maybe?"

"Bad??" His howling laugh pinballs around the canopy above our heads. "No, Cash," he says earnestly. "Smoking is good. A good thing. Good for men."

"It is?"

"Es. Very good for men. Men smoke." To emphasize this he crooks his arm and does a Spartacus muscle-clench gesture with it. Men smoke—grrrr!

Of course, *this* is where they'd benefit from television reception. Documentaries are handy for filling in the blanks. But for once I bite my tongue.

Still shaking his head in disbelief that we're even having such a ridiculous conversation, Tom stands up and vanishes into the trees, sidestepping a young woman bouncing a naked baby in her arms. As I watch him go, my eyes switch to the baby. In that moment, it expels a thick projectile of greeny-brown diarrhea from its ass, hosepipe-style. Then another. BLEEEEECCCCCHHHHHHH! A fecal torrent of such abundance that it cascades in a viscous stream over the mother's shoulder, down her arms and the backs of her legs.

Grossed out, Tasha takes in a sharp gulp of air behind me. Then, before it's even fully registered on any of us what just happened, a small dog, one of those emaciated bag-of-bones animals I saw roaming the village earlier, scurries out of the trees, clearly unable to believe its luck. Before the pigs can come running over, the dog wraps itself around the mother's feet and begins gobbling up the elasticated tongues of shit dripping from her arm.

Too stunned to recoil, too sick to throw up, I just stand there, staring, hand clutched to my mouth, thinking to myself, "*This* is the life? Seriously?"

5

Fat Kid

Coming up with the concept for *All Washed Up* turned out to be the easy part. Next, it had to be fleshed out into a full-blown TV series (the act of *watching* television taking a different set of skills to actually *making* it, apparently), and since I had no idea at all how to do that, a creditable production company needed to be found, one with experience making travel shows that could help me fully crystallize my vision.

"I've worked with these guys before," The Thumb said one day, calling from his office on the East Coast to tell me he was hooking me up with some old friends of his. *"They have an excellent track record. Always produce great stuff for us. Maybe you could go for a coffee with them, hang out, see how you get along . . ."*

He was confident he'd found a good match: the production company's many years of experience combined with my absolute confusion about what was happening to me being the perfect recipe for making quality TV.

"And what if we don't get along?"

"Hey, let's not be negative. We're gonna make a great show. I've given them your number. I'm sure there's gonna be a chemistry there. Let—"

"And if there isn't?"

"—me know how it goes. Always feel free to call me. Bye."

The meeting couldn't take place for two weeks. (According to my imaginary calendar, I was fully booked until then.) When it did, it happened in a Starbucks in Santa Monica.

I arrived first.

Soon after, The Thumb's friend showed his face. Turned out to be a real ball of fire, bursting through the doors in a typhoon of creative urgency, chest out, dagger eyes darting this way and that, looking like he'd just been hit by a car and flung twenty feet.

"HEY, CASH!" People glanced up from their coffees. "HOW'S IT GOING?"

An attractive man in his mid-thirties, he was five-foot-eight in person (seven feet or more in his own head), with a round Hawaiian face and spiky black hair pulled back from a dickering hairline that seemed undecided whether to stay or go. High-octane, intense, and driven, he was at once Goliath to my David, Argentina to my Falklands, Nintendo to my Etch-a-Sketch, and cartoonishly masculine, the way so many of these Hollywood type A guys tend to be, which I always find amusing. As if they've spent the past twenty years stockpiling testosterone, anticipating a shortage.

"I'VE HEARD A LOT ABOUT YOU. *A LOT!*"

"Really?" Stepping up to the counter, I took out my billfold . . .

"NOW, WHAT ARE YA HAVING?"

. . . and quickly put it away again. Well, you don't want to seem pushy.

Once we had our drinks, we retired to the smokers' patio, where the natural cacophony of the guy's voice would blend in with the traffic and not distract other patrons.

Clad in designer jeans and a figure-hugging black cotton V-neck—the kind worn by superheroes, and also by people who've been told "you look good in that" as a joke—his body was thin and serviceably buff while somehow hinting at an old weight problem. Not sure why. Just the way he handled himself—that classic fat-kid trick of being *extra*-extrovert to compensate for childhood insecurities.

"The network's VERY excited about this show," he said after we sat down. "And I love the concept as well. It's great."

It certainly is, I thought. That's why it's doing so well for CBS.

"What other programs have you produced?" I quizzed him.

"Oh, a whole bunch of great stuff."

He was a successful freelancer with irons in fires all over L.A., he said, reeling off a long list of shows he'd worked on, none of which I'd ever heard of. Nor can I recall anything about them, except that they ranged from (a few) mainstream ratings-winners to (mostly) low-end reality series with names like *Celebrity Tools, Splurge!, Extreme Dwarf Makeover,* or somesuch nonsense. I really wasn't paying attention.

TV is awash in programs like these. The kind of series where you'd swear they arrived at a campy title first, then somehow devised a concept to fit around it.[1] Cheap, mind-

---

1 Who among us, on a really bad night, hasn't almost fallen unconscious struggling through "fun-packed" home improvement shows called *Celebrity*

less, generic fluff that's fine in short bursts but ultimately forgettable, wheeled out by the networks each year to entertain . . . no, not entertain, *preoccupy* complete pinheads, and foisted on them for so long now that, numbed by mediocrity, especially the kids, they're no longer able to discern between quality and dross. Which is lucky, because dross like *Celebrity Tools* seems to be cheap and plentiful nowadays.

"Altogether . . ." a quick calculation on his fingers ". . . I have ten series in production currently. That's ten parties I can go to." His eager brown eyes slashed a triumphant Zorro *Z* across my face. "And I know *All Washed Up* is gonna be great too. Come on, drink up, I'll show you."

His office was located in Westwood, in a network of one-story buildings configured awkwardly like a badly thought-out puzzle. The moment I walked inside, my ears were assailed by a jangling timpani of slamming doors and rock rhythms blaring from TVs, like an electronic Middle Earth, a Tolkien netherworld of feverish endeavor. All around us, enthusiastic hobbit producers and hobbit technicians scurried back and forth, diving into rooms, out of rooms, shouting, laughing raucously. In cramped, twilit caves with their cur-

---

Tools or *Getting Hammered*? Or transparently sycophantic travel shows called *Backpakistan* (and its sequel *Backpakoslovakia*), in which some witless boob in shorts and a T-shirt hikes across whole continents without once being amusing, genuine, intelligent, insightful, funny, original, entertaining, or informative? Or game shows called *Matrimony, Acrimony, Alimony,* or *Battle of the Millionaire Amputees,* or, better still, *Phrenetic*! "Blindfolded experts try to identify celebrities by the bumps on their heads, with hilarious consequences." And the weird thing is, if you dare point out to producers or network executives that their shows are stupid, contemptible swill, they stare at you like *you're* the stupid one and you've simply failed to catch the many finer nuances of their truly excellent, groundbreaking, populist output.

tains drawn to make them seem subterranean, young, bleary-eyed hobbit editors sat hunched over keyboards, squinting at computer monitors while binge-eating Oreos and Frito-Lays. Lights flashed, pictures flickered, interspersed every so often with booming detonations of sound—snatches of dialogue or music—that would explode from speakers for an instant, then just as suddenly quit.

In public radio, we can boast nothing even remotely comparable. Our studios have a disturbing, almost sinister quiet to them. Confined to individual gray cubicles, armies of highly competent producers, reporters, and managers coexist for eight solid hours a day, crafting show after show, week after week, carrying out their work with almost catlike stealth, barely making a sound.

The same is not true in television. In *television,* where youthful urgency is considered a worthy substitute for being good at what you do, and making a great deal of noise is all too frequently mistaken for creativity in action, bedlam tends to be the norm.

In passing, I was introduced to the two owners of the company, seated in their respective caves. They'd be our show runners, Fat Kid explained, if the series got picked up. They seemed friendly enough, greeting me with exuberant cries of "Hiiiii! How are you? How's it going?" the way TV types do to people they've never met before.

"Okay! Great." Flinging himself down behind his desk with superhuman zeal, Fat Kid made up for lost time—hammered out an e-mail, scrolled down his BlackBerry, asked one of the hobbit PAs to fetch me a bottle of spring water, bit into an apple, glanced at an old black-and-white movie playing on a TV situated directly over my shoulder behind the couch, then finally, I guess once he'd run out of alternatives to actually speaking to me, turned his attention to the show.

"Assuming everything goes well with us"—meaning between me and him today—"then we have a go-ahead from the network to shoot a pilot. That'll be sometime in October. We've found this great little town in Central California. It's a Danish community called Solvang. Cute. Friendly."

"Is it on the ocean?"

"Er . . . no. No, it isn't. Why?"

"Then how can I be all washed up in it?"

"Ah. That's another thing. We're thinking of changing the title. The network wants you to arrive by a different means of transport every episode. Boats are too limiting. So one week a Chieftan tank, one week a plane, and so on . . ."

A Chieftan tank? Already I was nervous. I thought this was *my* show, so how come key decisions on *my* show were being made without consulting *me*?

"Cash, it's not your show," Fat Kid asserted commandingly. "It's *our* show now."

"It is?"

"Anyways, Solvang's a weird, weird little place. The people are very nice, though, so I'm sure, with your personality and your British charm, you can persuade someone to take you in, give you a bed for the night and some food."

Uh-oh. "You mean Danish food?"

"Yes. It's a Danish community."

"Does Danish food have lots of oil in it, d'you think?"

He had no idea. "Why?"

"Well," I said, "I have a problem with food."

"You can't eat food?"

"No, I . . ."

"All food?"

Not all food, *obviously,* you clown, otherwise I'd be dead. "No, just certain foods."

He directed a bemused, unblinking stare at me. "Such as?"

"Oh . . . milk, butter, bread, oats . . ."

I quickly rattled off the top ten "danger" items, reserving the biggest emphasis for my lifelong archenemy. "The *worst* one of all," I said, "the one I have to steer clear of at all costs, is oil. My body can't process oil or grease or fat."

"Why? What happens if you eat oil?"

"My cheeks and forehead break out in hives and I get sick."

It's true. Take two close-up photos, one of the moon's surface and another of my face after I've eaten a bucket of fried chicken, and I defy even NASA to tell which one is which. It's horrific. I can't go outside for days. Bane of my entire existence.

"Oh. Okay." With a worried "What the *hell* have I gotten myself into?" look, Fat Kid returned to checking e-mails.

"You know what?" I said, sensing I might have lost his interest. "Why don't I draw you up a list of things I can't eat?"

"Yeah, thanks," he said, typing, "why don't you?" And from there we quickly moved on. "Now, about shooting the pilot . . ."

6

Joe Versus a Volcano

After a great night's sleep at the hotel, I wake up with the larks. Or whatever the Vanuatan equivalent of larks is. Piglets, probably. Early anyway. Before five.

Following a filling breakfast of toast, tea, and grilled fish in the restaurant—plus another large bowl of raw grated cabbage, which I don't order; it just appears at the table—I drag on the same skanky clothes I wore yesterday[1] and make my way to the crew truck.

We have a new member joining our happy little band today. Joe, he's called, from the Vanuatan Tourism Bureau, a delightfully pleasant ni-Van native with a shy smile and a

---

[1] I'm given duplicates of every outfit, which I keep in my hotel room just in case, although for the sake of continuity it's considered best that I wear the same set of clothes for the whole show, however smelly, filthy, smeared, baggy, crumpled, creased, stained, or mutilated they might become.

whispery voice that brushes the ears like warm velour. Joe is bilingual, in the sense that he has a solid command of both English and Bislama-which-is-really-just-English-too-but-spoken-funny. His job on the show is to oil the wheels behind the scenes: help translate during interviews, explain to bystanders about the show, and, if needs be, to step in and bring calm to troubled waters in the event that the non-TV guy transgresses cultural boundaries and inadvertently offends the locals. Oh, as if!

First stop: a typical Tanna bush market.

The one Joe has chosen for us sits in a flat, stony recess at the roadside overlooking a narrow bay, with a dazzling beach and ocean view that, were I given to cliché, I would probably describe as idyllic. By the time we arrive, the place is rocking. People are sitting beneath the trees, chatting, gossiping. Kids play; teenagers, too cool to mix with their parents—some things are the same the world over—lounge in the hot sun, sheltering their eyes with cupped hands as they joke among themselves.

The main focus of everyone's attention seems to be a man with a bullhorn who is on his feet addressing the crowd, most of whom look like they rue the day that bullhorns went on sale in Vanuatu.

Eric sidles up to me. "So this is the idea." Feeling the heat, he runs a sweaty hand through his hair and adjusts his sunglasses up his nose. "It's the next day now. You've just left Yakel and you find yourself here in the market."

"You mean I just stumble upon the market?"

"Yep."

"Accidentally? The way I did with Yakel Village?"

"Yep."

"And you think the audience will buy that?"

"Yep."

I hope he's right. Even if you accept the possibility that

one man could have wandered through a foreign airport in this day and age and never shown a passport or visa; hiked fifteen miles over hostile terrain without food or water; spent a day and night with a lost tribe he just happened to come across in the jungle, then got up and walked another ten miles until he came, quite by chance, here, to this market, that still doesn't account for the fact that the whole thing was done without a single detour, map, or mishap, and without asking anyone for directions. Does nobody but me think that's weird?

Of course, I shouldn't be surprised. One thing I've noticed time and again while watching reality TV over the years is how there's usually one particular element missing from it, and that's reality. In order to make it work, the whole thing has to be shrouded in a gossamer of pretense and artifice, not quite lies and not quite truth, but certainly not reality, either—somewhere in between.

"Cash—*action!*"

Unsure where to begin, I saunter around the market with Camera Mark and Todd, his boom microphone held at arm's length above his head, shuffling alongside me.

The job of selling the produce seems to fall to the women. They spread a blanket on the ground in the cool shade of a tree, then lay out their wares, which sometimes might be as little as a single bunch of bananas, arranged in an eye-catching display. They then sit, supervising their stall, waiting for customers to drift by, while the men . . . okay, hands up, those who think this sentence ends with the words ". . . stand around watching them"?

Exactly.

An eclectic range of fruits and vegetables is on sale. Some I recognize: eggplant, cucumbers, taro, and I think papayas too. Others are oddly or obscenely shaped and a complete mystery. "What's this?" I ask, holding up a hairy, dirty stick.

Sadly, although I'm speaking Bislama—probably—the female vendors don't seem to understand a word I say. They simply stare up at me, baffled.

We stop shooting for a few moments to regroup and figure this out.

"Got it!" Director Mark has had a brilliant idea. "Where's Joe?"

Next thing he knows, the man from the tourist office has been conscripted into the show, and he doesn't seem too happy about it at all, especially since he's being forced to wear his dark blue Nike T-shirt back to front and inside-out to hide the logo. This is so that the network's sponsors back home won't start whining about how Nike's getting free air time and they're not. The result, however, makes Joe look slovenly. Not only are his seams showing at the shoulder, but the V of the neck is the wrong way round and the *Nike* check-mark logo is halfway down his back.

"Action."

And off we go. Take two.

On TV, Joe and I make convincing best buddies from the start, without any plausible explanation offered as to why, or where he came from. One moment he's not there, then suddenly he is, trotting at my side in his strange back-to-front shirt, smiling weakly, looking not the least bit excited by his meteoric rise from complete anonymity in local government to almost total obscurity on U.S. cable television.

"A bush market is the focal point of village life," he explains softly. "It serves as a meeting place, a place to find out what's happening in the community."

Today there's some kind of rally going on. A trestle table has been set up at the far side of the glade; behind it sits a panel of older men with serious expressions on their faces, waiting their turn. Another man, recently acquainted with the power of amplification and how it allows you to talk very, very loudly, drowning out anyone who disagrees with you, has been babbling for fifteen minutes or more through the bullhorn and sees no reason to stop now.

So what is this? What's going on?

"It's Women's Day," Joe elucidates. "We're trying to promote women's rights."

Well, what do you know!!! About time. *Finally,* someone is acknowledging the pivotal contribution women make to this society and campaigning to free them from their underdog—or, more accurately, underpig—status.

Curious, I ask, "What kind of rights do women have now?"

Thinking hard, Joe does his best to come up with an example, but eventually quits.

"Because," I help him out, "women are inferior to men here, right?"

"Yes, inferior," he nods, silently complimenting me on grasping the concept so quickly, and we walk on.

Shuffling from stall to stall, I sprinkle a fine dusting of ignorance over everything I touch, coming to rest by a heap of what appear to be lazily made cheerleader pompoms. "Joe, what are these?"

"Grass skirts. You wear them around your waist." Adding emphatically: "But *only* women."

"I know, because they're skirts. But what would happen if a man wore one?"

He's quite taken aback by this. "You'd . . . look . . . like a woman."

"And?"

Instead of replying, he visibly shudders, as if being mistaken for a woman, even as a joke, would be social suicide.

Moving on: "And what's this?" I pick up an ugly green bulb with tentacles that I recognize.

"This is the most important part of our *kastom,*" he explains, for the benefit of the audience. "This is kava. It's a traditional herb drink. See the roots here? That is the most important part of the kava. The young boys chew this . . ."

"Young boys? Why does it have to be young boys?"

"That is their job."

"So it's like homework?"

"Yes. Homework."

"Okay. The little boys chew the root. And?"

"And they spit it out onto a leaf, strain it into a coconut shell, mix it with water, and that's it, you have a delicious bowl of kava."

Wait a second. So kava, then, if I'm understanding this correctly, is a processed liquid that's first combined with the spit of little boys, then strained through an old sock or something, and finally served up in a shell to drink. Oh—my—God.

"And have you," I ask, indicating Joe, who looks too sensible ever to have put such a vile thing within three feet of his lips, "ever drunk any of this . . ."—unhygienic bilge—". . . stuff after it's been spat out by little boys?"

"Oh, yes," he says cheerfully. "Yes, I drink kava. Sure."

I think I may faint.

"What's the point of celebrating National Women's Day anyway?"

"They're trying to recognize women," Joe says.

"Who's trying?"

And then something dawns on me, something I didn't spot at first. Scanning the table at the head of the rally, I quietly count the number of female speakers on the panel.

Marking them off on my fingers, I estimate the total to be somewhere around . . . zero. The Women's Day committee is made up entirely of men!

"But of course!" Joe explains quietly. "Women aren't allowed to speak."

"Hang on. So you're telling me that the only people allowed to campaign for women's rights are . . . ?"

"Men. Yes."

Oh, that's just great.

"We would like to share everything in the home," one woman tells me. She's a gray-haired firebrand with a real sense of purpose about her. "So sometimes if the woman is sick, then men take over. Women is used to doing cooking morning, lunch, and dinner. We've decided we both have to do it."

"Good for you," I cheer.

"Women is used to being under men. We're starting to come up."

Excellent. "How long d'you think it'll take before you're the superior species?"

"Well, it'll be a long time, *obviously,*" she chuckles.

"Oh—why?"

"Well, we have just started last year."

"Last year?"

Oh God. Watching this great bulldozer of hope march off into the crowd, I turn to Joe and mumble despondently, "Nothing's going to change, is it?"

He gives me a strangely knowing look, but doesn't reply.

Farther along, in among the vegetables, we pass what for me is the most harrowing sight of the trip: a chicken trapped in a small cube-shaped cage made of sticks.

Let me define "small." First, imagine a chicken. Now

imagine a cage. Now shrink the cage until it's a lot smaller than the chicken, then lock the chicken in it anyway. For a culture supposedly in tune with Nature, the ni-Van abuse it a little too wantonly for my liking.

Distracted, I step out of the TV show for a moment and speak to Eric: "We need to release this thing."

"We can't release it, it's somebody's chicken," he says, and Joe agrees.

"So let's buy it. If we buy it, it's ours and we can release it. Please?"

Since, in the spirit of the show, I'm not allowed to have any money in my pockets, this makes me feel like a child asking for an advance on his allowance.

"You can't just release a chicken," Eric says. "It'll run into the road and get hit by a truck."

Yeah—so?

One part of me knows he's talking sense. The idiot part. The rest of me's with the chicken. I know if I were trapped in a cage with not a millimeter of latitude for movement, I'd probably fantasize the whole day about being hit by a truck. It's all I'd think about. It would be my dream. Anything but being inhumanely guantanamoed into a space no bigger than a cookie jar and left to die.

"But we can't just leave it here."

There follows a brief exchange of looks among the crew. It's a look I've seen before a few times. I spotted it first while we were shooting our Guadalajara show, when I was taken to a traditional Mexican rodeo, or *charreada*. Inside the ring, some cowardly men in stupid costumes were lassoing bulls with ropes, pulling them over, then dragging them along the ground for sport. I became so enraged by the despicable cruelty of it all that I started to cry—something TV hosts routinely don't do, I'm told—holding up filming for several minutes until I'd recovered my composure enough to carry on. So I know that look. It's secret crew language for exasperation. It means, "Uh-oh, the host is behaving like a baby again—what do we do now?"

What they *do* is placate me with sympathy, pretending that they are as concerned about the chicken as I am. However, these are the islanders' indigenous ways, and there's nothing we can do. "It's how things are. We mustn't interfere, and the chicken should be left to its fate."

"Aw, come on, guys," I find myself begging. "We can't just do nothing."

However, not only can we do nothing, but we're going to.

"Okay, then—what if"—I'm thinking fast—"we bought it and gave it away."

"Cash—it's a chicken!" Eric, already ruffled by the time it's taking to shoot this market scene, is losing his temper. "The person you give it to will probably eat it, so either way it's dead. Now, we're running late. Let's move on."

At my feet, unable to move more than a millimeter in any direction, the chicken, already half-dead in the baking sun, its head jammed against the bars, watches our argument with failing eyes. Eyes that say, "Just kill me. Please, do it now."

I hear you, pal. I work in public radio. Believe me, I know that feeling.

The remainder of the day and the morning of the next are given over to shooting B-roll, picturesque shots of the host ambling this way and that, up leafy slopes, through undergrowth, trekking along vast operatic beaches of black, volcanic sand that stretch all the way from here to a dark, jagged headland half a mile away, reducing me in the camera's eye to a mere polyp on the ocean's edge, as the two

Marks skillfully recapture the awe those original explorers must have felt in Historical Times when, thinking they'd found Australia, they rowed triumphantly ashore, expecting to be greeted with warmth and handshakes and beers and barbecued shrimp, but instead were showered with sharp stones and beaten with sticks. It's epic shots like these that, later on, will be cobbled into a montage and used to pad out the otherwise inexplicable gaps in the narrative between my arrival at the airport and—next minute—striding chirpily into Yakel Village, over fifteen miles away, with not a scuff mark or bead of sweat on me.

Another example: by all accounts, I'm in for a fabulous treat later this afternoon, though exactly what that treat might be is kept strictly under wraps. All anyone will say is that it's one of the things Tanna is famous for around the world, and it lies on the other side of the island, about twenty-five kilometers from our hotel, as the pterodactyl flies.

"No problem. And how do I get there?" I ask Eric.

Somewhat puzzled, he indicates the van.

"No, no—on the *show,* how do I get there? You said it's twenty-five kilometers away."

The logistics are farcical.

But for once Eric and I are on the same page about this. Transport, he tells me, will be provided.

Right on cue, a shiny green Toyota pickup rumbles to the curbside, one of our hotel's porters at the wheel. For a moment I find myself staring vacantly, first at Eric, then at the Toyota, then back at Eric again.

"This is Joe's truck," he explains. "You'll both be riding in back."

Ah, okay. "And is it *actually* Joe's truck?"

I mean, I don't claim to know too much about the guy's circumstances, but I *do* know he lives miles across the ocean on another island and therefore probably didn't drive here, even if the Toyota turns out to be amphibious, which I doubt. One of its windows is missing.

Wary that an ethical cul-de-sac may be looming, Eric pleads the Fifth. "Dude, look, don't worry, okay? Everything's super cool." And, with a disinterested flap of the hand, he walks off. "If there's a problem, you can fix it in post."[2]

Oh dear. Originally, I had higher hopes than this. I envisaged the series appealing to an older, more discerning crowd. Now, following a rethink, I'm reduced to praying that the bulk of our demographic is made up of idiots.

"Excuse me, is that an erupting volcano over there?"

One thing I didn't know about Vanuatu is that it has the misfortune to be sitting on the Pacific Ring of Fire, arguably the most unstable volcanic region in the world, a region, according to Science, that's been earmarked for cataclysmic destruction in the not-too-distant future. Good job we came here when we did.

---

2 TV talk. Postproduction is a period of controlled panic that takes place at the office after you're done filming a show. It includes editing, sound, voice-overs, digital effects, music, color correction, and so on. This is when you discover that half the stuff you shot doesn't make sense or won't fit together in an even semicoherent way, and as a result you'll be lucky to end up with even ten minutes of usable material to send to the network. When that happens, the director will blame the cameraman, the cameraman will blame the editor, the editor will blame the director *and* the cameraman, and, when still nobody can decide why the show isn't working, everyone will blame the host, who will run, crying, to the executive producer, who traditionally resolves the matter by firing everyone and bringing in a whole new bunch of people, who will go on to screw up the show too, but in different and previously unimagined ways. It seems like a very odd system, and not how I'd do things personally, but it works.

As evidence of this, there's some sort of steaming vent a mile away across the valley we're driving through. And not just any old steaming vent either—we're looking at Mount Yasur. I recognize it from the journey in on the plane. And also from *Survivor*! They made a whole episode about it. The ground shook, lives seemed to be in danger. It was very dramatic.

As we're watching, a couple of spectacular orange flashes light up the clouds around the peak, followed, a moment or two later, by a crackerjack bang that sends great gray cauliflowers of smoke outward and upward, joining earth to sky in a column of sulfurous gases that inspires at least one member of our party, I won't say who, to query out loud whether, given our easy expendability in the eyes of Nature, we really should be visiting a live volcano in the first place.

Just a thought.

Though not one that is heeded, alas.

To my dismay—okay, it was me!—minutes later we're right there on the volcano's eastern flanks, splashing across a shallow river onto a vast sloping plain of deathly gray ash, even as more violent explosions, like a series of quarry blasts, rend the air overhead, causing the earth to tremble.

Today's mystery destination, it turns out, is not the volcano per se, but a small village called Namakara, which cowers on its northern slope and is therefore, one might suppose, perpetually in harm's way. Clean and well laid out, its houses are solidly built of wood and volcanic soil, and appear to have been completed to the highest possible specifications, as laid down by perhaps the greatest master architects in history: the Three Little Pigs. As a result, the structures are able to withstand the force of a 120-mile-an-hour cyclone tearing through the jungle, or, to a much lesser extent, a wolf blowing on them. I would even go so far as to describe Namakara as quite charming and a good place to live.

Well, except for—

BOOOOOM!!!

—that. A guttural splutter-bang explosion flings a spray of red-hot debris into the sky, giving the crew a start. Nobody in the village even bothers to look up.

The inhabitants of Namakara have let go of the traditional grass-skirt-and-*nambas* look, succumbing to more progressive gear: light summer dresses for the women, shirts and long trousers for the men. At the center of the village, four tall flagpoles stand side by side before a neat wooden chalet. The flags hang limp. But even furled, I can tell that one of them, intriguingly, is the Stars and Stripes.

Joe leads me to the meetinghouse, a simple open barn structure with benches arranged along both sides, upon which a bunch of men are sitting quietly. The least prepossessing of them stands to greet us: he's small and middle-aged, with an endearing toothy smile when he does smile, but who otherwise boasts a dour countenance not uncommon among people living in the shadow of an erupting volcano. This is their Bigman.

"The chief will now explain the history of the village to you," Joe announces, getting ready to translate.

"Okay."

And, by golly, he does just that, fleshing out his story in the most phenomenal blow-by-blow detail, but in Bislama. Normally, this would pose no problem for me, of course. But out here in the more remote villages, everyday conversation tends to venture beyond the easy basics of *"alo," "tank yu,"* and *"banana."* People speak to each other in whole sentences, making it tough for foreigners to understand. Accordingly, seventeen hours later—at least, that's what it feels like—the last word he says is the only one that makes any sense to me at all. And that word is "John."

Huh?

"Er . . . I'm sorry, what?" I blink myself awake. "Who's John?"

A BRIEF SUMMARY OF WHAT THAT GUY WAS JUST SAYING

During World War II, Vanuatu, or the New Hebrides as it was still called at the time, was earmarked as a staging post for the U.S. military. At one point, three hundred thousand troops were stationed here at a base on the main island of Efaté.

On February 15, 1941, or so the story goes, an African American pilot from the Office of Strategic Services, on a mission to find places where the U.S. military could land their aircraft safely, proved why they shouldn't choose Tanna by crashing his, parachuting into the jungle like a flailing marionette, not in one of these newfangled chutes that refuse to open and let you hit the ground while you're still tugging at the cord, but with a real one, one that set him down gently in the vicinity of Namakara.

"Hi, how's everybody doin'? I'm John," he announced cheerfully to the gathering ni-Van, probably handing out tights and cigars. "John from America."

Awestruck, the natives instantly began fantasizing that he was the reincarnation of some ancient deity, possibly the rock creature Wuhngin, and started worshiping him.

Unfortunately for them, John's visit was short-lived. Just as they were thinking that their Dawn of Man existence was over and progress was within their grasp, the strange godlike airman was gone. No word on why. My guess is, his parachute got caught in a high wind and he was jerked up into the sky again. From here, as he was being yanked backwards through a chaos of undergrowth and branches, he yelled his lasting promise to the islanders: "Someday I'll return—ouch! Aaagh!—And when I—ouch!—do, I'll bring you—ow! Oh, God, that hurts so much—food and supplies, as well as—aaaaaaaaaghghgh!—twenty thousand soldiers, and we'll—OW! God*damn* freakin' nettles!—take y'all back—aaaagh, sheeeeeyit!!—to America with us—OW!—okay? Byeeeeeeeee—"

And away he went.

Now, why he would promise to return with twenty thousand soldiers remains a mystery. But many of the natives took him at his word. Fracturing into small religious groups, they raced to make lengthy preparations for John's return, building fake radio towers out of bamboo with tin-can microphones swinging from them, so that he could address his people when he got here; a runway for his aircraft with fake planes on it; and, just to be on the safe side, in case John came by sea, they built a harbor too. They even flew American flags. These are hoisted and lowered daily, while ni-Van men dressed as U.S. soldiers salute them with toy rifles. Finally, once the frenzy of preparations was over, they flopped down, breathless, on the grass, their hopeful eyes pinned on the sky, and waited for John from America to return to Tanna, bringing them his precious cargo of refrigerators and record players and deodorant and whisky, and possibly more tights.

And they waited.

And waited.

And continued waiting. For sixty-five years, and counting.

But John never came back.

Of course.

THE END

Six decades or so later, the cargo cults of "John Frum," as they're known ("Hi, I'm John *frum* America") are still waiting, their confidence not diminished one iota by the passage of time; still convinced that their heroic savior—who would be well into his eighties by now and probably on a walker—together with his twenty thousand elderly, decrepit storm troopers, and presumably a host of attendant caregivers as well, are up inside Mount Yasur, hiding in the crater somewhere, waiting for the right moment to emerge and distribute their largesse. (If you're interested, further details about cargo cults can be found in the book *John Frum, He Come*, by Edward Rice.[3])

"And did John Frum come?" I ask, once the story grinds to a close.

Silence. From Joe. From the Bigman. From the crew.

"Oh, I see. Well . . . never mind."

Once we're done interviewing the chief, one of the Marks floats the idea that we maybe should climb the volcano. That way, we can see if John Frum and his twenty thousand geriatrics are indeed up there loitering, can't we? And if they're not—duh!—then we simply come back down and break the news to the tribe, bringing their agonizing sixty-odd-year wait to an abrupt but long overdue end.

At that moment, behind us, an aerial river of belching smoke blocks out the sun.

"My Lord!" I gasp, too terrified to move. "Is it safe?"

---

[3] My own book refuting this—*Er . . . No He Not; It's All Made Up*—will be available in trade paperback next spring.

"Yes. It's safe." Joe nods. "The safest volcano in the world."

"The safest *about-to-erupt* volcano in the world?"

"Yes." He smiles and starts walking. "Come on."

Mount Yasur rises in a series of lurching terraces, scuffing the clouds at around a thousand feet or so. It's a daunting climb when you're not used to it—though, to be honest, it poses no problem for me and Joe. Following a brief saunter across the ash plain, we tackle the boulder-strewn slope for as long as is necessary to make us look butch and valiant; then, the instant the camera's off, we run back down the hill and drive the rest of the way by van.

After a short, jolting ride along a rough track, the driver draws to a stop in a parking area that's been leveled out of the hillside. From there we proceed on foot, pausing only when a particularly startling boom from up ahead sends dancing scree and gravel cascading past our feet.

"Are you absolutely sure it's not going to explode?"

I'm really having second thoughts about this.

Joe shrugs. "I can't guarantee it, no."

According to him, activity is about a Level 1 today. There are five levels altogether:

LEVEL 0: Practically dormant. Nothing to see here. Go back in your homes. (Its celebrity equivalent would be Enya.)

LEVEL 1: Normal activity. Occasional rumbles and tremors. Sounds dangerous, and alarmists are bound to overreact, but it's all for show. (Celebrity rating: Dixie Chicks.)

LEVEL 2: Moderate to high activity. Everyone, including alarmists, should start running. Evacuate the area, *don't* just hide under a table. (Think Rosie O'Donnell.)

LEVEL 3: Cancel your trip. We may have another Pompeii on our hands. Time to admit that the alarmists probably had a point. (Lily Tomlin.)

LEVEL 4: Run for your life! A full-on Barbra Streisand. Volcano making an unannounced comeback. Expect your charred remains to be featured on CNN.

Yasur demands respect. Tales abound of unsuspecting tourists who, paying no heed to its warnings, wandered up the side for a picnic, completely misjudging the peril they were in, and ended up being killed by lava bombs before they'd even unscrewed the lid off their Thermos.

BOOOOOOM!

Once again, the ground shivers. I make a grab for Joe and cling on to him, something he's clearly not used to. The ni-Van have been a little slow to embrace man-on-man action, even when it's quite innocent.

Following the all-clear, we rush up the last few feet of slope and emerge onto a path about four feet wide running a quarter of the way around the circumference of a crater four hundred feet across. And when I say the path is four feet wide, that's only in some places. In others it's as thin as a tightrope, skirting a one-hundred-foot drop.

B-BOOOOOOMMM!!

Several sharp blasts, like rapid pistol fire, launch mortars of fiery spume twenty stories into the air, creating phosphorescent wings of smoldering debris that shatter in every direction. Every direction, that is, but one—ours. Let's hope it lasts.

K-BOOOOOOM!

The sloping innards of the volcano are as barren as the moon. Inside the bigger crater, there's a smaller one, with a red-flaming fissure etched into the bottom that churns restlessly the whole time, as if the Earth has a bone in her throat and is trying to dislodge it, throwing up with each gargantuan belch a meaty phlegm of shimmering golden magma that splays through the air uncomfortably close to where we're standing.

B-BOOOOOOOOOOOOM!

"Whoah!"

Nothing emphasizes your insignificance, I find, quite as effectively as being close to some powerful object that could at any minute indiscriminately roll over and snuff you out.

"Walk this way," Camera Mark, completely unfazed, bawls into the wind, directing me to one of the narrower points on the rim. "Stand there. Then we can shoot the eruption as a backdrop."

"Nope. Sorry."

B-BOOOOOOOM! BOOOOOOOOOOOOOOOOM!

Pebbles and dust at my feet bounce in time with the detonations.

"Aw, c'mon. It's totally safe, just do it. Three paces back, then walk toward us."

"Nope. I'll fall."

There follows a Crew Look. Eric glances at Camera Mark, who glances at Director Mark. All three glance at Tasha. A round robin of disapproval.

"You *won't* fall, Cash. Come on, just three steps."

BOOOOOOOOOOOOOOOOOOOOOOOOOOOOOOOO OMMMMMM!!

"Aaaaagh!"

Loud cracks of what sound like thunder ricochet around me, as a bulging tongue of magma soars up in slo-mo, attempting to lick the clouds above us.

Excuse me—*hello?* Anyone feel like running for their life right now?

"Dude!" Bold, unshaken, as always, Camera Mark shouts, "Come on—hey, where are you going?"

His pleas are tinnitus in my head. I issue a few odd comments to Joe, for the benefit of the camera, about how awesome this all is. Then, gripped by blind terror, I race over the rim in precisely the opposite direction Mark's been pointing at, and down the hill again, to safety. My work is done here. I have what I came for. I can now say with incontrovertible certainty that there are neither angry spirits huddling in Mount Yasur's crater, nor twenty thousand American marines and their caregivers. I can't wait to see the glee on the faces of the John Frums when they hear that their hope all these years was false and their faith in America completely misplaced.

Wouldn't surprise me if they decided to reward me in some way for enlightening them, perhaps bestowing on me the status of god and savior. Y'know, now that the position is vacant 'n' all.

After sunset a slight wind picks up, rustling the leaves in ways that wouldn't sound creepy normally, only when an entire forest you can't see is closing in around you.

Darkness in the jungle falls faster than a collapsing highrise. When it does, your senses become drastically impaired. You find that your eyes, for example, which normally would adjust, don't at all, principally because . . . well, what are they going to adjust to? There's nothing out there.

About now is when Nature comes into its own and gets a little cocky. Suddenly, humans are the endangered species. We're surrounded by invisible movements and shrill screeching and nonhuman footsteps and barking and sniffing and, now and then, frantic wing-flapping overhead. Not far off, dusky zombies, seminaked, move sluggishly among the trees, sedated by the mystical soporific power of kava, their eyes reduced to gray pinpricks in the beam of a flashlight, staring blankly ahead. Some stop, disoriented. Others continue, playing out their eerie choreography for a final few steps until they find a space apart from everyone else, where they sink in a slow, fluid collapse to the ground and sit there, stupefied.

At the center of the John Frum village, there's a party going on. A small choir stands in virtual darkness, their happy faces lit by showers of crackling sparks from a small fire as they wail their discordant chants. Inside the meeting-house a guitar band pounds out an entrancing beat, surrounded by crowds of people singing and dancing, gyrating provocatively. For the sake of the camera only, and in an attempt to blend in, I join them, though it's plain to see I have no sense of rhythm. Most of the time I dance like I'm stepping on cockroaches, which is going to look awful on-screen. So I jiggle and wriggle about from foot to foot for as long as it takes Camera Mark to grab a couple of shots. Then that's enough. I'm done.

My first thought when I barge into these noisy festivities is that the tribe has caught wind of my amazing news already and they're celebrating being sprung from their decades-old straitjacket of superstition and ignorance. But according to Joe, who I think is beginning to tire of my wild theories, because he's not smiling as much as he used to, that's not the case. These dances are a routine, held every week, he insists. Furthermore, they're regarded as sacred religious events by the islanders, who are apparently more than a little upset by my ridiculous "prancing to the left, hopping to the right" dance technique.

And another thing, while we're at it, he throws in: the tribe *certainly* doesn't want to hear my news about John Frum not living inside the volcano and the whole thing being a hoax. That, he advises earnestly, is something I'd be wise to keep to myself—okay?

"Sure—but—"

"*Okay,* Cash?"

"Er . . . yeah, okay, okay."

On that peculiar note, I figure it's time to head on out.

"Before you go, though," Joe jumps in, "you should drink kava."

"Oh, no thanks," I reply very firmly.

After what he told me in the market about how it's made, not a single drop will ever be passing Sir's lips, of that I am certain. Kava is one aspect of the rich indigenous Tanna lifestyle that can happily remain a mystery. Sorry.

"Joe's right," Eric chimes in. "You can't leave without trying it. It would be a great way to end the show."

And blow me if everyone else doesn't agree with him! It would be the perfect way to wind things up, they insist. After all, how can I find kava at the start of the episode and not drink it by the end? The viewers will be so disappointed.

"So?" I dig my heels in. "They'll get over it. I mean . . ."

The bottom line is, I don't do drugs. I smoked weed once at my friend Len's condo in Santa Monica and it triggered a major paranoid episode. Within minutes, I became convinced I was trapped inside a photocopier and some seabirds were conspiring to kill me. I've never touched the stuff since.

". . . er . . ."

"But not here," Eric adds, somehow interpreting my "er" as a gung-ho yes. "We'll get some on the way back."

Our clandestine kava-drinking session happens an hour later at the hotel, in a spot in the grounds that Mark's rigged with lights to make it kind of look like the John Frum village if you're not paying close attention.

Kava bars are a staple of Tanna life. They're all over the island. Little wooden shacks set back from the roadside with lanterns burning outside to draw customers. On the way here, Joe stopped off to buy a small quantity of kava already prepared, which he now pours into a small bowl he brought from the hotel kitchen.

"Okay—*action*."

"Come on, Cash—drink," he says seductively, pushing the bowl to my lips.

After it's been dug up, sliced up, mashed up, chewed by prepubescent children, spat out, strained, mixed with water, and stirred, kava becomes an unattractive purple color, thin in consistency, not unlike emulsion paint. Because it smells of nothing at all, that makes it deceptively innocuous.

"Drink, Cash," Joe says again. "Driiiiiink."

Crouching anxiously by the roots of a tree, I can hear the surf beating on the shore to my left and staff members laughing in the restaurant, competing with the chatter of my conscience. "Don't do this," it's saying. "You know what happened last time."

The camera's rolling, all heads are turned in my direction.

Yet, despite the risk, I'm poised on the verge of following through.

Here's how I reason it.

It's about fitting in. I have a bunch more shows to shoot with these people. And if something as silly and as bold as swallowing a few sips of mildly hallucinogenic painty-looking liquid would help bridge the gap between us, giving them a small reason to accept me more, viewing me less as a wimpy host who's allergic to, scared of, and paranoid about everything he sees, and more as someone who's "on the team" and ready for anything, then that would not only be a feather in my cap but would stand me in good stead for the rest of the season, wouldn't it? That's what I'm thinking.

After all, it's only a bowl of liquid. How bad can it be?

"Take it, Cash," Joe whispers in a satanic growl, "and driiiiiiink."

So I do.

Sure enough, it is, without exception, the worst thing I have EVER put in my mouth! I try swallowing, but it won't go down, any more than brake fluid would go down, or donkey urine, or the sweat from a sumo wrestler's crotch. But before I can spit it out, and for want of somewhere better to go, it slowly starts to seep down my throat.

"Aaaagh, ugh!" Jesus Christ!

As I struggle to keep from vomiting, I hear Mark's characteristic high-pitched giggle behind the camera. Tasha's stuffing her knuckles in her mouth. Eric has turned away in case he laughs and ruins the shot.

"Keep drinking. Driiiiiiink."

I've consumed a third of what was in the bowl. That's quite enough.

"Now, just relax. And wait."

"Okay."

It's this, the waiting part, I find the scariest. Luckily, the narcotic effects of kava roll over you super fast. First thing that happens: your tongue loses all sensation, followed by your lips and your throat, as, bit by bit, a creeping numbness rises to engulf you. Anyone who's tried watching the entire *Lord of the Rings* trilogy at one sitting knows this same feeling. In under two minutes I'm rendered immobile. That's how quickly it tightens its grip. If you're standing up, then you must sit. If you're sitting and you had plans to go somewhere, you should probably call and cancel.

Instantly I understand why the men on this island spend

so much time lounging around on the ground doing nothing. Once this stuff's in your system, you not only lose your get-up-and-go, but even flopping down idly against a tree twiddling your thumbs begins to feel like a delinquent waste of effort. It's as if you're dead, but you can't remember what killed you. The curtain comes down on the headlong scrum of life and you're lulled into a blissful state of resignation that leaves you soothed, unrushed and, yes, partially paralyzed too, which is scary, but that's only temporary.

When you're in this state, it's better, according to Joe, to stay where you are, cocooned within a deliciously cozy, tranquil shell of delirium, and just . . . sit it out. Indeed, a large part of the kava experience seems to consist of waiting for it to be over.

"Will you be okay?"

An echoing voice seeps through the invisible mist.

Twenty minutes have gone by already. Joe's left for his hotel. Mark and Todd are dismantling the lights. Tasha's grabbed her backpack and is heading off to her bungalow. That was the final scene of the show, and whatever the camera captured just now, it must have been TV Gold, because everyone leaves smiling.

"Sure," I tell Eric, sounding wobbly. "Sure. It's all fine."

I'm floating, leaving my body behind, happy in my new world of qualified consciousness and drug-induced quadriplegia. Seeking space and time to savor these feelings, I say good night to the others before navigating an uncertain course through the darkened gardens in the direction of the hotel bar, my legs moving with the slowed-down swagger of a diver bobbing along the seabed.

It must be very late. The dining room is empty, the staff long gone. Fresh white dust sheets, spread across the furniture, gleam translucent, giving the place a shadowy, spookily abandoned feel. Don't know how I do it, but somehow I waft my way into a chair on the veranda, where I sit for the longest time, motionless, deliciously warm, letting a fresh wind off the ocean noodle with my hair. As my brain swims, the crash of the tide on rocks not ten feet away writes a symphony of foaming melodies that swish inside my ears. Up above, a damp smudge of a moon filters halfheartedly through clouds of stretched lint, obscuring billions of stars that I badly want to reach out and touch. And would, too, if the wretched kava hadn't sapped all the power from my arms.

This, I hear myself saying, each word punctuated by infinity, is amazing.

To think, there are Buddhists the world over who at this very moment are closeted away in hilltop sanctuaries; maybe they've been there for their entire adult lives, meditating in solitary silence in an effort to glimpse a fraction, a tiny speck of the nirvana I'm experiencing right now, when really, honestly, they're wasting their energy. The answers they've been searching for were right there waiting for them from day one. All they needed this whole time, it turns out, was drugs.

Lots and lots of lovely drugs.

Who knew?

7

Solvang

You know what a pilot show is, right? We're talking a low-budget dry run of a series idea. A tease, a presentation. Taking it out for a spin to see if it flies.

As Fat Kid promised, ours was shot in the scenic town of Solvang, north of Santa Barbara, deep in California wine country. Fascinating place. Founded around 1911 by a bunch of sour-faced schoolteachers—you should see the photos!—who left Denmark to build a new life in America, but then, when they got here and saw what America was actually like, changed their minds. "Screw that," they cried, "let's build another Denmark instead." So that's what they did, laying cobbled squares reminiscent of the ones they'd left behind, and surrounding them with cute windmills, half-timbered gingerbread houses, and tea shops that are still standing today, many of them owned and run by descendants of those original settlers, who, despite being several generations along, still find themselves stuck with Danish names, such as Lars and Bent.

Anyway, for three days I romped carefreely around town with a film crew of six people—frantic, buzzing electrons to my nucleus—pretending to be lost (first essential element of the concept), shuffling from square to museum, museum to café, café to windmill, chatting with pastry-shop owners and smorgasbord restaurant waitresses, wangling free food off them wherever possible (second essential element), and ultimately finding a local baker to offer me a bed for the night (third essential element). And I carried it off very successfully, I thought, without insulting anyone, or casting their dull, quiet, annoyingly eccentric little town in anything but a positive light. All in all, it was tremendous fun. Doing TV was a darned sight easier than I'd imagined.

The result was pretty different from other travel programs. Funny, insightful, and innovative—everything most reality shows are not, in fact—an initiative that paid dividends. Two months later, our fourteen-minute mini-episode about Solvang was a monster hit when it was shown to focus groups in Las Vegas.[1] Every measurable demographic right across the board warmed instantly to the *All Washed Up* concept. The only one that didn't, I believe, was the "people who

---

1 TV Talk. Many TV executives today have no idea what will make good television or what shows should get made. And those that do are often too scared to back their hunches. After all, they have mortgages, car payments, and kids to put through school. So, as a rule, and rather than endanger their family's security, they outsource the really important decisions to focus groups. Focus groups are ordinary people who know absolutely nothing about television either. But they are *very* good at telling TV executives what to think. Synergy, I believe this is called.

live in Solvang" demographic. Apparently, they were in an uproar.

Just saw the episode of your show on Solvang, my hometown . . . you appear to be a brainless, soulless, blithering no-talent hackjob. . . .
—Gerald.

Mr Peters!
After viewing your travel segment, i find u 2 b, a total fucking idiot!!
What ever happened to having talent to be able to be on tv.
—Ryan.

Well, if you're going to be picky, whatever happened to using grammar, punctuation, good English, and manners to write e-mails? Hah!

Later, a friend of mine spotted this article in a Santa Barbara newspaper.[2] I was stunned. Here's just a fraction of it:

Traveling Buffoon Stranded in Solvang
Cash Peters . . . embarrassed everyone he met in Solvang with boorish behavior and willful stupidity. . . . Peters badmouthed those who helped him, insulted their heritage and their wives, and played at falling down drunk, before he hightailed it out of town. . . .

Actually, that's not *quite* true; I didn't hightail it out of anywhere.

---

2 The *Santa Barbara News-Press*. This excerpt is reproduced with their kind permission.

It was the last night of the shoot. Late. We were in a men's lodge called The Danish Brotherhood, and I'm sorry to say I drank way too much of something called aquavit, a clear, watery liqueur made from fermented potatoes. Three shots was all I had, but that's enough. Enough, I suspect, to tranquilize a bear. In fact, I got so wasted that I broke loose while the camera was still rolling and started hugging every Lars and Bent I could lay my hands on—another groundbreaking departure in TV, one from which other travel hosts could learn a great deal, and which would surely set our series apart from the dozens of mediocre ones hosted by insipid, milquetoast men in pastel golfing sweaters who never kiss or hug *anybody* during their shows.

Well, the Solvanistas thought otherwise, obviously. They hated it. The way the news article described things, you'd think I stopped just short of raping their town. Somehow, with my peculiar knack in life for taking lemonade and turning it back into lemons again, I'd riled up enough of the townsfolk to warrant an outcry. The reporter went on:

> . . . [T]his was a crass, foolish pack of lies from the get-go.[3] Peters should be stranded permanently, off the air,[4] so he can't afflict other communities with his moronic antics.
>
> Cash Peters tossed down aquavit with the boys until he was reeling, then staggered off to sleep in [Bent] Olsen's guest room. He grabbed Bent's wife like a *Titanic* survivor grabbing a lifejacket,[5] and wouldn't let go.[6] He made fun of Bent's piano skills.

---

3 No it wasn't. A crass, foolish pack of factual oversights possibly! Not lies.

4 No I shouldn't.

5 No I didn't.

6 Yes I would.

"The drunk act was a put-on,"[7] Mrs. Olsen revealed. "He can't drink.[8] He's a diabetic."[9]

Well, at least the focus groups liked it. A lot. Which meant the American public probably would too. Plus, hey, a little controversy's a good thing, right?

Furthermore, I was sure that, with some canny British ingenuity, we could reframe this terrible review, tighten it, pick out a few choice phrases, and turn it into something that didn't defame me quite as much as the original. Let me see, now . . .

"Cash Peters helped . . . their heritage . . . with his . . . antics."

Perfect.

So that's how we got picked up for a series. Putting the Solvang minirevolt behind us, and with the wind of confidence filling our sails, we embarked on this one-year project. During that time I would be dumped in a whole new set of places, including Greece, Mexico, Kenya, Russia, Vanuatu, Romania, Alaska, Dubai, Colorado, Turin, and the Idaho wilderness. There was to be no obvious link between any of these destinations. Each episode would start afresh in a new location. The only common element was that all the places should offer us a unique and very different culture to explore. Cultures that would help turn *All Washed Up* into a winner.

No, better than a winner—TV Gold.

---

7 No it wasn't.

8 Yes I can.

9 No I'm not.

8

ΞυχηΔΔΔΔΨΧςψώΫ

The phone rings. A crisis meeting is being called.

When I finally track down Eric he's in the cavernous white lobby of our hotel, agitated, pacing up and down, wearing his usual uniform of plain T-shirt and cargo shorts, pale anorexic legs rattling around inside them like bell-clappers. Tasha's off to one side, hunched on a couch, chin resting on a clipboard, Director Mark beside her.

"Dude, this town is super boring." Eric sighs. "Tasha went out yesterday and scouted around, and there's . . ."

". . . nothing," she picks up. "It's a quaint little coastal village, but that's all. There are churches, hotels, bars, a monastery, some ancient ruins . . . I mean, it's a vacation place. Really beautiful, and quiet and stuff, but . . ."

Not enough to fill a thirty-minute TV show.

Deep in thought, Eric migrates to the bay window, juggling his cell phone between hands, tossing, catching, tossing, catching, as he squints out into blinding sunlight at a sweep of unbroken olive groves descending to an oceanscape of such improbable blue that it looks like it was painted indiscriminately by an ungifted child, the way it does in cheap postcards.

Tasha's right about the quiet. It's suffocating. The entire town is in a round-the-clock coma. Nothing moves in the heat, except maybe a lizard or two, or a bedraggled peasant plodding along the lane outside with a donkey and cart piled high with cheese. Evidently, we've been sent to a place that, to someone in a cubicle in L.A., must have sounded like dynamite, positively packed with promise, only to find that many of the things we came here for don't exist, and the ones that do are too boring to make a show about. As a holiday resort, a place to rest and unwind, this would be ideal. As a location for an entertaining adventure travel show, it's pure anesthetic.

Stifling a yawn, I collapse into a chair.

These are early days, but already the workload from shooting this series is starting to catch up with me. Tanna Island left us for dead. And that was only our fourth trip! Since then there have been seven more, including New Zealand, Moscow, and Transylvania, all of them shot rat-a-tat, one after the other in rapid succession, and it's utterly exhausting.

To complicate things further, I was so busy at the start, impressing on everyone my prohibitive list of food sensitivities, that I completely forgot to mention my prohibitive list of phobias too. These include heights, enclosed spaces, spiders, high speeds, authority figures, flying, wild animals, large dogs, genitalia,[1] snakes, horses, and, ever since a time

[1] Any genitalia, really, including my own. People laugh when I tell them this, but I swear I'm not lying. In particular I am highly vaginaphobic (technically known as *eurotophobic*). Back in my youth, I remember a friend opening a porno magazine in a shop in North Wales and showing me a close-up

years ago when a psychic told me I would someday die by drowning, water. Of course, none of these things figures very much in my world back home in Hollywood, where life is comfortable, bordering on luxurious, and I have total control over my environment. But out here on the road it's a different story. I'm confronted almost daily with one ghastly hazard after another. For instance, despite repeatedly underscoring my phobias to people and insisting I be pampered without cease, already I've been forced to walk through untamed jungle (spiders, dogs, snakes, germs), been crammed down a tiny, stifling mine shaft in Australia (enclosed spaces), sent jet-boating on a turbulent river in New Zealand (speed and water), made to stand on the rim of an erupting volcano in Vanuatu (heights), and taken snowboarding on a mountain in Colorado (heights and speed). As if that wasn't enough, I ended up getting stoned in one episode, hideously drunk in three others—this is becoming my calling card—was stripped completely naked in our Navajo Indian show, then again in our Moscow show; and on our trip to Guadalajara, a Mexican wrestler gripped me so tightly around the neck that my contact lenses almost popped out.

As you can imagine, this, plus the rapidfire turnover of destinations and activities, coupled with insane working

---

of a vagina. This came at the beginning of puberty and changed my life. Hot, dizzy, and nauseous, I stumbled into the street and collapsed to the ground, denting a car on the way down and chipping one of my front teeth. And exactly the same thing would happen today too. The cause has yet to be satisfactorily diagnosed. However, it's no worse, I'm thinking, than people who suffer from *aulophobia* (an irrational fear of flutes), or *lutraphobia* (a fear of otters), *ostraconophobia* (a fear of shellfish), *automatonophobia* (a fear of ventriloquists' dummies), or, possibly the worst one of the lot, *Walloonophobia*. Although, quite honestly, when you get down to it, who among us *isn't* afraid of the Walloons?

hours and flight schedules, is monumentally wearing. Other people wait their whole lives to visit just one of the incredible places we've been to. Me, I've seen the whole lot in under two months, and quite honestly I'm whacked. Clinically whacked. And ask any doctor; he'll tell you that clinically whacked is the worst kind of whacked. Even jet lag has no effect on me any more. Day or night, my body never has any idea where the hell it is.

Eric's still tossing his phone from hand to hand by the window.

"So you're telling me," I address the back of his head, "that there's nothing about this place or this culture that's fun? Nothing at all?"

"Well," Tasha says, hesitating slightly, "there is *one* thing . . ." she's giggling already, ". . . it's *kinda* known for."

"There is? Great."

"The *only* thing actually," Eric continues. And he smiles broadly.

So does Mark.

"Excellent," I say. "Let's start there, then. What is it?"

Pelasgia, one of this place's many names, is in the Aegean Sea. It's the third-largest of the Greek Islands, and, viewed from above, is male-pattern-baldness-shaped, like a horseshoe, or one of those inflatable pillows people use on aircraft to rest their neck. To reach our hotel we traveled through the southwest region in a two-hour white-knuckle ride across spectacular mountain scenery, to the village of Skala Eressos (pronounced Shkala Erreshosh), a dreamily pleasant matrix of narrow streets, dazzling white facades, blue doors, and red-tiled rooftops that ooze history from every cracked shutter and broken drain.

Pelasgia has been inhabited since Time Immemorial (see

footnote on page 55). By 6 B.C., during Ancient Historical Times, it was regarded as the center of global civilization and was the birthplace of many notable Greeks, who obviously considered it just as boring as we do, because most of them packed their bags the first chance they got and hoofed it to somewhere else instead. These included:

- **Terpander.** Musician. Couldn't get away fast enough. Moved to Athens, where he became famous for inventing a seven-note scale that could be played on the lyre. A lyre is basically a hollowed-out tortoise with strings, and possibly THE most annoying musical instrument ever. That's why you've never heard of Terpander.

- **Arion.** Poet. Left Pelasgia as soon as he could and moved to Corinth. Most noted for (*a*) developing an ancient type of hymn called a dithyramb, and also—because nobody gives a rat's ass about dithyrambs—(*b*) being rescued by dolphins after he was thrown off a ship by pirates, which is far more interesting.

- **Theophrastus.** Known as the Father of Botany. Doesn't sound like much now, but back then it could get you the best table in restaurants. Author of the book *Enquiry into Plants,* he too left the island ASAP. Famous for saying, "We die just when we are beginning to live," shortly before he died.

- **Phanias.** Eminent historian. Inventor of Thermopylae, the Greek board game, and friend of Theophrastus. Spent years writing a book about music, but forgot to make a backup copy. Then he lost it and, well, that was that. Died before Thermopylae caught on. Bit of a loser all round, really.

- **Sappho.** Ah, now you're talking! Highly strung female aristocrat in 620 B.C. Made homosexuality cool and acceptable by writing erotic gay love poems. But there was political unrest. Fear-filled pre-Christian Christian-types destroyed her work by setting fire to the parchments or, worse, crumbling them.[2] Bastards. Exiled to Sicily. Fell in love with Phaon, a ferry boat operator. But it didn't work out. Well, of course not: *he was a man!* Distraught and confused, Sappho threw herself off a cliff and died, ending the "Will she, won't she commit suicide?" speculation once and for all.

Over the centuries, as I said, the island's name was changed repeatedly (depending on which invading nation had control of it at the time) from Pelasgia to Aeolis to Lassia to Makaria to Mytonis, and a whole bunch more, most of which, because they sounded like brands of cough syrup, never caught on. Eventually, though, the locals did manage to agree on a name, and that's the one it's still known by:

Lesbos.

Since Sappho's day, the island has been a place of pilgrimage for lesbian couples vacationing in Europe, same way penguins congregate in Antarctica, and people who can't get laid attend MacWorld. In fact, after olives and cheese, homosexuals are probably its most widely available natural resource, much to the consternation, I gather, of the Lesbian government, whose members, being incredibly hetero and butch—grrrr—would prefer their homeland to be famous for something a little more wholesome. Oh, and one other thing: if it's all the same to you, the islanders dislike being referred to as Lesbians. Particularly the men, for some

---

[2] Probably.

reason. They much prefer the drearier, less amusing term "Lesbonians."

Shame nobody else does.

So, Lesbians it is!

Rrrrrrrrrrrrrrrrrr. Rrrrr. Rrrr. Rrrrrrrrrrrrrrrrrrrrrrrrr.

Braving a 95-degree morning high, and with the crew at my heels, I stride into the heart of the village in search of something worth making a TV show about.

Rrrrrrrrrrrrrrrrrrrrrr. Rrrrrrrrrrrrrrrrrrrrrr. Rrrrrrrrrrrr-rrrrr.

My first task as host is to pretend I've just been washed up on a mystery island, but with absolutely no clue which one. Every episode starts that way, and I've developed a special look to handle it: I call it My Mystified Look. It's more of a sequence of looks, really. Glance left, glance right, frown, squint, purse my lips, then walk out of shot at a brisk pace, as though intrigued by something off-camera.[3] Works like a dream every time. Catch me wandering around on-screen with that look on my face and you instantly say to yourself: "Now, *there's* a fella with no clue where he's at."

We make a sharp right onto the main drag, a sleepy, paved conduit of blinding white walls running parallel to the shoreline, dotted with restaurants and pokey little coffee bars that are very inviting, and seem all the more so when you're busy working and can't go in them. Outside each is a chalkboard menu, either balanced on a chair or hooked onto the wall, listing a bunch of specials in Greek: items such as *noykanikoxopiatix* and *kotonoyoeoy.* That's how they spell

[3] And before you go copying this in *your* TV show, I'm currently applying for a patent to protect it. So back off.

stuff over here, in code. Makes their language very difficult to pick up, and their Scrabble games a nightmare, I should imagine.

Seated at tables along the sidewalk, old men—and I mean *old* old, their bodies pickled by ouzo, tobacco, and a lifetime living in an unrelenting furnace—sit playing backgammon, or in some cases Thermopylae, with their shirts off, unself-consciously exposing their hunched, leathery Crypt Keeper physiques to the public. And if they catch you laughing and pointing, they merely laugh back, lips hitching up like badly creased theater curtains around a proscenium of crooked brown teeth and raw red gums.

There are lots of old men in Lesbos; lots of weary middle-aged housewives, too, lugging heavy shopping bags up hills to their homes; and lots and lots of statuesque youths tearing up the streets on motor scooters . . .

Rrrrrrrrrrrrrrrrrr. Rrrrrrr. Rrrrrrrrrrrrrrrrrrrrrrrrrrrrrrrrrrrrrrrrrrrr.

. . . wimples of flowing brown hair straight out of a Clairol commercial rippling godlike in their slipstream, along with their baggy white shirttails.

Rrrrrrrrrrr. Rrrrrrrrrrrr. Rrrr. Rrrrrrrrrrrrrrrrrrrrrrrrrrr.

But, oddly, no lesbians.

Given its reputation, I expected the village to be teeming with them, strolling along, holding hands, openly enjoying the free expression of their love in an environment which, if not exactly endorsing of it, has yet to find a way to stop it. But so far we haven't seen a single one, and that's not good for the show. Maybe they have a herd mentality, I'm thinking. Find one, and you'll find a thousand of them. It's just a matter of time.

So I set off on a sort of minisafari, dropping in on butcher's shops and bakeries along the way to scrounge scraps of food, exactly the way someone who had just been stranded on this island with no money might—only in my case with significantly better results.

In fact, this is becoming a problem. There's a worrying inauthenticity that comes with having a camera with you. Something none of us foresaw when we started. It's virtually impossible, we now find, to be "all washed up" in any place in the world and not survive quite adequately, and probably in considerable comfort actually, when there's a TV crew and two producers following you around. Everyone you meet goes out of their way to make a good impression. Nobody wants to be the one to refuse hospitality and look like a total jackass when the program goes out. And although I'm very grateful, obviously, since it makes my job so much easier, their eagerness to please defeats the purpose of the show, removing any real element of challenge or struggle.

I mean, not to malign people's generosity or anything, but in real life it's nonexistent. Fact. They simply don't give stuff away to strangers. If you doubt me, try it. Try walking out of a Greek patisserie carrying four muffins and an onion pie you've not paid for, see how far you get. So to watch them being magnanimous on-screen is not only highly irregular, but it's bound to set alarm bells ringing in the viewer's mind.

Example: I step into a cheese shop and tell the man behind the counter that I have no money. Instantly, he wraps a large chunk of local sheep's cheese in paper and hands it to me. But of *course* he does, he's on television!

Another example: I saunter into one of many breezy bars lining the ocean's edge, and the waitress, straight out of the gate, volunteers to make me a free cocktail. Just like that! "It's a special promotion we're running today," she announces.

Well, how lucky that I happened to stop by, then.

"We call it a Hula-Mula Wonder. Would you like to try one?"

A foaming pink vodka shake slides from the blender into a frosted glass big enough to hold a bunch of carnations, topped off by a quarter-moon of cantaloupe.

"Hula-Mula is a village in Australia," she says, handing it to me.

I have a sneaking suspicion that the place she's really referring to is Woolloomooloo, but who cares where the drink comes from? I only know where it's going. And I chug down half of it and instantly order another, refusing to pay for that one too.

See what I mean? It's disturbingly easy.

Every bar and restaurant skirting the beach has its own little private cabana, sheltered from a harsh sun by some kind of tiki thatch, or else a colored tarp that puffs and heaves in the wind. Today, a noticeable air of desolation hangs over the place. Most of the bars are empty, the streets are quiet. It's the height of the tourist season, too.

"So how come everything has a chilly funfair-in-winter feel to it?" I ask Joanna.

We have three extra women working with us on this episode. Joanna's one of them. A brunette in her midthirties; runs a travel agency in town; helped set up our flights and hotel; knows everybody. A bit on the small side, a *lot* on the loud and bossy side, but a real pistol. Heaps of fun. She's also very overtly sexual, with pouting lips and ramekins for eyes. Seductive, green, mirrored ramekins, big as solar panels, that would, in his day, have been the downfall not only of Jason, but of half his Argonauts as well; eyes that one suspects could be put to far greater use than merely seeing out of.

"Why is nobody in the bars today?"

"Well, it's still early," she explains, but with a worried look that tells me this probably isn't the whole story. "Also, our . . ."

I knew it!

". . . numbers are way down because of the Games."

Ah yes, the Games.

The Olympic Games.

After lesbianism, cheese, and ouzo, they're the biggest thing Greece ever gave us.

The event of Summer 2004, though, turned out to be disastrous for some of the islands. Drawn by the celebrations, thousands of tourists were sucked away to Athens, ripping a great hole in the local economy. Hopefully it's only temporary, but right now Joanna's not so sure. Her business is still suffering.

"Some people, they come back to us year after year. But new people," she sighs, "they are not coming. And we *need* them to come. That's why your show will be so good for us. It'll bring tourists back."

Er . . . well, you might want to watch an episode of it before you go leaping to crazy conclusions like that.

As she talks, she stares with undisguised lust toward the ocean and two athletic young guys mindlessly tossing a white beach ball back and forth in the surf.

"Okay, Cash," Director Mark says. "Here's what's happening. You've arrived in this bar, you've been given a drink, and you see a woman at the table over there. So you sit beside her, the two of you get talking—chat chat chat, whatever you want to talk about about—and she invites you to a restaurant for dinner."

"She does?"

"Yup."

"So . . . I just run into her, and she immediately invites me out to dinner?"

"Yup."

Hm, okay. Nothing unnatural or forced about that.

"Action."

When I next turn around, by the magic of television, the cabana is no longer empty. There's a solitary barfly sitting at one of the tables, sipping a beer and staring lustfully at the two muscular guys tossing their ball. The woman's name is . . .

"Oh . . . hello."

. . . Joanna. *Our* Joanna!

Joanna is now also doubling up as a colorful local character, apparently, since this bar is one of her regular haunts.

Caught off guard, I do my best to pretend I don't know her. "So are you a—" I begin.

"Yes." She smiles before I can finish. "I *am* a—"

"—lesbian?"

"—local."

"Oh."

Joanna is most definitely not a lesbian, I can vouch for that, because I overheard her recounting her long, turgid life story to Tasha earlier, including how she's secretly in love with two men right now but can't decide which of her two paramours to run off with and which, by default, to make suicidal.

Rigid with nerves before the camera, she first pretends she doesn't speak English, which brings the scene grinding to a halt straight away. Then she starts bantering with someone off-camera and giggling. Finally, on the retake, she blows every last ounce of believability this chance meeting between two complete strangers might have had by saying, "Hello, Cash" before I've even introduced myself and by being far more friendly than she'd ever be in a bar to a man she's never met before. Or maybe not. Maybe if she were a little less open and friendly to men in bars, she wouldn't be in the trouble she's in now, paramour-wise. Just thinking aloud.

Anyway, a special event is being held tonight at a restaurant nearby, she explains woodenly in her thick accent. "It's a very nice Greek night—a bouzouki night."

"What's a bouzouki?" I ask.

"It's the most fun instrument in Greece."

Remember the lyre? Well, you hollow out your tortoise in much the same way, only this time you give it a longer fret board. Played correctly, it sounds like a grand piano being thrown down two flights of stairs. Very traditional.

"We drink ouzo," she continues, "we dance on the table, we dance under the table, we smash plates. Do you want to come?"

Not really. But our show is desperately short of material and I've always wanted to see someone dance under a table, so yes, I'd *love* to come.

"The Blue Sardine. End of the boardwalk. 7:30 tonight."

Great.

"See you there," Joanna says.

"Okay," I say, and step out of frame as if I have somewhere else to go, which, as we know, is most certainly not the case at all.

"Cut!"

Congratulating ourselves on a successful morning's work, we break for lunch and head for a boardwalk restaurant Joanna picked out for us. En route, she eases in close to me and begins asking questions, some about the show, others more personal.

"Back home, are you famous, Cash?"

"Famous? Hm, let me see. I've been broadcasting nationally on public radio in Britain for fifteen years and in America every week for ten years . . . so no."

"But once this program is shown . . . ?"

"Oh, probably. Depends how things go. Why?"

Bobbing alongside, she's looking up at me, a little starry-eyed.

"Just asking." She grins impishly, then clams up.

How very odd.

"Hmmmmm," I hula-mula-wonder to myself, "what's *that* about?"

The most difficult aspect for me of continually being on the road is—big surprise—finding food to eat. Specifically food that isn't swimming in oil. And never more so than in Greece—the clue's in the name, really—a country where olives grow in profusion and olive oil is so integral to the national diet that I'm surprised they don't just serve it neat in a pint glass and be done with it.

Waiters become quite offended, I've noticed, if you dare to suggest that your food be cooked without it.

"No *oil*??" they gasp, forcing me to explain the reason, using my hands to mime boils bursting all over my face. Psh, psh, psh!

The best compromise most times is the soup, once the waiter has assured me very begrudgingly that there's only "the *barest minimum* of olive oil in it" (by Greek standards that means about half a liter or so), plus some grilled fish fresh caught that morning, a specialty of the islands. Good, that'll do.

Lunch, once you've ordered it, takes forty minutes to arrive. Nobody rushes to do anything in Lesbos. It's either too hot or they're too lazy, not sure which. So while I'm busy keeping my eye on the chef, the crew wanders off to do some clothes shopping in nearby stores, taking Joanna along with them to translate.

As the group walks away, I hear her mumbling to Tasha,

"It's a big problem. I don't know which to choose. I love them both. What shall I do? What would *you* do?"

In the clear absence of lesbians today, we abandon our search of the bars along the seafront and switch our attention instead to filming B-roll of the Bewilderbeest sauntering idly along the beach wearing nothing but a T-shirt, shorts, and his special Mystified Look:[4] glance left, glance right, frown, squint, a purse of the lips, then—"Uh-oh, what's that interesting thing over there?"—and walk out of shot at a brisk pace. Never fails!

Skala Eressos has one of the best beaches in Europe, or so they say. It's even won awards. Hard to say why that is, because parts of it are truly horrible. *Horrible!*

"Ow, ow, ow, OWWWW!"

This used to be miles of golden sand. But then something terrible happened: a ruinous storm, according to Joanna, that hauled in a bunch of shingle from somewhere, doing to parts of the beach what the 2004 Olympics did to the rest of Lesbos, leaving it volcanic gray in color and pebble-strewn, and turning a pleasurable paddle in the water into one of the most unendurably painful experiences of my entire life. Like walking barefoot over crushed beer cans.

"Ow, ow, ow, ow, ow, ow, OW! OW!"

Afterwards, I hobble back to the village square to meet with Yorgos, the owner of a local motor-scooter shop.

Having come to this island apparently to see the lesbians, only to find that they're a bit thin on the ground, and with nothing else seemingly going on, we're reduced to improvising, shooting on the fly, filling the show with things we've

---

[4] Patent pending.

just thought of, *immediately* after we've thought of them. It's very laissez-faire, and a lot more enjoyable for being so.

Yorgos, a jolly, middle-aged man with a gray mullet and substantial girth that spills over his belt like sandbags, and who would no doubt benefit from giving up riding mopeds and walking a little more, volunteers to drive me to an old monastery located several miles inland. I dare say that, if I didn't have a camera crew with me, he would never do this, but I'm not about to turn down such a kind offer, so . . .

Rrrrrrrrrrrrrrrrrrrrrrrrr. Rrrrrrr. Rrrrrrrrrrrrrrrrrrrrrrrrrrrr.

. . . we mount one of his scooters. Fearing I might slide sideways, I wrap both arms around his waist, fingers interlocked on the other side in the deep crease between his gut and nipples, giving me unlimited free access to the rich man-musk of his underarm, then we set off out of the village into open countryside.

Rrrrrrrrrrrrrrrrrrrrr. Rrrrrrrrrrrrrrrrrrrrrr. Rrrrr. Rrrrr. Rrrrrrrrrr.

If Lesbos were a drop-leaf table, Skala Eressos would be on the bit that folds down after dinner. The rest would be a broad, flat plain littered with mulberry trees, potato farms, and acres of flourishing olive groves. It's quite delightful. Great for riding.

After a few minutes, we cruise over a gentle hill and—

"Oh my God, look out!!!"

—nearly hit an elderly pedestrian who's halfway across the road—

"Woooooоah!"

—missing him by inches.

Yet Yorgos doesn't even flinch. He clearly enjoys running into people he knows.

As we speed away, I shout an apology over my shoulder at the old man. "Have a nice day!" But he doesn't understand. "Yorgos, what's the Greek for have a nice day?"

Twice he pronounces it. Both times it sounds like "pajamas." And "good afternoon/evening" is, apparently, *"kalispara."* That's what I'm hearing.

"Kalispara!" I shout back to the old man we almost killed. "Pajamas."

"*ΨєπΥΤ ΤΗΨєξζξ,*" he yells back in Greek, waving his clenched fist—the international symbol of forgiveness.

Rrrrrrrrrrrrrrrrrrrrrrr. Rrrrrrrrrrrrrrrrrrrrrr. Rrrrrrrrrrrrrrrrr.

As the sun succumbs gamely to evening, burnishing the hills behind the town a fiery orange, that's when Skala Eressos starts to show signs of life. The same pickled old men I saw in the street earlier, hunched over backgammon boards, drinking ouzo, and smoking, have been home for a few hours to escape the worst of the heat, and now, rested after a short nap, they're back, hunched over backgammon boards, drinking ouzo, and smoking again. Families graze the streets. Children play and perform cartwheels in cobbled lanes. Young lovers in every acceptable sexual permutation speed by on scooters, swerving now and then to avoid hitting the last few bathers stumbling up from the beach—"Ow ow ow ow ow!!"—as they head back to the hotel to put Neosporin on their cuts.

Along the narrow boardwalk that bisects the promenade, dividing the patios of various restaurants from the kitchens that serve them, strings of fairy-lights jiggle and clink overhead in a faint ocean breeze, dousing their patrons, many of them parties of women, in shifting smudges of ochre. The individual establishments are fenced off from each other by lattice windbreaks decorated with octopuses stretched out like roadkill, a traditional Greek way to ward off Satan, unless I'm mistaken.

"Yes, you are," Joanna corrects. "It's to dry them out before they're cooked."

Oh.

I tried octopus once. In Sicily. Never again. Next time I crave something rubbery with creepy suction cups all over it, I'll eat the mat in my shower.

The Blue Sardine turns out to be the very last restaurant on the boardwalk. I steer a course toward it using the rhythm of the bouzouki band as my sextant.

Something I forgot to tell you: earlier in the day, before the monastery trip[5] with Yorgos, I struck gold, lesbian-wise.[6] Quite by chance, I found a small cluster of them in a bar on the seafront eating breakfast. Clare, Liz, and Mary. All from Manchester, England—my hometown, as it happens, so of course we bonded instantly. Clare—who's the ringleader and the most rosieodonnellish of the trio—and Liz are an item, whereas Mary is single and looking for love. "Or whatever I can get," she says, giggling. Ecstatic at breaking our run of bad luck on the lesbian front, I pressured the three of them into coming to The Blue Sardine with me, though not before Clare had grabbed me by the face and planted a huge tonguey kiss right on my lips.

It was my own fault. I take full responsibility. I'd asked

---

[5] Another disaster, by the way. The Monastery of Pithariou, an isolated twelfth-century relic up in the hills, was closed when we got there, with its gates chained up, and no amount of loud heckling or throwing stones at their chapel windows would bring the monks out to greet us. It was a huge disappointment.

[6] I don't want to spark mass panic, but I fear the world's lesbian resources may be running out, and it's a real worry. I'm doubtless not the first to blame global warming for this, although I probably *am* the first to advocate rationing them as a result. At the very least we all need to come together and conserve as many lesbians as we can, before they become as rare as bald eagles, bees, and Republican senators without some kind of secret sexual past.

her a question I had always wanted to ask a lesbian about lesbianism.

"Tell me," I said, "is it a man-hating thing?"

Once Clare had stopped laughing pityingly at my ignorance, that's when she grabbed me and kissed me. It was like drowning in quicksand.

I emerged disheveled and gasping. "Wow!" I cried, wiping bits of her breakfast off my lips, "you kiss like a demon."

"No," she corrected quickly with a throaty laugh, "I kiss like a man!"

Manchester girls are the best fun!

At the restaurant, I find that Joanna's brought people too. Mostly family members eager to be on TV, including her diminutive, rather confused-looking mother, a small, bespectacled woman with unfeasibly brown hair. Following quick introductions for the benefit of the camera, Joanna goes about pouring ouzo for everyone.

Ouzo's the big thing around here, and has been since Historical Times, after a previous fad, absinthe, was found to have dangerous side effects, including tremors, hallucinations, dry mouth, cramps, and possibly internal bleeding. By contrast, ouzo's only real side effect is that it gets you crazy-blind-messed-up drunk, which is the one you're looking for anyway, so it was quickly dubbed a worthy substitute. Lesbos' home-produced version is considered one of the best in the world. A clear, smooth liqueur flavored with anise, it turns from transparent to white the moment you add water, and is generally served with appetizers called *mezedes,* which tonight are carried to our table by an eccentric Disney caricature of a Greek man with a dark ponytail and a thick, straggly beard. This is the restaurant owner. For some reason, he's turned up wearing nothing but two white tablecloths, one safety-pinned at his hip and the other knotted around his shoulders to make a crude toga. He has no underwear on, something he verifies by cocking a leg and flashing his nuts, to loud oohs and aahs from the crowd. Except for Mary, I notice, who looks away in horror.

"Heeeeeeeey, my frieeeeeeends, weeeeeeellllcome!" he roars, laying down tray after tray of *mezedes* before us.

Very soon the table is heaving with traditional island food: sweetbreads (cooked using oil), stuffed tomatoes (leaking oil), something lurid swimming in oil that looks like stuffed tomatoes again, only regurgitated; fish (sauteed in oil, I believe); vegetables, brushed with oil; honeyballs that have been deep-fried; and a delicacy called *sardeles pastes:* basically, fresh sardines doused in salt. And *oil*!

Distressed, I round on Eric. "I'm sorry, I know this stuff is probably delicious, but I can't eat any of it."

"Well, try," he says abruptly. "Do it for the show." He grew tired of my food issues several episodes ago. Despite the fact that I drew up a comprehensive inventory of all the things I can't eat, he doesn't seem to be taking my complaint seriously any more.

"But there's oil on *everything*."

My continued protest inevitably draws a Crew Look. Remember the Crew Look? The one that means, "Uh-oh, the host is being difficult *again*"?

Tasha rushes in to smooth things over. "Hey, babe," she whispers in my ear, "do what you can, okay? You don't have to eat the whole lot, just try some."

For her sake I give in, and cautiously pick and nibble. Some of the sardines are not *that* oily, I guess. But just in case, I knock back a couple of extra glasses of ouzo to anesthetize my system. So does Joanna. So do the three token lesbians, who are lapping up the free hospitality. "Cheers to queers!" Clare shouts, raising her glass, and soon we're all pretty wasted.

"We'll drink one more bottle of ouzo," Joanna tells me after a while, slurring her words, "and we'll dance the *zeibekiko*." If that's how you spell it. In Greek, it's probably something like *ΞζφξηΔΔΔΔΘθΩ*.

"What's a zebiki . . . ?"

"The zeibekiko . . ." She rests her head on my shoulder, ramekin eyes ogling me, ". . . talks about love and sadness, about death, about life . . . everything."

"Oh, does it now?" I say, pushing her off me. To show interest at this point, I sense, would be courting disaster.

There's nothing to Greek dancing really. It's very simple, and almost impossible to get wrong. Basically, several people form a line with their arms strapped across each other's shoulders and can-can their way around the room like boozed-up Rockettes. That's it.

Once we're ready to go, the four-piece band of three bouzoukis and a drum strikes up with a new version of the same melody they seem to have been playing all night, the one that sounds like a grand piano being thrown down two flights of stairs, and everyone starts to move around, with me at the end of the line doing my best to keep up.

A zeibekiko is basically a slow tantrum. But we've barely started when an interesting thing happens. I find myself hijacked by Joanna's mother, a buxom dwarf who dances with all the grace of someone who can't. She's wearing a shin-length black skirt and a blue nylon spangly top, inside which two pendulous breasts pursue their own line in choreography independent of the rest of her. A hostage to the bouzouki's terpsichorean rhythms, she advances and retreats several times around my body without ever looking at me, obviously following a blueprint in her head that reduces her partner to a colorful but unimportant accessory. Back she comes, and away she goes, hands held aloft, turning east, then west, swirling and twirling, repeating the same sequence many times over, like one of those robot vacuum cleaners when it gets wedged under a dressing table. But then, once it's over, after the music rises to a rousing, out-of-tune flourish, eliciting loud applause from around the restaurant, something strange happens. Joanna's mother, yanked from her trance and suddenly realizing whom she's been dancing with all this time, shoots me an odd look, one of utter disgust, and charges back to the table, scowling.

What the *hell* was that about?

Before I have chance to ask, the band starts up again. Same out-of-tune tune, only faster. Fingers skitter over strings. Drums pound. The lead vocalist mumbles a song, taking a drag on a cigarette between verses and letting the smoke dribble from his lips as he sings.

"This is a dance for strong men; for hard men," Joanna growls earthakittishly, staring up at me, projecting pure sex. "It talks about pain, about love, passion, and despair."

Oh, *does* it, now?

Obviously, Eric or Mark put her up to this, because, without being asked, she leads me from the floor to a bench, then onto a table—*onto* it, not under it, note; she hasn't mastered that move, after all—where, caught in the thrall of the primal rhythm, she abandons all pretension to dignity by crushing herself against me, grinding at my crotch with her ass, and running her fingers up and down my body in a jitterbug of seduction, squeezing my buttocks to the beat, clawing at my shorts, and fumbling with my shirt.

For the record, here's how a woman might end up with two boyfriends she can't get rid of!

"Okay, cut. Thanks, everyone." Director Mark steps in to save me, signaling the end of both the dance and the entire Lesbos shoot.

Not our best show, it has to be said—it would need to

have actual content and subject matter for that—but more entertaining than we expected, certainly.

Still panting, and leaving the crew to mop up shots of the band, I throw myself down at the table, where I begin picking at the food. Apparently, this affords Joanna the opportunity she's been waiting for, because she sidles in like a horny crab beside me, her usually neat blonde-streaked hair more than a little askew. I don't know how many ouzos she's knocked back by now, but the woman's hammered, and, trust me, she makes a maudlin, broody drunk.

"What am I going to do about my two men, Cash?" she sighs after a moment, pouring herself another glass. "It is a big problem. I wish you would advise me. I have no clue what decision I should make."

"Why not dump them both?" I suggest playfully, giving it the minimum of thought.

"What are you talking about?"

"Why make a choice at all? Dump them and start again with somebody new."

"But *I can't do that.*" Tears spring to her eyes. "They both love me."

Uh, good grief.

Sliding a sardine between my fingers to squeeze out the excess oil, I pop it into my mouth, even though I know I shouldn't, followed by a tomato—ohmygodohmygod, has anything on this planet ever tasted so good?—and put an end to this discussion with a curt "I'm sorry, dear; I don't know what else to tell you." Then, after giving her a super-sized hug because she's looking so downcast, I quickly return to my plate of sardines. Mmmmmm. Mmm.

Luckily, Joanna has the attention span of a two-day-old puppy. Realizing this is all the sympathy she's going to get from me, she's already put the paramour situation behind her and is on to a new topic. A topic she's obviously been thinking about for a while, and which is troubling her just as much.

"I have something to ask you." She puts down her glass and fixes me with those large olive-green eyes.

"What's the matter?" I'm busy squeezing sardines, only half-listening.

Casting a quick defensive glance in both directions in case her weirdly petite mother is within earshot, she places a hand on my arm, rubs it gently, and says:

"Cash, please, will you let me have your baby?"

Wha???

Like a torpedo, the sardine I'm holding flies from out between my fingers and shoots across the table onto the floor.

9

More Crew Looks

"So what did you say?"

"About what?"

"When she asked if she could have your baby."

Tasha is goggle-eyed with shock next day at the airport when I tell her.

"I said no, of course."

Alas, to a desperate, unmarried woman whose biological clock is ticking fast, a definite no, even when it's accompanied by a wagging oily finger and a stern glare, clearly still leaves wiggle room for negotiation, because Joanna continued arguing for some time.

"I want a baby that's as tall as you, with your beautiful blue eyes and your sense of humor."

"And let's not forget the glorious hives I'm bound to get all over my forehead after eating oily sardines," I thought.

"It would be wonderful."

"Yes, it would—for you. But *I don't want a child!!*"

Even a firm refusal, though, wasn't enough to put her off.

"It's okay," she assured me, knocking back another drink and moving on to Plan B, "we wouldn't have to have physical contact, actual penetration. You could just donate your sperm."

Oh—my—God.

I was due to leave Greece the following morning, so I could afford to be honest with her. Therefore, as tactfully as I could, and to spare her feelings, I blurted out, "No frickin' way. There's not a bloody chance in hell that that's ever going to happen."

No offense.

After which, I took one last swig of ouzo, and left.

Returning to the office following the Lesbos trip—following most of our trips, actually—was an odd affair: a jarring clash of cultures, pitting those who'd flown to distant continents, stayed in fabulous hotels, eaten exotic food, and mingled with amazing people, against those we'd left behind sitting at their desks. In a short number of weeks the crew and I had seen the world, our horizons and frames of references expanding exponentially with every new location, whereas for the hobbits in the office nothing much had changed at all, and I guess they didn't want to be reminded of it.

Unfortunately, most times, as soon as our plane touched down in L.A., I would burst in through the office door, looking tanned and jet-lagged, regaling everyone with wild tales of my adventures: of almost drowning during a river-rafting expedition in Idaho; of almost falling to my death while opal mining in the Australian Outback; of being stripped naked and whipped with wet twigs in Russia; of almost losing a leg when I fell off the back of a snowmobile in Colorado; of almost snapping my left ankle in Massachusetts after I tripped getting out of the crew truck and it rolled right over my foot, putting me in the hospital; of almost being arrested while dodging guards in Moscow's Red Square; and of how I'd come *this* close to sliding headfirst down the full length of an icy ten-thousand-foot-high mountain because the daffy wardrobe woman had bought me boots with no grips on the soles.

"Wow. That's excellent," the hobbits would coo, delighted that filming had gone so well and we had a show, but on a personal level a little envious, I'm sure. "Good for you. Nice job. Great to see you back." Then they'd drop the subject at once and return to staring at the same computer they were staring at when I left a couple of weeks before.

That said, everyone remained professional and it never became a huge issue. Although, once the seed of unrest is planted like that, particularly in a close environment, grievances can sometimes escalate, and even, if you're not careful, mutate into something far more serious. And that's what happened here.

With each passing trip, the mood in L.A. became worse somehow. Looking back, there must have been a tipping point, though I was too busy making the show to notice what it might be. From my point of view the production seemed to be in good shape, the crew and staff were happy, the early episodes were turning out just great; then . . . well, I don't know what happened. I left for a week to shoot two U.S. domestic shows and by the time I got back things had gone south. A troubling and very palpable unease had developed around me as the host, but with no immediate signposts pointing to why, nothing to connect the dots. Instead of smiles and handshakes, I was met quite often with glum or embarrassed frowns. Or people would look the other way and begin a conversation with someone else. Or, worse, they'd spot me coming along a corridor, duck into rooms, and close the door. It was like living with my parents all over again.

Not long afterwards, the puzzle unraveled slightly when I was summoned to Fat Kid's cave for a pep talk. One of those special little pep talks that, in the wrong hands—his, for instance—can leave you feeling ten times more miserable than when you went in.

"Look at it like this, Cash," he said with his characteristic bombastic firmness. "It's our job to bring your genius . . ."

I'm sorry???

". . . your *genius* to the screen. We know you're good at what you do. You're *very* good at what you do. So how about you let us do what we're good at? You have to trust us. Don't fight it. Let us guide you. We're all on the same team here."

Aaaaaaaaaaah!!!

Suddenly, a light went on. Hearing that word—team—it came to me: now I knew why everyone was so upset. It was because of my well-advertised aversion to, and undeniable feebleness in the face of, danger.

Ever since Australia, when I'd resisted going down the opal mine on a faulty winch that was only marginally safer, according to the guy operating it, than hurling myself into the fifty-foot shaft headfirst, rumors had filtered back to Los Angeles that, somewhat bizarrely, the star of this major global adventure travel series: (*a*) didn't seem to enjoy traveling very much; and (*b*) was not adventurous in the least. If nobody believed me at the start when I told them I was a totally new breed of daredevil, the kind who's not remotely daring and takes no risks whatsoever, they were sure believing it now.

In television, where people will do almost anything for money, even if they can't then spend it because of being dead, self-preservation is seen as pure heresy. Whereas in my world it's Priority Number 1, which merely proves how ahead of my time I am.

In hindsight, if I had to nominate one incident that best illustrates the problem, and which, in some people's jaundiced eyes, spoiled the show, it would probably be the one in New Zealand.

A breezy March morning. I was fresh off a ferry boat in Queenstown on the South Island. Billed as the Adventure Capital of the World, Queenstown cowers before a sweeping amphitheater of mountains arranged like banks of snow-capped throw pillows on the shores of Lake Wakatipu and reflected in smooth waters of cobalt blue. But here's the problem: you can't go calling your town something as bold as the Adventure Capital of anything without subsequently attracting a broad spectrum of type A daredevils hell-bent on killing themselves, if they can only figure out how. Luckily, whatever your self-annihilation needs may be—parasailing off a perilously high peak; jet-boating along turbulent, boulder-strewn rivers; bungee-jumping—Queenstown has it all. Especially the last one.

The thing they don't tell you about bungee-jumping is that it involves throwing yourself off a ledge at a great height and tumbling at enormous speeds toward the ground. Or maybe they do; I didn't read the leaflet.

The sport originated in Vanuatu, and continues there to this day on the island of Pentecost, where it's called *naghol*, or land-diving, a timeless ritual in which teenage boys attempt to prove to their tribe that they've matured into manhood (and possibly don't want to get any older) by building a rickety seventy-five-foot tower, then tying vines to their ankles and leaping off the top. Done right, the boy's head skims the earth, fertilizing the soil for the upcoming harvest. Done wrong, *his whole body* ends up fertilizing the soil for the upcoming harvest.

Now, I need hardly tell you that jumping off rickety towers isn't an exact science. Many times the practice results in catastrophe. Either the vines snap and the kid plunges to the ground, breaking his neck. Or the vines are too long and he slams into the earth and is knocked unconscious. Occasionally, things go a little better and the boy merely feels his spleen burst open on impact. The whole thing's a lottery, really.

Anyway, back to the story.

New Zealanders Henry Van Asch and his business partner A. J. Hackett were the first to see the potential of land-diving as an extreme sport. If only there was a way to reduce that pesky death-toll thing, they thought, which research showed might deter repeat business and be a turnoff to certain customers. So over the next two years they worked diligently in tandem with the University of Auckland to invent a super-strong cable that wouldn't snap under pressure. This became the bungee they use today.

No sooner had I walked into his office and met Henry, a cheerful, strapping, curly-haired shortcake in a padded anorak with his company's logo on the back, than he decided to take the morning off work and drive me to his best site, at Nevis Bluff, the highest bungee jump in the country. Do I have the luck of the Devil or what? The Nevis setup is an engineering marvel. Somehow, Henry's team of wizards has managed to magic a large metal gondola the shape of a blunted acorn across the gorge on four wires and suspend it midway. You reach it by means of a small, fragile-looking cable car, though I'm unable to confirm this since I closed my eyes the instant someone mentioned the words "cable car" and told me I'd be going on one. When you get there, the gondola feels a lot sturdier than you'd imagined. It's made up mostly of windows, to be scenic, but then totally bucks the idea of the fourth wall by only having three of them. On one side of the main platform, a yawning gap opens up to a dizzying, uninterrupted 134-meter drop to the Nevis River below.

"Eeee-heeeeee." Mark grinned upon seeing it for the first time. "That's sick!"

Indeed.

"Why on earth would you do this?" I asked a frightened young girl as she was being harnessed up.

"I need the buzz, the excitement," she trembled. "I'm always trying to find something that excites me a bit more."

"So learn to play the cello."

"Oh no, no, no, no. Not quite the same thing!" And on the count of three she dived over the edge and disappeared.

My God.

It's an eight-second plunge to the bottom. So, after thirty seconds, when she hadn't reappeared, not unnaturally I assumed we'd lost her for good. "But hey, we should all move on with our lives," I told her friends. "It's what she would have wanted."

I spoke too soon. Before they even had time to begin the grieving process, the giant winch was already grinding into action, hauling her up again. A minute and a half later she was back, shaken, red-faced, screeching with delight, and definitely not as dead as some of us had been predicting.

"Regret it?" I asked.

"No. *You* should do it."

One of her friends even taunted me. "You want to do it, but you're scared."

"No, I *don't* want to do it," I corrected him, "*because* I'm scared."

"It's nothing to worry about," another guy chipped in, shortly before he grabbed three oranges and stood on the very edge of a little diving board, juggling. "It's such an awesome system that's in place and you've got to put your faith in something. So I put my faith in the system itself, the bungee, the training, and all the engineering that goes into it." Then, yodeling and juggling, he jumped. What a madman.

"Dude, you *have* to do it," Director Mark told me when my turn came.

"No. Not a chance." I dismissed him brusquely, making to go.

"But you can't come all the way to New Zealand and not jump."

"D'you wanna bet? Just watch me."

Well, the whole crew was stunned. Even Henry was a little at a loss for words. But I'm sorry, that's just how I felt. For a start, I'm terrified of heights; there was no conceivable way I'd be jumping out of a bloody gondola into a gorge. But beyond that, I've never understood the ballyhoo about conquering your fears and "being all you can be." It's such a silly alpha-male thing. The rest of us, luckily, are secure enough in ourselves to stand firm. Why not be *less* than you can be? That's what I say. Why not do what makes you feel comfortable, especially if it also means you stay safe, happy, unstressed, and in one piece? I told them this from the very start: when it comes to refusing to do things, consider me your go-to guy.

"But dude . . ."

"I'm not jumping, Mark! That's final. End of story!"

Well, you can probably guess what came next: a Crew Look.

Jeez, how I wish they'd stop doing that.

It was Eric who broke the impasse. "Okay, I wouldn't

ask you to do anything I wouldn't do," he said, then promptly threw his weedy, middle-aged, entirely-dispensable-as-far-as-I-was-concerned body off the platform into the unknown. Minutes later, he too came back, disheveled, thrilled, happy.

After him it was Camera Mark's turn to be hooked up to the harness. Mind you, I'm surprised he didn't simply do away with the bungee cord altogether and just jump, hoping for the best.

Then Director Mark went, followed by Todd, who dumped his sound equipment on the floor and leaped carefreely from the gondola, whooping loudly.

And finally, when it looked to them like I was still balking at the prospect, brave Tasha got harnessed up. Biting her lip and laughing, but with deadly worried eyes, she nevertheless dug up the courage from somewhere, counting down from three to one, and went for it, skipping off the platform and flinging her body into the wind, plunging freestyle 134 meters toward the river below.

"Oh my God. OH MY GOD!!!!!" she screamed moments later, her face packing in a thousand emotions all at once, as the winch pulled her into the arms of shortcake Henry Van Asch once more. "That was so *amazing*! Oh, Cash, you *have* to try it."

"Okay," Henry said, placing his hand on my arm. "You're up next."

And all eyes turned in my direction.

"But it's my show," I told Fat Kid back in the office weeks later, in response to his pep talk, which was not going well, "and if I don't want to do something on my show, why should I have to? Real, ordinary people don't bungee-jump.

Most people are like me; they're scared. Why should my show not reflect how . . . ?"

I got no further. His olive cheeks began to glow red and, as if triggered remotely by a cell phone some distance away, his rage blew up in my face.

"It's NOT . . ." Sparks flew from his eyes. ". . . YOUR show."

"It's not?"

"No, it's OUR show, okay? OUR show," he yelled, rubbing a manly hand through his gelled spiky hair. "Yours, ours, the network's show. NOT yours. Understand?"

Every superhero has a dark side. But this transformation—BOOOM—this switcheroo from light to dark, meek servant to dark overlord, was quite extraordinary. I was so shocked by it that I almost swallowed my gum.

"TELEVISION IS A *COLLABORATIVE* EFFORT." He was at full volume now. "IN RADIO, YOU OPERATE ALONE; YOU'RE A ONE-MAN BAND. AND THAT'S GREAT. BUT THAT'S NOT HOW TV WORKS, CASH. TELEVISION IS A TEAM EFFORT. AND IF YOU CAN'T ACCEPT THAT AND WORK AS PART OF OUR TEAM, THEN YOUR SHOW WILL FAIL."

Deep down, I knew he was right. Flustered and frustrated beyond measure at what he saw as an insufferably lame host who lived for comfort and ease and never took risks, he was at a loss for what to do. The very idea that the presenter of a TV adventure show would travel to an opal mine in the Australian Outback, then be too afraid to go down it; or climb a volcano in Vanuatu, but leave almost immediately because he was afraid of heights; or stand shivering on a ten-thousand-foot snowy mountain, unable to move because he found the ice too slippery; or fly halfway around the world to New Zealand, the home of bungee-jumping, then refuse outright to bungee-jump,[1] even after the rest of the crew had done it, was unheard of, and a catastrophe for the show. The whole production was being thrown for a loop by these minor acts of rebellion.

"WHAT YOU HAVE TO ASK YOURSELF IS THIS." And he lunged at me from his seat. "AM—I—A—TEAM—PLAYER?"

Well, maybe in the competitive, ego-driven type A world of television that he inhabits I do, where life is all politics and scoring points and proving how great you are, and where you never want to be seen to stand alone, or be the odd man out, or do the unpopular thing. But in my world, where you plod along on your own, working at your own pace, rarely competing with anyone but yourself, such factors are much less vital.

"SO?" he prompted after a long pause. "ARE YOU? *ARE YOU A TEAM PLAYER, CASH?*"

Er . . .

"No," I muttered, matching his pause moment for moment. "No, I'm not."

His eyes almost exploded from their sockets.

"THEN I'M SORRY," he proclaimed in a voice loud enough to steer ships away from rocks in a fog, "*BUT YOUR SHOW WILL FAIL.*"

And on that grim note of foreboding, with a face as dark as raked-over embers, he launched himself across the room,

---

[1] Oh yeah, I forgot to tell you. Of *course* I refused. Are you crazy? No freakin' way! The instant the camera was off, I removed my harness, traveled back to safety on the side of the gorge again, and retired to a café for a glass of wine and a long sit-down. The lesson? Never give in to peer pressure, kids. Go your own way, even if it means sabotaging your TV career to do it.

and even looked for a moment like he was going to fly out of the window and away. Instead, he dived back behind his desk and started typing.

The pep talk was over.

Relieved to be out from under his acetylene gaze, I slipped into the corridor, shaking slightly, and put in a call to The Thumb to inform him of the news, that the show was going to fail, bec—

"AND ANOTHER THING: *PLEASE* STOP CALLING THE NETWORK EVERY TIME YOU HAVE A PROBLEM."

—oops.

Soaring

10

The Girl with No Nose

"Well, Cash, good night. I wish you many blessings."

I'm lying on the floor in a *stupa*.

Not a stupor, a *stupa*. Some kind of Buddhist meditation building with a raised platform at one end.

Four timid young monks in saffron-colored robes stand over me, each one an expressionless mannequin, elevated by love and light and infinite patience into a state of lofty indifference that sets them above life's minor tribulations. Which is how we'd all like to be, I'm sure, only some of us have bills to pay.

It's around 8:30 P.M. Almost dark outside. Lit by a couple of bare bulbs high in the ceiling, the meditation room is murkily uninviting, although thankfully the temperature, which has been in the 100s all day and sticky, has dipped a little. Now it's just oppressively claustrophobic. Fairly typical, I dare say, for a Cambodian summer.

While I wait and watch, fumbling hands unroll a thin

mattress onto the bare wooden boards and rig a simple tent of blue mosquito netting over it.

Buddhist monks are by tradition nonviolent, honest, patient, effortlessly kind, and sober. So, of course, you'd never want to hang out with them socially. But here at Wat Bo Monastery it allows them to be very accommodating hosts, eager to welcome passing travelers to share their basic ways: eating simple food, wearing simple robes, and spending the night on a simple bed. And quite honestly, beds don't come much simpler than not having one.

"Our temple is open for the public of the world," the head monk told me on the way here. His name is Preah Maha Vimaladhamma PIN SEM Sirisuvanno, which unless I'm mistaken is also the chemical name for aspirin, and a bit of a mouthful, even for a Cambodian.

"So I can come and stay for free?"

"Yes. For one, two, three days," he said.

"Wow, this gets better and better!" The word "free" has the same effect on me that a hefty tax rebate has on others, or finding a neighbor's expensive magazines stuck in my mailbox by mistake. Nothing can quite beat the rush of exhilaration I feel on learning that something is to be handed to me on a plate with absolutely no effort on my part. "And where will I be sleeping?"

"This way."

Down on the floor of the stupa, I find myself addressing Vim's bare ankles. (I call him Vim for short.) He's a slight, round-headed man with the permanent strained expression on his face of someone who's expecting a balloon to be popped close by his ear at any second. Despite his calm-enough-to-be-mistaken-for-dead demeanor and the noble position he holds within this young spiritual community, unfortunately for him he also possesses the voice of a fiendish supervillain, a creepy nasal monotone drone emitted through barely open lips, like an English tavern sign creaking in the wind, the way they do in old werewolf movies—*nyeeeeeerk nyeeeeeerk nyeeeeeeeerk.* Somehow within that sound, words are formed. Fiendish-sounding words.

"Well, Cash, good night . . ."—*nyeeeeerk*—". . . we wish you many blessings. Tonight you are sleeping here alone. Is it comfortable for you?"

"It is very comfortable," I respond through the netting. "So what do I do tomorrow?"

"You get up to have breakfast with us."

"And what will we be eating?"

"Rice porridge. It is traditional for Cambodian monks to eat it."

Rice porridge, eh? Hm. Maybe I'll sleep in.

The monks press their hands together, give a little nod of the head, then shuffle from the platform in single file, while I turn over and make as if I'm going to nod off.

"Okay, cut," Jay says, rushing in. Jay's our supermotivated new director for this show, taking up where Mark left off. "How was that, Kevin?"

Oh, yes, and we have a different cameraman.

After a quick check of the tape, Kevin shakes his head. Not enough light.

Back come the monks, pattering softly in loose sandals, to fan around my sleeping bag for a second time, looking amused at the idea that reality can be relived. Though why that would bother them I don't know. Isn't it the very essence of reincarnation?

This time a brighter indoor lamp is positioned in one corner and we go again.

"Well, Cash,"—*nyeeeerk*—"tonight you will sleep alone here. Is it comfortable?"

"It is. Thank you very much. I'll see you in the morning

for breakfast. Good night." Relieved, I close my eyes and roll over.

The room I'm in seems to be some kind of run-down auditorium. Intimate and musty with a high, raftered ceiling and a small raised platform at one end, it's like something the Southeast Asian touring company of *Call Me Madam* might rehearse in. The platform is where I'll be sleeping tonight. Or trying to. Because, after a few seconds of snoozing, I realize that the monks haven't gone away. They're still outside the mosquito netting, staring down at me.

"No, no, cut!"

Jay circles the room in big purposeful strides and explains again. "After Cash says good night, you all need to move away from him. Go this way,"—he outlines a path to the door—"the way you did the first time."

Vim translates for the others. *Nyeeeeerk.* They get it.

"Good. Let's go again. Action."

"So, Cash, tonight you sleep here alone. This place doesn't have any . . ." *nyeeeeeeerk* ". . . sound to disturb you. We will see you in the morning for breakfast."

"All right, thank you very much. Good night."

Through the wall of my makeshift sarcophagus I see four shaven heads bob this way and that, each checking to see what the others are doing, before maneuvering themselves with anything but certainty toward the door.

"Aaaaaand . . . cut!" Convinced that mild confusion is the best he can hope for from these guys, Jay puts us out of our agony. "All right, that's it for today. Thank you."

Yay!

The lights are switched off, along with the camera. Hot but relieved, everyone disperses into the fresh air, leaving me lying on bare boards in the dark, because I have to stay here for the entire night now—that's the new rule. Previously, we didn't think this was important. We weren't making a survival show, it was entertainment, remember? But then I started to hear rumblings. Rumblings and grumblings.

"Don't question me about it," a slightly testy Tasha said when I asked, running a hand through her bleached ends to flatten them, then giving three sharp tosses of the head to make it all look wild again. "I'm not allowed to say. All I know is, you have to spend the *whole* night in each place from now on."

"Really? Who said?"

But she wouldn't be drawn. Nor would the rest of the crew, nor anyone at the office when we got back. How frustrating. This whole TV production process is so threaded with intrigue and secret lines of communication, I doubt anyone fully understands what's going on. But if they do, then they're not leaking any of it to me. However, if I had to take a crazy stab at a guess, I'd say that Vanuatu is at the back of this somehow, and here's why.

The week after we finished shooting on Tanna, I came across a short puff piece on a Vanuatan news website, proclaiming in its own peculiar form of English:

> The program . . . has ended with a positive note for a visitor to experience reality on an island. For this episode, the host is dropped off at a location unknown to him. Over the course of the show, Cash and the viewers at home experience a new place together with Cash showing viewers how to survive in a tropical island, what to do, what to eat, what one is expecting to see and what not to do on the island.

The article carried on to say that the show:

> . . . represents a terrific promotional opportunity for the tourist destinations, which features the reality of an island and the experiences in Vanuatu.

Hm.

As nice an idea as this was, that's not quite how things turned out. We planned to show viewers what life was like in an unspoiled tropical paradise: exciting, dangerous, sweaty, and full of bugs. *Full of bugs.* Bugs that suck holes in your legs. In other words, we intended to tell the truth. What could possibly be wrong with that?

At some point I even recall giving a short interview to a newspaper in Texas, which appeared under the banner "Itinerant Traveler Has One Tip: Avoid Vanuatu!" in which I'd summed up in two words my advice to anybody planning a trip to Tanna: "Don't go."[1]

Kidding, of course.

Well, okay, half-kidding.

So here's my theory: what if this silly little article found its way onto the desk of someone important in Vanuatu? Not the part of Vanuatu that's without trousers or phones, or even desks, but on Efaté, for example. The capital, Port Vila, is a modern growing city of mod cons: web access, cars, and refrigerators, food that doesn't run away as you're trying to fry it, and electricity. They also have lawyers—uh-oh. Lawyers who, because they're not fleeing in terror all day long from erupting volcanoes, have plenty of time on their hands to read foreign news articles about their country, which everyone is desperately anxious, for economic reasons, to promote to the rest of the world as a must-visit

[1] Which I still feel they should adopt as their promotional slogan. It's a winner. Call me, Vanuatu, we'll talk.

tourist destination. And what if this unnamed, and possibly nonexistent, lawyer discovered that I'd told people "Don't go!" to his lovely country (or, worse-case scenario, he'd watched the actual Vanuatu episode on his magical flickering light box), and freaked out? The way the people of Solvang freaked out.

"Hey, wait a Wuhngin-damned minute!" he may have said to himself in Bislama. "This program, she is not 'a terrific promotional opportunity for the tourist destinations, which features the reality of an island and the experiences in Vanuatu.' No, man, *this is bullshit.*"

And, oh my God, *what if* he instigated a top-level inquiry and Joe spilled the beans that I'd not spent the whole night in Yakel Village, only part of a night, and the nonexistent lawyer had threatened to reveal this to the world?

As I say, it's all guesswork and I could be way off the mark. But even if it wasn't that, something serious must have happened to compel us to play by these new sleeping rules.

While the crew is packing up outside, Jay and I hold an impromptu meeting.

"So how long do I have to stay here, d'you think?" I ask, wriggling to find a comfortable spot on the hard floor. "How many hours?"

Through the veil of my tent, Jay, a mercurial wisp of a man whose face in repose invariably sags into gloom, stands like a red-haired phantom against a darkening sky. "Five," he volunteers.

"We're saying a night lasts five hours? Really?"

His eyes sparkle mischievously. "Well, some people only sleep for five hours a night, don't they?"

Sure. Parents of newborn babies. People passing kidney stones. Fugitives.

It's an audacious stretching of the truth, but we're running with it. From now on, all I have to do is sleep or rest in a place for five hours, and that apparently counts as the whole night. Agreed.

Cambodia is not what it was. And thank God for that! Because what it was, and we're talking only a few years ago, was a bottomless swamp of Communist tyranny, war, and genocide; a place you could fly to and, within a short time of your arrival, pretty much count on having your ass blown off.

In the early 1970s, the political situation here was ugly. Not only were they having serious problems controlling an unruly group of rebel commies called the Khmer Rouge, but there was also a right-wing military coup going on, trying to declare Cambodia a republic, a move planned and funded in part by the U.S. government.

As you can imagine, this coup was a source of major upset to their neighbors, the North Vietnamese, who were enraged. "How *dare* you!" they fumed, and straight away expanded their military presence in Cambodia, building camps and joining forces with the Khmer Rouge to destabilize the republic, which in turn enraged the United States. "No, how dare *you*!" President Richard Nixon blustered at them from his office back in Washington, safe from all the fighting[2] and ordered U.S. troops to attack the camps and kill insurgents using land mines. And in case you're thinking, "But how did any of this make things better?" It didn't. Wars don't, generally. Their only real purpose is to thin out the global population and keep it at reasonable levels. In due course, anyway, such blatant antagonism enraged the North

---

[2] Funny how that works.

Vietnamese and the communist insurgents further, to the point where they too began planting land mines in an effort to kill Americans.

From here the situation spiraled into hell. When the republic fell finally in 1975, the Khmer Rouge was left running Cambodia under the rule of a guy called Pol Pot.

In photos he's quite the charmer, with a smiley, kind face. The sort of guy you'd let babysit your grandkids or count the collection money at your church. Whereas, in reality, he was an odious psycho-madman who'd kill one and steal the other.

As prime minister, he banished thousands of city dwellers into the countryside, where they perished of disease and starvation. He confiscated and destroyed private cars, made it illegal for anyone to wear jewelry or glasses, and stomped out any religion he didn't happen to care for, including Buddhism. Random atrocities became the norm. People were shot on the spot for being gay. Others were made to dig their own grave, then beaten unconscious with a hammer and pushed into it. Whole families were run over with tanks and flattened. Children were tied to posts, where they were whipped without mercy. Horror upon horror upon horror. It was one of the worst bouts of ethnic cleansing in history. Furthermore, Pol Pot set about mass-murdering as many eminent teachers, politicians, librarians, police officers, intellectuals, monks, and social leaders as his attack-dog soldiers could get their hands on. Anyone senior enough, enlightened enough, or literate enough to recall the good old days before the Khmer Rouge rose to power, and who might, God forbid, pass on stories about those days to others, maybe causing the young folk to rebel against the obvious joys of life under Maoist Communism and demand freedom, was slaughtered.

Nobody's able to pin a final total on the carnage, but a

conservative estimate has 25 percent of Cambodia's 7 million inhabitants dying at Pol Pot's hands during those years; 1.5 million have since been recovered from mass graves. Statistics that are impossible to comprehend and that left a dark stain not only on the region, but the world.

I read recently that roughly one million antipersonnel mines were laid during the civil war days, and in the most innocent of places too—places ordinary people might walk: in forest glades, on footpaths, in the vicinity of small villages, alongside rivers. Yet, despite concerted clearance efforts, thousands of them, not to mention antivehicle mines, booby traps, and bombs left over from multiple air raids, remain scattered across the countryside.

This makes the job on a show of this sort that much more difficult.

In other locations, when we're shooting B-roll, the cameraman simply points and says, "Okay, Cash, see where I'm pointing? Go stand over there and start walking toward me," and that's what I do. But yesterday, when Kevin, our zippy new camera guy, tried this, ordering me to amble through a sunlit forest glade (check), along a footpath (check) that passed close by a village (check), beside a small, lazy river (check), for obvious reasons I freaked out and refused.

"Cash, you'll be fine. There are no land mines around here," he said. "Siem Reap is a major tourist destination. I'm sure somebody—the government—cleared them away."

"How sure?"

"Well, er . . ."

Precisely. He's not *that* sure. Not sure-sure. Nobody is.

In the past few years, millions of square meters of land in Cambodia have been cleared, coordinated by the Cambodian Mine Action and Victim Assistance Authority, or CMAA for short (which, cruelly, also happens to be the last sound you hear after you step on a mine). Princess Diana was involved at one point in raising awareness, as was popular actorvist Angelina Jolie. For that reason, and because there is no greater natural force on the planet than the force of celebrity, progress is definitely being made.

Which is great news. But I'm still not budging.

Since the late 1970s, there have been almost sixty thousand land-mine or bomb casualties in Cambodia. *Sixty thousand!!* And 98 percent of the casualties are civilian. Which is why, before I'll walk anywhere, on-camera or off, Jay or Kevin or one of the others has to stride ahead of me, covering the same ground, while I stand far away with my fingers in my ears, cringing. Of course, I pay for this cowardly reluctance with another Crew Look, but so what? I don't care how many mines the CMAA has cleared, I don't even care if Angelina Jolie went out there personally with a chimpanzee and a big long stick and exploded them herself; there are still thousands more to be found, lying in wait to ambush the unwary.

On a brighter note, and all nightmares aside, Cambodia is as stable nowadays as any culture with a history of genocide, invasion, and protracted political turmoil could be. Stable enough at least to have become a popular stopping-off point for thousands of backpackers and other wandering souls as they go zigzagging through the backwoods of Southeast Asia and who come here to experience one place above all else: a monument just outside of Siem Reap whose staggering mystical grandeur will haunt them for a lifetime—Angkor Wat.

"Angkor Wat temple is one of the Seven Wonders of the World," a young rice trader called Rith informed me yesterday in the *p'saa,* the market in Siem Reap, shocked that I'd not heard of it.

"So how do I get there? How do I reach Angkor Wat?"

"Sorry?"

"Fleuv naa teuv Angkor Wat?" (That's your actual Cambodian.) "Is there a bus?"

He shook his head. No bus. His best suggestion for reaching the temple complex was a *tuk-tuk*.

"What's a *tuk-tuk*?" I asked.

"It can take you to Angkor Wat, ten miles," he replied in truncated English. "Is one of Seven Wonders of the World."

"Yes, yes, I know. You told me that. But what is it?"

Running ahead of me, Tasha found about a dozen *tuk-tuks* lined up for hire at the roadside, their drivers chatting in a huddle, fanning themselves with newspapers.

Basically, a *tuk-tuk* is a motorized rickshaw. Take a seat from a disused Ferris wheel, glue it to the back of a moped, and hey presto!

Once we'd picked out a vehicle, its owner came running.

"Me want *tuk-tuk*," I said. (Damn, I inadvertently slipped into Bislama there. Sorry. It's the jet-lag.) "I want to go to Angkor Wat."

The driver watched as I took out my money.[3] All fares are negotiable, so you're encouraged to haggle, either in U.S. dollars or in their local currency, riel, it's up to you.

---

[3] Rare for me to have any money on these shows, but back in L.A., anticipating that I wouldn't be able to pay for the *tuk-tuk* otherwise, the office had thought ahead and given me a wristwatch, to be used for bartering. With Rith's help I exchanged this in the market for thirteen dollars, which for an object with such profound sentimental value doesn't seem like a lot, but by Cambodian standards it's a fortune. I went in with nothing and came out as the new Bill Gates. Flush with cash, I bought a hat with a brim to protect me against the thrashing heat of the sun, as well as some weird sticky rice and bean banana-leaf burrito thing that Rith recommended as a local delicacy but which was *disgusting*. Ever eaten warm cavity wall insulation? Or *laplap* straight from the ground? It was like that.

"Teuv Angkor Wat th'lay pohnmaan?"

That's your actual Cambodian for "So how much might the fare be?"

Without thinking, he said: *"Muy lian"*—one million riel. And of course I laughed in his face. *In his face,* I tell you! What am I, an idiot?

"Er, how about four?" I offered instead. *"Buan."*

"Four?"

This standoff lasted . . . oh, all of three-tenths of a second.

"Okay, four," he nodded, deciding to take it in dollars instead, which in this town is almost enough to retire on, and we set off.

Rrrrrrrrrrr. Rrrrrrrrrrrrrrrrrrrr. Rrrrrrrrrrrrrrrr. Rrrrrr.

My *tuk-tuk* ride, though brief, was packed with incident.

At one point, two motor scooters buzzed by, the drivers carrying a long bamboo pole between them balanced on their left shoulders. Dangling from the pole, roped by its feet, was a whole dead pig.

A man to my left staggered along the sidewalk with ten plastic chairs stacked on his head. Someone else had a gong.

An old woman carrying a baby stepped into the road, then scrammed back to the curb with a yelp, a millisecond before a bus roared over the very spot where she'd been standing.

And this stuff is going on all the time. It's as if you're living in a Keystone Kops movie, only it's less funny because people could really get hit and killed.

Siem Reap has two distinct sides to it: a detached, elegant side—which is charming to look at, but not quite real somehow, given the rest of the place—and *then* the rest of the place, a dusty ghetto like the Old West, at once rough, tumultuous, and exciting. One minute you're in the back of your *tuk-tuk* bouncing past towering pagodas along a wide leaf-speckled avenue of splendid Colonial-style houses bathed in rich golden sunlight; the next, a mere block or two farther along, this brief idyll has evaporated and you descend into pandemonium, swallowed by a shimmering cacophonous typhoon of honking cars, mopeds, *tuk-tuks*, buses belching smoke, carts overloaded with bales of flopping hay tied into enormous spliffs, and wobbling cyclists of all ages who, if you're a pedestrian, don't necessarily *seek* to mow you down, but if it's a toss-up between hitting you full-on or braking suddenly, causing two thousand cyclists behind them to jackknife off a bridge, there's every chance you'll be a goner.

Horns *parp*, bicycle bells ring, shopkeepers unload trucks, calling out to each other as they do so and laughing; feral children—almost babies, it seems—homeless but happy, skitter unsupervised along the roadside, dusting off discarded fruit and licking it, before taking their chances and diving onto the highway into perilous traffic. I tried crossing a street myself and it's not easy. You just hold your breath and run. There are no lights or intersections, no particular code of conduct, beyond a general consensus that killing innocent pedestrians is uncool and might come back to bite you in the ass in some future lifetime. Basically, the only way these motorists will stop for you is if you're on their hood with your body scrunched up against the windshield and they can't see out. Luckily, drivers and cyclists seem to make an exception for children, navigating between the tiny trotting obstacles, graciously allowing them to make it to the other side untrampled.

Careening around corner after corner at speeds of up to twenty miles per hour, we passed terraces of odd-shaped shops piled carelessly one on top of the other like rickety beer crates. Every so often, through the haze and confusion, I'd pick out a cheerful starburst of reddish orange. Monks. A graceful flotilla of them, out for their daily constitutional. Instantly, the grimy roadside became a catwalk spectacle as they pressed on in single file against a rogue wind that threatened to drag their saffron-colored robes up about their shoulders, bald heads shielded from a merciless sun by saffron umbrellas. Nine of them in a bobbing row. Nine dancing orange pontoons. How marvelous. And how wonderfully savvy of them to coordinate their outfits with their accessories. Mind you, they were young. Additionally, in a lot of cases, meditation seems to have put them very much in touch with their feminine side—ahem—so maybe their fashion sense was not too much of a surprise. I'm guessing that the elders, having long since outgrown their obsession with style's dos and don'ts, and too old to make this daily trek into town, allow the novices to go unsupervised, keeping their fingers crossed that, by doing so, they don't fall in with the wrong crowd while they're out. After all, you know what monks are like!

Rrrrrrrrrrrrrr. Rrrrrrrrrrrrrrrrrrrrrrrrr. Rrrr. Rrrrrrrrrrrrrrrrrrrrrr.

"ANGKOR WHAT?"

It's a joke. The name of a bar. Someone at the office tracked it down, thought it might make for an extra story beat if I stopped off on my way to the temple.

A lot of streets in Siem Reap don't have a name. Well, why bother, really? But Bar Street does. One of the most popular thoroughfares in town, it's calm and laid-back by day, convulsing with excitement and doused in neon by night, the sweet smell of curries drifting from the kitchens of tandoori restaurants along with the thumping beat of European music that pumps continuously out of odd windows and doorways. Located not far from the main market, this short, dusty avenue is a big draw to tourists, and, by extension, to dozens of beggars as well. The sidewalks swarm with them: small kids mostly, cloaked in the grime of the gutter, their hands outstretched, and also adult land-mine victims doing the same thing—when they have hands, that is, which is not always. Altogether, they're the country's restless conscience, hard-to-overlook remnants of past atrocities. There's still no welfare system in Cambodia, and no other safety net to catch the destitute when they drop off the social ladder, so panhandling is all that's left.

I'll be honest, some of the beggars' injuries are hard to deal with if you're squeamish. Sometimes even the cup they're holding is broken,[4] that's how badly off they are, placing you in the worst dilemma imaginable. Sheer human decency demands that you give them something, brother to struggling brother. A few coins, a dollar bill, what the hell! How can you withstand such dire need? Yet you must. Show compassion, and you start a stampede. A dozen grasping urchins, sniffing a payout, descend upon you to claim their share. Rith the rice seller did his best to shoo them away from us,[5] but to no avail. They simply regroup, coming back at you with even greater persistence than before.

---

[4] How much worse can things get than that? You're a limbless beggar confined to the gutter in Cambodia and now your cup is broken, so the money drops out. Seriously, is there a God? You tell me, because I'm not sure any more.

[5] Yes, he was still with us! He followed us around everywhere like a stray dog, mesmerized by the whole TV thing. Try as I might, I couldn't shake the guy off. Indeed, Sir was all for calling the cops—until I discovered he was now doubling as our translator, and I'd be doing the show a disservice if I went out of my way to have him arrested.

"Pliss, mister, pliss!" Grubby hands claw at your shirt. "Pliss! Pliss, mister!"

It's heartbreaking. But also, if I'm being absolutely truthful, the most terrible nuisance, especially if you dare give money to one but not the others. At that point those angelic little faces turn quite nasty, shouting and cursing you out. Luckily, they don't speak enough English to cause real offense. All they seem to know are some generic brush-offs—the prime one being "Go fuck yourself!"—which, unless *Frommer's* has dropped the standards of its glossary drastically to snag the youth market, I assume they picked up from angry backpackers trying to outrun them.

The whole scene on Bar Street was quite difficult, anyway, and I'm glad I had Tasha close by to protect me.

I come across a delicate dark-haired girl in Cambodian national dress—that is to say, a dress—standing in some trees beside a board with prices on it.

"Hello, good morning, I'm looking for Angkor Wat," I say to her. Adding, for clarity, "It's a temple, you know," in case she's new. "D'you know where it is?"

"Yes. Angkor Wat is over there. One kilometer and a half. You want to take trip on elephant?"

In real life, she'd know never to ask me anything so ridiculous. Of *course* I don't want to ride on an elephant, what a silly question. Not only are they dangerous, they're also a lot more menacing up close than they look in movies. A guy could quite easily fall off one and break something. So no—no, I don't want to take trip on elephant, thank you very much.

But, unfortunately, I'm no longer possessed of the rebellious spirit I once had. A few weeks and five shows ago, maybe. Back then I'd have refused, same way I refused to go bungee-jumping and waltzing around the rim of erupting volcanoes, but not now. To begin with, there was Fat Kid's alarming pep talk: "Be a team player OR YOUR SHOW WILL FAIL," which, to be honest, has kind of spooked me. I've always believed that thoughts are things. Put thoughts of failure out there and you draw them back to you ten times over. The series hasn't even premiered on TV yet, but on that basis alone it already feels doomed. More than this, though, I'm weary. A creeping fatigue, sprouting from equal measures of overwork and sleep deprivation after so much intensive traveling, has left me a beaten man. Also, Jay's very persistent when it comes to these challenges. Generally speaking, by the time I've stood my ground and argued with him about why I shouldn't do something—riding an elephant, for instance—I could have gone ahead and done it already, sparing myself a whole load of red-faced frustration and Crew Looks. So:

"How much?"

"Fifteen dollars per person from here to Angkor Wat." The girl smiles.

Interesting.

Handing over a wad of bills with the firm expectation that it will be handed back again once the camera's off, and leaving Tasha to explain to her why, and how television works,[6] I scale a wooden staircase that leads to the branches

---

6 Before you say it, I know fifteen dollars is more than I made from selling the watch in the market. And yes, I've also bought a hat since then, plus that slimy burrito thing and a *tuk-tuk* ride, out of the original money, leaving me with about two dollars. "So how can you afford fifteen dollars for an elephant ride now, then?" you're asking. "It doesn't make sense." To which I would say, "Good point. Well spotted. But this is TV. Let's not ruin it with logic."

of the tree, and from there onto a rickety wooden platform only slightly different from one of those tray tables you eat your dinner off while you're watching *Jeopardy*!

Here, using some perfunctory acrobatic skills I didn't know I had (hurray, those days at clown college are *finally* paying off!), I splay my legs over its spine and settle in, faking one of those maharaja poses I've seen a dozen times in old movies: head erect, back straight, limbs loose, allowing my entire body to undulate and sway in sync with the elephant's lumbering gait.

The driver, a young boy—seems no older than twelve—pivots nimbly on the creature's giant head and steers it to left or right by hitting it with a stick and repeatedly kicking its ears. Of course, if elephants had any wit at all, they'd unionize and put a stop to this. But they don't. Like me, they've been knocked down too low to stage a rebellion.

With the first drops of rain from an approaching storm spotting my face, we lollop along at tree height onto an ancient causeway lined with squat, weather-worn statues: fifty-four gods and demons, stretching from one end to the other in long snakes. Beyond them, a crumbling stone arch is set into a wall over twenty-five feet high, the entrance to the temple complex.

Kevin and Mike, his soundman, are up ahead, filming me from a different elephant.

"So what's the next step up on the career ladder as far as elephant-driving goes?" I shout to the boy. "Do you get a faster elephant?"

"Huh?"

I see Mike wince. Oops. Was that the wrong question to ask? A little tactless? Condescending?

As it is, the kid has a poor grasp of English and doesn't understand.

Maybe that's just as well.

A REFRESHINGLY BRIEF HISTORY OF ANGKOR WAT

In 1100 A.D., the ruler of the Khmer Empire was King Suryavarman II. To honor the Hindu god Vishnu, "creator of all beings, sustainer of the universe,"[7] he began construction on a new sandstone temple in Angkor, his capital city. This he called Angkor Wat, an ambitious sprawling layer cake of a thing, epic in scale, with a rectangular moat almost two hundred meters wide, pools inside and out, and all manner of cupolas, statuary, and colonnades to divert and enchant the eye. Estimated completion time: seventy-five years later.

Shortly after it was done, in 1177, the Chams, from neighboring Champa (later South Vietnam), came thundering in to kick the Khmers' imperial ass, looting homes and temples in Angkor and setting fire to anything that would burn, which was basically everything. Everything but Angkor Wat.

Once the Chams had been chased out, in 1181, a new king, the powerful and audacious Jayavaman VII, found himself with a problem. Many of his people, faced with a decimated city and their homes and livelihoods in ruins, began to question whether the gods they'd put so much faith in all these years, and who were supposed to protect them from harm, were real. *Maybe,* they argued, the gods were fake: a brilliant ruse concocted by clever minds to keep society in check by instilling fear and superstition in the gullible. Maybe religion was, after all, nothing but a made-up bunch of old hooey.

Uh-oh.

---

7 Probably.

Quickly, Jayavaman gathered his generals. "Damn, they're onto us!" he said.

Then, after a little thought, he did something very clever.

Rather than risk an uprising, which would have cost him his throne, he switched religions. Just like that. Dumped Hinduism, which was very god-driven and quite strict, and adopted Buddhism instead, on the grounds that it was loose and joyful and free, and you got to wear orange all the time.

Well, miraculously, and bizarrely, this simple act was enough to quell the tide of discontent in the city of Angkor and reignite religious fervor.

"Oooh!" the people said. *"Orange!"*

Without wasting a second, they began building a bunch of new temples,[8] this time honoring Buddha, surrounding them with a ravishing new city called Angkor Thom, which would eventually become the center of Jayavaman's empire, including a great wall, an impressive moat, and with the commanding and beautiful temple of Angkor Wat at its center.

THE END

I stumble blithely through the gate of Angkor Wat without paying the twenty-dollar admission fee (natch), drawing to a stop in front of one of the most stunning monuments on Earth, a vision too big, too grand, too complex, too elaborate, too multifaceted, and too overwhelming to sum up in mere words, although, I must admit, big, grand, complex, elaborate, multifaceted, and overwhelming do come pretty close.

---

[8] Two hundred and twenty in this area alone. It's all people did in those days, apparently. That, and tear them down again.

What it's *not,* though, is one of the Seven Wonders of the World. That punk Rith, the rice seller, he was dead wrong. I knew there was something odd going on there. Immediately after I spoke to him, I went out of my way to check several lists, including the Seven Ancient Wonders list, the Seven Modern Wonders list, and even, for the sake of completeness, the Seven Underwater Wonders list, and Angkor Wat is not on any of them. A calamitous oversight in my view, since, thanks to continual restoration work, Angkor Wat has remained pretty much intact, which is more than can be said for some of the other temples around here.

There's one up the road, for instance, called the Bayon, that dates back to the twelfth century and, from a distance, looks as though it was left out in the sun too long and melted. Pathways sag. Archways crumble. Musty, sharply rising staircases, treacherous if you're wearing heels, lie in wait to help less-focused tourists twist their ankles. They're held together nowadays by little more than good intentions and air, their stone blocks, carved with beautiful symbolic dancing figures, strewn discarded across the grass like Lego. It's highly precarious. One misstep, and you could bring the whole thing crashing down around you.

Within minutes, a pelting rain sets in, chasing five thousand tourists back to their buses, cheap guidebooks spread over their heads, at the same time sending a dozen or more guidebook sellers scurrying for cover beneath the trees in the parking lot.

"I wasn't expecting it to be as crowded as this," Jay sighs, upset.

Good, clear shots are hard to come by. Kevin, a lean runner type with etched bones and a deep, knowing eye, scoots from plinth to column to window frame to crumbling doorway, grabbing what he can, mostly in vain. No matter where he points his camera, anything from a student with a backpack to a whole herd of South Korean holidaymakers, hundreds strong, gets in the way, wandering idly across the background, streaming up broken steps, along corridors, through courtyards, posing for pictures and jabbering excitedly.

Click. South Korean coach-party group photo on causeway with temple in background.

Click. French coach-party group photo with bas-relief in background.

Click. French coach-party group photo with South Korean coach-party in background.

The rain is coming down in sheets now. Scampering for shelter, I hide inside the broad stone casing of what used to be a window, and watch as, all around me, storm clouds weep gently upon the temple ruins, in a warm, timeless drizzle that somehow, and quite uncannily, bridges the centuries.

Without realizing it, I find myself standing beside a small girl panhandling for change like so many others. She can't be much older than eleven or twelve, with long, slightly scrappy dark hair falling across the shoulders of her cute floral dress. A dainty creature ignored by tourists, her large, dejected brown eyes eventually lock into mine, pleading with me to give her something.

"Me?" When this happens I'm so horrified that I turn away immediately. Though it's not the glum intensity of her eyes that troubles me so much, it's her nose.

More specifically, she doesn't have one.

I swear. There's nothing there. A blank space.

And now I'm picturing this sweet, innocent creature running through a forest glade one day, down a footpath, or alongside a river in the vicinity of her village, when—

CMAA!—she steps on a land mine. Possibly an American land mine at that. The very thought of this tears a black hole in my stomach.

At that moment, forty sodden South Korean tourists come to my rescue, splashing along the causeway, hunched under umbrellas, and barge on through the doors of the temple, oblivious to anyone or anything.

Half of me—the dark, pathetic half—is hoping that they'll whisk the little girl away with them in their rush to get indoors, so that I won't have to deal with this situation or feel the depth of survivor's guilt that I do. But that's not the case. When the crowd dissipates, she's still there, in her pretty lace-trimmed floral summer dress, leaning against a stone balustrade. And we're right back where we started.

Doe-eyed, she rattles her cup, surveying my awkwardness calmly from behind the flap of pale grafted skin that connects her top lip to her forehead. I guess she's used to moments like this, to rejection, double-takes, revulsion, the slow drip of pity from passersby, and is inured to them. But knowing this doesn't make it any easier to deal with, or alleviate the profound sadness I feel as I try to avoid staring at her.

"No," I plead silently, "please don't rattle your cup at me. I have nothing to give you."

I want to explain that I'm making a dumb, gimmicky TV travel show where I visit foreign lands without money and pretend I'm hungry and desperate and poor. Christ, what a feeble concept that's seeming right now; what a miserably lame idea for a piece of so-called entertainment. I don't even carry loose change. Whatever money I have is given to Tasha between shots for safekeeping. As proof, I drag the lining out of my trouser pockets, mumbling under my breath, "I'm sorry. I'm sorry."

Then, badly shaken, and stung to the point of tears, I do what everyone else seems to do to the girl with no nose: I dive through the temple doors and run off.

If you can work it that you visit Angkor Wat in the early hours of the morning while the tourists are back at their hotel eating breakfast, or in the evening while they're having dinner, it's a blissful, entrancing experience. Or so I hear. As it is, I arrive midafternoon and find that the reverie of traveling through time is almost impossible here, marred as it is by Swedish babies crying, Argentinean camera shutters turning over, German students scrunching together for a group photo, and the infuriating nonstop clatter-patter of sensible English walking shoes echoing down the dark stone passageways. It's utterly depressing. Like watching ants dismantle a dead bird. I mean, if you can't be alone even for a couple of seconds in a place that was constructed for that very purpose, then you can't find peace, and what's a temple without peace? It's just a building.

Curiously, even if you take the initiative and walk against the flow, somehow you end up in the same place as everyone else: a giant, scalable stone tower on the roof. Shaped like an elongated pyramid, it rises steep and looms ominous, and is supposed to represent Mount Meru, home of the gods in Hindu tradition. It was here, at its summit, that King Suryavarman erected a giant golden statue honoring Vishnu, who, though acclaimed as "the creator of all things," appeared, when it came to constructing this tower anyway, to be very much dependent on mankind to knuckle down and do the heavy lifting for him.

The statue was placed at the tip of some thin stone steps, more like little ledges really, numbering around twenty-five in all, rising to a point some thirty feet high. Think of it as an early Cambodian escalator, one that's broken and no longer moves.

Cowering in an alcove out of the lashing rain, I watch amused, along with a crowd of eager spectators, as several elderly robust grandmothers from the American Midwest tell themselves that you can't come all the way from Ohio to the greatest Buddhist temple in the world and not see the golden statue of Vishnu, can you? Of course not. So, goading each other with clucking noises and cries of "chicken," they take a deep breath, adjust their plastic rain hats, smear water off their spectacles, and brave the downpour to begin their mission.

"Don't look down!" some wag shouts at them when they're still on the first step.

"Martha! Martha, over here," someone else cries, waving a camera. "Smile."

But Martha is in no mood to smile. Gutsily, she soldiers on against the raging elements, scaling a further seven steps before pausing for breath, at which point a vexatious westerly wind, sensing an opportunity for comedy, rushes in to lift up her pleated gray skirt, exposing a flash of senior buttock-flab to the crowd below. More senior buttock-flab, I'd say, than any human being with a gag reflex ought to be exposed to.

"Okay, off you go," Jay manifests out of nowhere and hisses in my ear. "Give us five minutes, then start climbing. I'll tell Kevin."

"Excuse me—are you *out of your freakin' mind?*" Fat Kid's rousing pep talk is suddenly a distant memory. "Have you seen how high it is? I am not—repeat, NOT—going up there!"

But Jay's a different directing animal from Mark, harder to dissuade. Faced with any obstacle—a reluctant TV host is the first example that comes to mind—he adopts one of those long-suffering expressions he does so well, of a mother supervising a petulant three-year-old whom she loves dearly, but not today, not right now, and sighs heavily.

"Cash," he groans, "you'll be fine. If a bunch of old biddies can climb it, I'm sure you can. Now—go." Then, without even allowing me the common courtesy of arguing with him, he plows deep into the crowd, shouting over his shoulder, "Don't bother about where the camera is, Kevin will find you. Just keep climbing."

Two steps from the top, Martha has staggered to a premature halt. Aware now that two hundred people are looking up her skirt, she tries to grip it between her knees, a move that could be her undoing. Several shaky squeals are lost amidst the laughter and general hullabaloo in the courtyard, as still more people, teased into joining this folly, each of them thinking, "Well, if the old bag in the pink bloomers can do it, so can I!," tie on rain hats and start their own ascent.

As I watch their feet slither and slide across the watery ledges, the same ugly, gnawing fear I felt staring into that 134-meter gorge in New Zealand and Mount Yasur's fiery crater, begins eating away at my intestines once again.

I hate heights! Is nobody listening to me when I say this? *I hate heights.*

And remember, my definition of heights is pretty modest, too: anything higher than a bar stool, really. Yet, even as the tension is choking me, I recall Fat Kid's admonitions: teamwork, collaboration, it's not just about me, and so on. And as I do, in some peculiar way it weakens the grip of my terror a little, infusing it with an unexpected surge of resolve. Maybe I can do this. If I just focus my mind and ignore the drop.

Besides, I reason to myself, if I do lose my footing on the

steps, there'll be enough old women in rain hats coming up behind me to cushion my fall, won't there?

Good thinking.

Considerably cheered by this, I wait five minutes, then run through the rain to the base of the pyramid.

As it is, my worst fears prove to be groundless. The climb is a breeze and takes me a mere ten minutes top to bottom. I even overtake Martha and her slow-coach friends on the way up, as I make it, damp, dizzy, out of breath, and with pins and needles in my feet, to the top step and the very summit of Mount Meru.

Yay!

Who would have thought that? Sir contained his anxiety for long enough to climb a pyramid! If I had a baton I would twirl it. Indeed, so slap-happy am I at this rare triumph over one of my phobias that I perch jauntily on the edge for a while to allow the camera, which I'm unable to spot in the scrum below but I know is there somewhere, to record and savor this valiant accomplishment.

Then, once I've left enough time for Kevin to get his shot, I head off in search of the giant golden statue of Vishnu.

That's when I realize two things: first, there is no statue. It was apparently looted centuries ago, leaving one big dark empty space thirty feet up in the air that, take it from me, is not worth all the effort it takes to reach it. And second, once you grow tired of looking at a big dark empty space and decide to take the back stairs down to the bottom again, *there are no back stairs* either. I thought there might be, but there aren't.

I hunted for several minutes, pacing the missing-statue area five times, like a small kid lost in a department store, traipsing disconsolately in rectangular circles, becoming more agitated with every circuit.

"There has to be a back way," I thought. "There's always a back way."

But King Suryavarman, when he built this thing, it appears, had no exit strategy. The tower was the home of the gods, and the gods, because they were invented by man as a means of holding a primitive society together by fear, never came down to mingle with their subjects. How could they? They weren't there in the first place.

Instantly, my body registers how high I am off the ground—which is really, *really* high—and freezes. A rush of vertigo sends chills fizzing beneath my flesh. My feet feel light. The hair on my neck is bristling. And, oh God, my scrotum is starting to *tingle*—like it's full of champagne bubbles. In my world that's a sure sign something is about to happen. Could be bad or good, I'm never sure—my scrotum doesn't differentiate.

All of a sudden, the wind renews its efforts to dislodge me, tossing fresh squalls of warm rain into my face. I'm quite a way from the edge, eight feet or so, yet convinced I'm about to be blown over. Wrapping both arms around a pillar, I hug it tight, helpless, wet, and paralyzed with terror, as streams of people—Martha and her friends among them—double back, threading their way through the deluge, down the steps to roof level again.

It's then I hear a familiar voice. "Cash, what happened?"

Oh, thank Vishnu!

"I . . ." I turn to find Jay standing behind me. "I . . ."

"We've been waiting for you. Are you okay?"

"I . . . can't get down."

"Of course you can. Follow me."

"Jay, I can't."

"Yes you can." Man, this guy doesn't brook any objections.

"It's too high. The steps are too thin."

"Come on. I'll go first and I'll make sure you don't fall, okay?"

There's a rope. A flimsy, ever-shifting rope. You're meant to hold onto it the whole way, hugging the right-hand side of the steps to avoid colliding with those climbing up. The plan is to create order out of chaos, but as far as I can tell it actually halves the order and quadruples the chaos. Everyone's sliding and shouting. Arms flail, toes dangle, seeking something solid to grip onto and occasionally finding it, but just as often slipping right off the wet stones into the back of the person below them, knocking them forward into the next person in the chain. In my case that person would be Jay, who nonetheless soldiers on stoically like he always does.

Eventually, with his help, and also of course by the good graces of Vishnu—I don't care if he is fictional, Vishnu's the man, baby!—my feet land on solid ground once more and I'm free.

Gasping, unsteady, relieved.

"So how did it all look?" I ask afterwards, pausing to get my breath back.

Jay takes out the clock he always carries with him. We're behind schedule. Gotta go. At the same time he's shaking his head and glances up at me forlornly.

"What? Something's wrong? What happened?"

"We didn't get it," he says. "That's what I came up to tell you. Kevin wasn't ready in time."

He . . . there's . . . I'm . . . what??????

All that turmoil—the climbing, the danger, the sodden clothes, the panic—and he shot no footage at all of my resounding victory?

"I'm afraid so."

Jay shrugs. Adding, "Oh," as we push through the crowd, "and another thing: your microphone gave out halfway, so there's no sound either."

It—but—how—I mean, I—

"Sorry."

11

A Gift from the Network!

When a reality TV show is set to launch, a whole bunch of extra last-minute duties are piled on the host. One of these, I discovered when it was already too late to wriggle out of it, is called "attending the up-fronts."

The up-fronts are a blast. Almost every network has them. It's an annual shindig where nervous TV executives, anxious to know whether they'll still have a job in a year, fly to key cities throughout the United States to parade their latest programs before potential advertisers and the press. Of course, left to me it would be a very simple affair indeed. Everyone would receive a DVD in the mail, and maybe a Starbucks voucher for a free latte to prove we're not cheap, and that would be it. If they liked the shows on the DVD, great; if they didn't—pah, screw 'em! And quite honestly, you can't get more up-front than that!

Trouble is, advertisers love junkets. It's their Achilles' heel. Their financial affections must be wooed, *teased* out of them. They want glamour, they want to be fêted and plied with free booze and snacks. So, with that end in mind, what in most industries would amount to a routine twenty-minute PowerPoint presentation with a leaflet to take home at the end, gets fleshed out into a splashy two-day bonanza in a big expensive theater filled with TV stars, musical numbers, and skits, *anything* in fact that might persuade world-weary marketing people to reach for their checkbooks and reserve a bunch of advertising spots "up front." In other words, before the new season begins.

And so it was with our little effort. Since the series was to be a linchpin of the network's summer schedule, I was sent a first-class ticket to the East Coast and told to break off from whatever I was doing—which happened to be making a TV show; duh—and go peddle my wares like an Edwardian knife grinder at the up-front in New York.

The hotel the network booked me into, the Trump International on Columbus Circle, turned out to be a very classy place indeed. One of those high-end hotels where the staff nannies you and fusses with almost obsessive enthusiasm. For instance, they all remember your name. I don't know how they do this, but they do. During my brief stay I must have made five surprise visits to reception for five different reasons, and, each time the girl on the desk looked up and said instantly, "Yes, Mr. Peters, how may I help you?" without consulting a book or a screen, or having someone hold up cue cards, or *anything*.

And my suite was terrific. Three rooms: bedroom, well-stocked kitchenette, and a large living room with automatic drapes—ooooh!—that opened to reveal a quick glimpse of the Manhattan skyline and then closed again like one of those old amusement arcade slot machines, leaving me wanting more. Once I'd done playing with those—and I'll be honest, it was a while—the porter showed me how the lights worked and where the remote for the TV was, slipping in at the end that "every suite at the Trump has its own personalized phone and fax number, it's *not* an extension."

How about that!

"Oh, look, there's even a business card here with my name already printed on it!"

"Yes, sir."

Excellent.

Thin and cheap-looking, admittedly, but excellent. I still have a stack of them. Next time you meet me, ask for one. We can keep in touch.

Also, on the nightstand I found a bag with a free iPod in it. A present from the network, apparently. Well, how very generous of them.

Anyway, I slipped the porter two bucks, which he stared at for a moment, before thanking me, but in a neutral tone perfected after years and years of not being impressed by things, and left.

The moment the door closed, I leaped to my personalized Trump phone to call Mandy, an old friend of mine from London, who was in town for a couple of days, and invited her to come see my swanky New York pad.

A beautiful, diminutive ball of love wrapped in a black knee-length leather coat and topped off with an explosion of fiery red hair, she was suitably impressed by the suite, though less so by my business cards, which she surveyed with discerning peppermint green eyes, doubtless thinking, "But they're so thin and cheap-looking," before putting them down without comment.

Once we'd chatted for a while and caught up, I went off to play with the drapes again and make a couple of extra calls on my personalized phone, while Mandy occupied herself out of sight in the kitchen, where she cracked open a complimentary can of peanuts and stuck a corkscrew into a complimentary half-bottle of Chardonnay, pouring herself a generous glass, maybe even two. In fact, I only know she did this because, two days later, when it came time to check out, I received a whopping bill for incidentals. The wine and peanuts weren't complimentary at all, it turns out. Far from it.

But hey, that's okay, I thought. It's the network's problem. Those guys were footing the bill, so what did I care, really? That's what expense accounts are for—right?

Er . . .

Shortly after, I discovered a letter. It was stuffed into the bottom of the same bag that the iPod came in, and explained in very clear legal terms that the room was being paid for by the network, *but the incidentals most definitely weren't.*

I don't fully remember, but I think my hands began shaking at this point.

Bottom line: that's the last time I ever let a friend of mine out of my sight. If I'd known Mandy was going to switch inadvertently from the free stuff to the stuff hotels make you pay through the nose for, believe me, I would have thought twice about inviting her up to my swanky pad in the first place. I'm serious.

The show premiered four weeks later. On my birthday, as a matter of fact, June 6. A coincidence everyone was quick to label a lucky omen.

It's hard to encapsulate in a single word the myriad feelings that surge through you when you first appear on TV in your very own series, but, after much thought, I can honestly say that "YIPPPPPPPPPPPPPPPEEEEEEE!!!!" probably comes the closest.

Quick off the mark, The Thumb sent me a congratulatory note. In it, he went to the trouble of listing some other significant events that had taken place on the same date throughout history, which I thought was a wonderful gesture.

Were you aware that June 6 is Memorial Day in South Korea? I wasn't. Or that some people celebrate the Feast of Saint Norbert of Gennep on that day? Or that it marks a number of epic watersheds: the D-Day landings in Normandy (1944), the death of Robert F. Kennedy (1968), the launch of *Soyuz* 11 (1971), and Roosevelt's New Deal (1934)? Not to mention the birth of Tony Yeboah, Ada Kok, and James "Munky" Shaffer? (Just thinking aloud, but it's possible I may be the most famous person ever born on June 6. And I'm not famous *at all*!)

Then, at the very bottom, tagged onto these momentous events, was a personal note: **"Cash, congratulations on the launch of this incredible endeavor!!"**

He even called me at home as the initial episodes were about to air, very excited as always. *"Did you get my gift?"*

Oh boy. My own show *and* a gift, too!

"No," I said, "I didn't. Is it a car?"

I'd read about networks handing out Porsches to stars as a thank-you for taking time out from their busy celebrity schedule to show up to work . . .

"No, it's not a car," he replied, shocked.

. . . just not *this* network, evidently.

Still hopeful, in case he was kidding, I hurried downstairs to the front door and found, waiting for me on the step outside . . .

An envelope.

"Oh."

Inside was a gift voucher. For four free massages at a spa in West Hollywood.

Hm. Okay.

Sweet gesture.

Please don't think I didn't appreciate it, because I did. Spas are lovely. I like spas.

And anyway, it's the thought that counts, right?

But . . .

Actually, there is no but. Spa treatments make a great gift.

It's just that . . .

A car would have been nicer, that's all I'm saying.

Now, let's move on and put this ugly scene behind us.

12

The Emir's New Clothes

In the beginning, when we first embarked on the series, our plan was to break new ground in reality television by being authentic, honest, and courageously laissez-faire. That is to say, we'd turn up unannounced in a place, mingle for real with the community, befriend interesting strangers, visit their homes, and generally improvise our way from pillar to post without a plan, letting the whole thing develop organically, the way life does, to see how it all worked out. Then at least we could say we were remaining true to our brief of being a genuine people show filled with knockabout spontaneity.

Unfortunately, by the time we reach Dubai, all of that has flown out the window.

The backbone premise, "guy arrives in strange culture with no money and scrounges meals and assistance off complete strangers" won't fly in the Middle East. In fact, the idea of knockabout spontaneity is not only frowned upon here, it can earn you a lengthy prison sentence.

"Dubai is a benign dictatorship," our fixer, Nick, warns grimly at the hotel on the first day. A scruffy young Londoner with a baby face, he's freelanced on several TV shows out here as a producer and has been hired to help us negotiate this, the trickiest of cultures. "The country is ruled by Sheikh Mohammed bin Rashid Al Maktoum and the Maktoum family according to Islamic law, and what they say goes, mate."

It wasn't always like that. At one time this region was run by a group of feudal clans. Back then, the Al Maktoums were part of the Bani Yas clan. Then, in 1833, they broke away and took over Dubai, where they've been in charge ever since. They own it, they run it, it's theirs. If you don't like it, then take your ball and leave.

"Whatever happens," the show's senior coordinator, Rick, told me before I left L.A., "watch what you do and say in Dubai. That means *no* innuendo. *Don't* touch or hug people. And most definitely no, repeat no, religious, risqué, or gay jokes of any kind—okay?"

No hugging or gay jokes? Jeez, that's a bit harsh.

Seems Islam has yet to embrace the fun, vivacious side of homosexuality. Despite Dubai's outward pretense to Western-style openness and freedom, the people are extremely uptight. It's certainly no Lesbos, that's for sure. Anyone flaunting the love that dare not speak its name could easily end up in prison, then deported.

In other news: Under Islamic law, if a man walks up to a woman he doesn't know, the way I frequently do, and starts talking to her without being invited, as I also frequently do, he can be jailed for a year, I'm told, which I'm not up for at all. In fact, you can be jailed in Muslim countries on a whim for almost anything: having sex out of wedlock, getting drunk, being a pothead, and all manner of other playful acts that we take for granted in our culture and that really don't count in the bigger scheme of things, but which these people take very seriously *indeed.* I heard of a man in Saudi Arabia, for instance, who left his wife after she was caught in front of the TV watching a program starring a male host. Merely seeing this guy *on television* was in itself considered adultery and sufficient grounds for divorce. In Iran, I hear, you can be flogged or stoned for having a copy of the Bible in your home and put on trial for calling your teddy bear Mohammed. In Dubai, a straight guy who was anally raped by a gang of closet homosexuals was instantly deemed to be homosexual himself and banged up in the slammer. Elsewhere, thieves may be punished by having their hands chopped off. Panhandling is illegal. Bums are thrown in jail, too. Etcetera, etcetera, etcetera. It's all very eye-for-an-eye and gratuitously barbaric.

Luckily, Dubai has moved on a little these days. It's no longer considered quite such a haven of narrow-minded intolerance as other Islamic countries are. Still, you can't help worrying for your safety, and I'm taking no chances.

Having already put the fear of Allah up me, Nick has more. "I mean, I don't want to influence you editorially or anything, mate,"—meaning he does—"but there are certain things you shouldn't ask people."

"Such as what?"

"About money and . . . well, certain other stuff," he adds mysteriously.

Oh, okay. Well, thanks for clarifying.

"And when you write the script for the show, *please* only say nice things."

"Why is that?"

He looks nervous. "Because if you don't, mate, they'll come after us."

"Who will?"

"They'll find out who 'elped you, who made the arrangements, and they'll shut down our company."

"*Who* will, Nick?"

Too scared to name names, he clams up.

"And anyway," I persist, "why would they shut *your* company down for something *I* did? It doesn't make sense."

As he's about to answer, a man wearing the traditional Arab white robe—the *dishdasha*—and the white headdress—the *gutra*—saunters by with a laptop—*asonyvaio*—looking for a wireless connection. Nick stalls, waiting for him to pass, then two earnest blue eyes round on me. "My point is, mate," he lowers his voice, "watch what you say or you'll get everyone into trouble."

And Tasha agrees.

The three of us are huddled conspiratorially in fancy leather armchairs in the ultra-plush, oak-paneled lounge of a private club at our hotel, eating cake. The club is "members only," reserved for elite guests—that is to say, those staying in the more expensive suites on the tenth floor and up. Sadly, we're booked into budget rooms on the ninth and below, so we don't qualify. However, reading the hotel brochure last night, I noticed in passing that the club offers afternoon tea each day in its lounge. Well, who doesn't love a spot of tea in the afternoon? It's a very British institution. More to the point—and here was its main appeal as far as I was concerned—the tea was *free.* So I swapped my jeans and T-shirt for a smart designer number and slacks to make me look less ninthfloorish, slid a little mousse into my hair, took the elevator up to the club, and defined myself as a member simply by walking in, quite brazenly grabbing a corner table and a plate of scones and refusing to leave until I'd eaten them all.

I also went to the trouble of putting the receptionist on notice that I was expecting guests for a business meeting, a piece of news she received with snake-eyed skepticism and a "Yes, sir" so chilly I was able to see my own breath for a moment.

Unfortunately, Tasha and Nick have blown my cover wide open by arriving in sweaty T-shirts and shorts. Tasha even put her old backpack on the table, *in my private club!* Totally letting the side down. We can be only minutes away from the receptionist calling security and having us all thrown in jail for five years. Anticipating this, I grab another couple of scones from the tray while I still have hands to hold them with.

"And there's something else," Tasha says.

Nick brushes wisps of fair hair from his eyes, trying to figure out the most tactful way of framing it. "We've arranged for you to meet a very senior member of the government. 'E's major, mate. Close connections to the Maktoums. You're lucky to 'ave 'im on the show. It'll make for a great segment. Nice guy. Friendly, but . . ."

"But . . ." Tasha echoes ominously.

"But what?"

". . . he's very high up, very important, and if you upset him, then . . ."

Before the threat can be fully fleshed out—though I'm sure it probably entails being arrested and thrown in prison for five years; call me psychic—Tasha chips in with a curt "Just *don't* upset him, okay?"

"Alrighty . . . and what exactly would I have to say to upset him?"

She stands up and makes to go. "Just don't."

❧

If you're wondering where Dubai is, it's at the eastern end of the Arabian Peninsula. And if you're wondering where that is, well, you could always buy an atlas—hm?

Basically, we're talking about the Middle East, but not the part where people slaughter each other daily for no good reason; rather, the relatively nice part of the Persian Gulf where the lifestyle, because they have the buffer of vast oil reserves and the high-minded good sense not to squander them on war or nuclear weapons, is peaceful, and steeped—*steeped*, mind—in five-star opulence. That's Dubai.

"Safest country in the world," Nick trumpets.

Thousands of people agree with him and have set their sights on living and working here. Unfortunately, most arrived before Dubai was quite ready for them, and the city is struggling to keep pace.

"Why is it the safest?" I ask, as we crawl an inch at a time through bumper-to-bumper traffic along an unfinished four-lane highway en route to our first location, an unfinished tower block. "You mean there are no terrorist attacks here?"

He shakes his head.

"But why not? Surely, this whole place is one great big bull's-eye for Al Qaeda."

Same way Las Vegas is. Stands to reason. If anywhere in the world has Great Satan written all over it, it's Vegas. Or it did, until Dubai came along, which will soon be bigger, glitzier, more lavish, and a whole lot *satanier* than Vegas could ever dream of.

"The earth has a new center," a giant billboard screams at us from the roadside. And what extremist wouldn't welcome the chance to bomb the center of the earth?

Yet Nick remains adamant. "Won't 'appen, mate."

"But why?"

For the second time this trip, he turns mysterious and lowers his voice, even though there's only me and the crew here.

"It's rumored that someone in the government is related to one of Bin Laden's cousins, and they've . . . y'know . . . done a deal, sort of thing. 'We'll scratch your back, mate, and you don't bomb ours, okay?' And that's what we think 'appened."

"So . . . is it true?"

He shoots me an alarmed glance via the rearview mirror. Already said too much.

"Safest country in the world, mate."

And the topic is quickly dropped.

By Nick, at least. Me, I'm nowhere near done yet.

Dubai nowadays is a modern marvel. That's how far it's come. Half a century ago there was almost nothing here, except for a modest fishing port renowned for its flourishing trade in precious pearl oysters. Everything else was just a very large patch of sand. One of seven similarly large patches of sand known as emirates, or Arab sheikhdoms, bordering the Persian Gulf.

For a while in the nineteenth century, the region was under threat of attack from the ever-expanding Ottoman Empire, centered in Constantinople (now Istanbul). Luckily, in 1873, the British came along and put their foot down (which was a shock: normally people only put their feet *up* on Ottomans), offering protection to the sheikhdoms and their trade routes. Until 1971, that is, when the Brits grew tired of daddying the Gulf region, with all its attendant troubles, and went home, throwing the Arabian Peninsula once again to the wolves. That's when the emirs, the shrewd rulers of the seven large patches of sand, decided to do something radical: they ganged together and formed a single country, called the United Arab Seven Large Patches of Sand, which was changed *the very next morning,* after the man who'd suggested such a stupid name was thrown in jail for five years, to the United Arab Emirates.

"So what's this, then?"

I'm standing on a hillock of freshly excavated soil before a jagged skyline of unfinished metal and glass towers stretching as far as the cynical eye can see.

"What you're looking at, mate, is what Dubai's all about," Nick explains proudly.

"Half-assed construction projects?"

"No. Sheik Mohammed wants this city to 'ave the biggest and the best of everything. He wants to be a player and put it on the map, bringing in more and more people. See those condos over there? Every one of 'em's sold already."

Shrouded in cranes, a dozen huge towers gnaw at the clouds like punched-in teeth. Most have their upper floors missing, though not for much longer. Buildings like these are shooting up all over town at record speeds—which hardly gives me confidence that they'll stay up, quite honestly—thanks to a reservoir of imported labor flooding in from the Indian subcontinent and willing to work for minimum wage. A rate of four dollars a day is not uncommon.

The guy behind the construction splurge was Dubai's forward-thinking ruler, Sheikh Maktoum bin Rashid al-Maktoum. In the 1970s he came up with a daring vision: to take this primitive Muslim country of fifteen hundred or so square miles and transform it into one of the premier free enterprise economies and tourist destinations in the world. Unhampered by cumbersome bureaucracy (being a dictator, Sheikh Mak *was* the bureaucracy), and tapping into substantial revenues he'd pulled in from oil, he began devising the infrastructure for a wondrous city of the future, then gathered a bunch of architects and engineers together, clapped his hands, and said, “Make it so!” exactly the way Aladdin did when he lived here.

But here’s where the plan got to be really audacious: the city wouldn’t be built piecemeal, he resolved, the way the rest of us would do it, a little bit at a time to see how things go, because that could take forever. No, everything would be put up more or less *simultaneously,* at a total cost of around $400 billion.

Clap, clap. “Make it so!”

Well, you’ve never seen as much frenzied activity in all your life. Before long, there were more people building the city than actually living in it, 80 percent of them from overseas. And I don’t know how many cranes there are in the world right now, but I do know, because Nick told me, that at any one time 25 percent of them are to be found in Dubai.

Anyway, by the time Sheikh Mak died in 2006, he’d performed a miracle, bringing this large patch of sand firmly into the twentieth century, exactly as he’d promised.

Unfortunately, by then it was the twenty-first century. So it fell to his younger brother, Sheikh Mohammed bin Rashid Al Maktoum, who thankfully was also a visionary with deep, oil-lined pockets, to grab the baton and take the plan even further, expanding Dubai into a prime residential location, a thriving business center, and, someday, the number one tourist destination on the planet.

Agog at the ambition of it all, we retreat from the crushing heat to the safety of the van, and, with the AC cranked up to “January in Reykjavik,” set off into town along a wide, dusty, unfinished highway.

“This,” Nick says, leading us to a broad stretch of sand on the Gulf called Jumeirah Beach, “is an iconic building, the one that really put Dubai on the map.”

On the other side of a concrete wall we find the Burj Al Arab, the Tower of the Arabs, hogging the horizon to our left. The world's tallest hotel at the time, at 1,053 feet high, it was built to look like an old merchant sailing ship, called a *dhow,* and is sculpted out of glass and white-painted steel. Inside, it claims to have its own microclimate in the 590-foot atrium, plus a restaurant with a floor-to-ceiling aquarium, and even its own submarine. Not that I can confirm any of these things: leaning over a wall is about as close as we're allowed to get to it. According to Nick, a vigilant security detail guards the gate at all times, keeping riffraff like me from mingling with guests, in case it reminds them that poor people really do exist in the world and freaks them out.

"Want to know something funny?" Nick asks chirpily. "The architects were British, right? And when they were designing the building they included a gigantic white crucifix."

"They did? Where?"

"You can't see it from 'ere. It's on the ocean side."

How wise.

Seems the white cantilevered shelf the hotel uses as a helipad cuts across a white vertical steel rod at just the right point to form a cross. I wonder how long it'll be before someone important finds out, and, when he does, if in a fit of rage he'll have the whole place torn down and indiscriminately order someone to be thrown into jail for five years.

"The company has never admitted it was deliberate, of course," Nick tags on, "but if you believe the rumors, it was their big F.U. to the Muslim community." And he laughs again.

Don't you just love this guy? His corner-of-the-mouth gossip, his candor. The sort of candor you'll only get from the British, who have a nose for the truth and tongues unafraid to speak it—contrasting starkly with Dubai City, which somehow, to the nonpartisan observer, feels like a very big fat expensive lie, a pricey diamond half-blinding you with the many-faceted brightness of its riches, while never quite allaying the suspicion that what you're looking at is really just a huge dazzling chunk of Diamonique. Mutton dressed as lamb. The Emir's New Clothes, if you will.

"The Burj is reputed to be the world's only seven-star hotel," Nick throws in. Seven stars! Wow! That's two more than they could ever need.

If true, such braggadocio is typical of the city's juvenile clamoring for the world's attention, by breaking records, putting up buildings that graze the stratosphere, and generally being the biggest and best at things that the rest of us don't really care about.

Tallest flagpole in the world, anyone?

Largest number of men called Mohammed assembled in one place?

And on it goes. One shameless ploy after another. Extremism for its own sake. Underscoring a broader principle: "If you can't see us, then we may as well not exist."

The $400 billion that continues to be pumped into making this the center of the earth has produced other important firsts: the world's tallest free-standing structure, the largest housing development ever; the largest shopping mall containing the world's largest aquarium, the glitziest financial and media center; the sprawlingest airport; the biggest amusement park—Dubailand[1]—and the largest working refrigerator, which, because nobody has any use for a refriger-

---

1 One billion square feet of attractions, including a real full-sized snow dome and a "City of Wonders" featuring re-creations of the Taj Mahal, the pyramids of Giza, and the Leaning Tower of Pisa, which will be better than the originals because they'll be new. And at least one of them probably won't lean over, the way the old one does.

ator that big, they turned into an indoor ski slope twenty-five stories high instead.

We stopped by Ski Dubai briefly. An enclosed alpine wonderland of chairlifts, pine trees, and frosted railings, it boasts five different runs of varying difficulty, plus what's hilariously called a Freestyle Zone, reserved for those whose technique could broadly be described as "wanting." Mainly it amounts to falling over and slithering the rest of the way on their ass. All in all, then, a totally self-contained and convincing world, as long as you don't look up at the ceiling, which is studded with lights and also vents from which showers of real snow fall every morning.

Afterwards, I was chatting with a stunning Jordanian model called Samar. I met her in Starbucks. Though, since we're in Dubai, no way could I just meet her, as that would be against the law. Our accidental rendezvous had to be set up in advance. And not in any old Starbucks, either. Theirs turned out to be a grandiose, sprawling coffee mosque-type affair, crowned with a magnificent domed blue ceiling worthy of Versailles. I have photos.

"I don't understand," I said. "Why would they build a ski slope in a place where nobody skis?"

Her answer was trite but true, and went a long way to explaining everything else about this country in a nutshell. "Because," she said, "they can."

That's it. Three words.

Because they can.

A basic fact of life when you're loaded. The rest of us just have to accept it.

Once the Ski Dubai shots are over and done with, we're slated to visit the world's largest flagpole. Another outlandish white elephant that someone here thought they might as well build "because we can." Yet for some reason our enthusiasm, already tepid to begin with, wanes to almost nothing the closer we get. And by the time we're half a mile away, some of us are even feeling pangs of hostility toward it. Seems nobody cares about the world's largest flagpole. Nobody cared before they built it, nobody cares now. So instead we do something far more interesting: we take a detour to Nick's favorite vegetarian café for an early lunch.

Much of the food in Dubai is wonderfully westernized. The best of any of our trips so far. Whatever your diet—including special weirdo demands such as "no oil on *anything*"—they'll accommodate it here, and in unwieldy portions. Although be warned, it's pricey. Last night at the hotel restaurant, for instance, I got into a squabble with my waitress after she tried to charge me thirty-one dollars for a side salad from the buffet. And just so you don't think I was being obnoxious for the sake of it, let me define side salad for you: two pieces of lettuce, three cherry tomatoes, and a couple of slices of cucumber. That's all I had for thirty-one dollars, a price they charge, no doubt, once again "because they can."

Well, Sir wasn't standing for it.

"I'm sorry," I said, after calling over the maitre d', "there's been a mistake."

"No, my colleague is correct," he intoned with forced politeness, inspecting the check. "It says here 'thirty-one dollars.'"

"Yes, I know it says it there, but that's outrageous." I moved to the buffet table for a full demonstration. "What you're telling me is that if I take a plate and eat everything here, *everything,* all of this stuff"—pointing—"until there's none left, you'd charge me the same price you did for a tiny fraction of it, namely some lettuce, three tomatoes, and a couple of slices of cucumber."

I may appear to be a wimp in certain circumstances—when asked to sleep in spider-ridden huts, for instance, or while digging holes with sticks in the jungle or going down opal mines—but on my home turf of a first-class hotel, I am invincible. A fearless conquistador *demanding* fair play.

"Does that seem fair to you? Does it?"

And I glared—something I don't do lightly.

"Well . . ."

Five minutes later, a smallish fat guy, with more mustache than any man could possibly have use for, came charging into the room with some urgency. The manager. Suddenly, I was trapped by a black-tied cabal of forced-smiling hotel employees circling my table. Yet did I give an inch of ground? Not likely.

"I *insist* you change this at once," I commanded to all three, waving the check.

By now, more guests were drifting in, watching this unpleasant scene escalate. Feeling the heat, and tired, obviously, of dealing with a cheapskate who couldn't see that being ripped off by high prices was part of the whole "Dubai experience," their resistance collapsed like a faulty card table, as begrudgingly—you should have seen the ire on their faces; it was Solvang all over again—they took the bill away and made a suitable adjustment.

"Thank you. I appreciate it," I said coldly, handing over five bucks or so, and left.

Frankly, I'm surprised they get any return business. Next time, to hell with them all. I shall dine in my private club. For free.

Time to shoot some B-roll.

"Now . . . 'til you . . . come . . . spot . . . top!"

Huh?

"Okay, we're rolling!"

Under a blazing noonday sun, I'm stumbling along the ridge of a flawless golden dune shaped like a croissant, one of thousands stretching in every direction. From this lofty vantage point I can make out a shifting smudge of shadows in the far hazy distance, inching south across the sand. Camels. Driven from behind by a solitary bearded Bedouin herdsman in flapping white robes. Otherwise, I see nothing, neither another living soul nor another set of footprints, and even my own are eroded within seconds by the wind.

It doesn't take much to picture the rulers of Dubai a long time ago traveling across this exact patch of desert, feeling thoroughly depressed at how desolate it all was, how empty, and thinking to themselves, "Let's face it, fellas, the tide's never coming back in again," resolving there and then to put their crowned heads together and figure out something interesting and unique to do with their country.

Once I'm finished walking across the ridge, I stop to mop my reddening forehead and to check back with Kevin, who's some distance away, naked from the waist up, with a floppy hat on protecting his face, to see if my walking bit was okay.

It wasn't.

From behind his tripod, he shouts more orders: "Top . . . ridge . . . beat . . . curve!"

I cup my ear, but I still can't make out a word he's saying. The wind's against us. And his crazy arm gestures don't help. Nevertheless, I return to my starting point and try again, a little further to the left this time. Pure guesswork, and obviously nothing like what he had in mind, because moments later I see him throw a small fit—first time he's done that, *ever*—and come sprinting over.

"Jesus, Cash, are you deaf? Go *behind* the ridge!" he calls up to me. "Wait ten seconds, then start climbing. Walk over it toward me—okay?"

Aaaaaaahh! So that's it. "Sorry, Kevin."

By now I have sand inside my shoes, my ears, my armpits, my foreskin, and crunching between my teeth. After a brief pause, I do as instructed and clamber up to the top of the ridge again. Taking no chances this time, I reach into my box of well-tried expressions and pull out the ultimate crowd-pleaser: my Mystified Look. I squint across the wide-open landscape as if to get my bearings, glance right, glance left, glance right again, then bumble out of shot with the brooding air of a man who, if he's asked to do this one more time, may fly off the handle and punch someone, even if it means risking a spot of jail time.

"And . . . cut. Great."

Kevin's not the only one showing signs of cracking. Everyone's testy today.

I blame Dubai. Something about this corner of the world screws with your mind, I think. It's in the air. Even on a good day, you're on edge the whole time. You know that frazzled feeling you get when, halfway to work, you suddenly think to yourself, "Jesus! Did I turn the oven off?" Well, it's a bit like that. Nothing too major, nothing you can put your finger on exactly, but enough to cancel out most traces of good humor during your stay and make every molehill feel like an unassailable mountain.

Good example: this morning, first thing, the normally quite unflustered Kevin had a run-in with Jay over camera angles. And then Jay had a run-in with me in front of the whole crew about some continuity point or other. All very fleeting, and easily patched up, but unsettling at the same time. As it is, we're already making big allowances for Jay. Before we came on this trip, he blew out one of the discs in his back and is currently half-crippled with sciatica, poor guy. Though this is a mere blip on the sonar compared to the real firestorm we're facing right now.

Mike—Kevin's soundman—has lost his gear.

THE gear. The fifty-pound sound-mixer box of tricks he wears around his neck during filming, together with his microphones, cables, and whatever else he uses to record interviews. All of it failed to turn up on the carousel at the airport, which was a staggering blow to the production, because as wonderfully sumptuous as Kevin's pictures may be, they're not strictly television unless they make a noise. (These aren't my rules, it's just the way it is.) So until he finds it, he's forced to lease or borrow equipment in every location we visit.

Numerous calls throughout the day to American Airlines by Mike at his most charming . . .

"Hey, buddy, how's it goin'? Cool. Listen, dude, I wonder if you can help me?"

. . . have failed to produce the breakthrough he's hoping for. As of now, nobody, least of all the airlines, has any idea where the equipment went. And I say "airlines," plural, because these trips rarely involve direct flights on a single carrier. Too often, in the name of being economical, we're booked onto multiple carriers, which means multiple layovers in multiple airports before we reach our destination. Sometimes the layovers are really out of our way, too. In the past month alone, for example, I've visited Madrid four times. *Four times!* Which would be fine if even one of our shows was set in Spain, but it wasn't.

Over lunch, Mike calls American again, angling for an update. Still they're unable to say what happened. "Stolen, probably," is their best guess. Unhappy, he follows this with a call to the office in L.A. to take up the matter with them.

I can't tell you what Fat Kid's response is to these concerns, because I can't hear it. All I know is, by the time Mike hangs up, he's very, *very* unhappy. Furious even. Which is highly unusual for him. Bear in mind who we're talking about here: a California surfer dude. A cool, mellow Buddhist who practices yoga every morning. His elfin face, with twinkling gimlet eyes, is generally awash with good humor, revealing a man wonderfully at ease with himself and his world . . .

"Man, this is all such bullshit."

. . . just not while he's working on this show.

"I've never come across a crew more at war with its own producers," Nick admits to me later that night at his townhouse on the outskirts of the city.

True to Fat Kid's new edict, I must sleep in someone's home each episode for a minimum of five hours. To prove that I did, the crew has been given a Sony mini-DV camera equipped with night vision. Called "the Tuck-in Cam," it's rigged up at my bedside to make sure I really lie down and sleep, in case anyone challenges us later. However, the tapes usually run out after an hour and the machine switches off automatically. That leaves me free on this occasion to get up again, trot downstairs, and wait out the remaining four hours with Nick and his wife, and grab a beer or two 'til a taxi arrives to ferry me back to the hotel.

Unfortunately, this being Dubai, alcohol laws are so strict that you have to apply for a license to drink in your own home! So I settle for tea and nibbles, while Nick stands out on the patio smoking, one of the few vices you don't get jailed for around here.

"Why are your people at the office being such pricks?" he asks, exhaling into the night sky.

"I don't know that they are. It's hard coordinating all of this, the trips, the flights. I'm sure they're doing the best they can. It just doesn't seem that way when you're here."

Off duty, Nick's chipper-Dan raciness lifts like a burka to

reveal a degree of glum dissatisfaction beneath. The way he tells it, he's one of thousands of people who left England for a new life here—80 percent of the labor force is made up of ex-pats, a lot of them British—only to find that the new life they'd run away to wasn't all it was cracked up to be.

"You get 'ere, and everything seems wonderful," he explains, "and yes, sure, mate, there's tons of money to be made. *Tons.* It's very lavish. Plus, the weather's great, and everything's new and exciting, know what I mean? But then after a while it . . . I dunno, something 'appens. It starts to get on your nerves, wears you down."

"What does?"

"The chaos. The temperature. The unfinished roads. The language. Culture barriers. Just the general atmosphere here. You must have noticed it."

I admit that I have, and that I too find it subtly menacing. Their gargantuan malls, ski slope, perfectly landscaped racetrack, ritzy airport, their art gallery to rival the Louvre—a thousand dazzling baubles and novelties heaped up and brimming over and meant to be so very enticing, when all they do really is transmit a shrill cry of warning, letting the rest of us know that Dubai, one of the tiniest countries on earth, has possibly the most terrifying Napoleon complex ever, like a needy, insecure child jumping through hoops, clamoring to be the center of attention after centuries of being ignored on the world stage.

"Dubai tries to be as westernized as any place can be, but first and foremost it's a Muslim country and there are limits. Myself, I reckon," he says, stepping inside and closing the patio door, "I've got another year to go here. Maybe less. Then I'm off."

"Oh yeah? Where to?"

"New York. I've always wanted to live in New York."

"Ah. A real city, you mean."

We exchange looks and laugh. "Yeah, a real city."

The final showdown has arrived. Time to meet the monster everyone's been warning me against. The top-ranking government official who, with a few words in the appropriate ear and a "clap-clap make it so," could have the lot of us evicted from Dubai—which, strangely, is something I would actively welcome by this point. It's nothing anyone's done specifically, just that, after everything Nick told me about life here, all the dos and don'ts, the way the rich treat those who aren't as fortunate as they are, I can't help feeling jittery and vulnerable. It's only been a couple of days, but I'm ready to scram and never return.

Jay comes limping over, stoically soldiering on despite the constant nagging pain of his sciatica. "Remember, you can't needle this guy the way you do other people." Last-minute instructions. "Don't ask him any difficult questions. Go easy on him."

I won't. I will. Stop worrying.

We rendezvous inside an elegant creamy-white showpiece auditorium that someone has striven to make perfect, and in so doing scrubbed it clean of all personality, like so much else around here. It's reached by crossing a bridge decorated with towering palm trees made from beaten copper. These are continued in the interior.

On the shout of "Action!" from Jay, I enter, wearing My Mystified Look again. As I do so, a cultured and charming man with an easy smile steps out to greet me, his frame concealed beneath a gleaming white *dishdasha*.

"Hello, Cash, how do you do, I'm Hamza."

Conveniently overlooking the anomaly of why a senior

figure in Dubai commerce would be just standing there in the room, ready to talk about his projects to a guy he doesn't even know, wink wink, we shake hands and do our spontaneous interview.

Actually, he's agreeable enough. Certainly not the ogre he's been painted. Tasha and Nick needn't have panicked. I guess they were expecting a grizzly bear. In fact we got Yogi. The real reason everyone walks on eggshells around him, I quickly discover, is that he's the general manager of Dubai's most audacious project to date: the Palm Jumeira—you've probably seen reports; it's been all over the news—a splayed peninsula packed with villas, hotels, and shops, built on reclaimed land in the Gulf and shaped like an elegant palm tree. Constructed by fourteen thousand poor people to enable a few rich ones to enjoy an even better life than they have already, it includes marinas, beaches, cafés, lavish spas, a monorail, and an artificial reef for divers and wildlife, created, I read somewhere, by sinking fighter jets into the ocean. They're already calling the Palm the Eighth Wonder of the World. Which is a shame, because, the way things stand, this will push poor Angkor Wat down to ninth. That's bound to make somebody mad.

What's more, it turned out to be such an off-the-wall crazily marketable idea that Nakheel, the construction company (owner: Sheik Mo), built two even bigger ones farther along the coast: the Palm Deira and the Palm Jebel Ali. But then—*then*—guess what! Even as these were getting under way, Sheikh Mo, who I'm guessing never sleeps, hatched his greatest brainchild yet. This required another impressive model, which takes pride of place in the showroom, depicting a wondrous archipelago of three hundred manmade private islands individually fashioned into a map of the earth's continents and countries, and called The World.

Ooh, *The World,* I'm thinking—that's where *I* live!

There's even a video.

"Choose your island, choose your opportunity," a narrator purrs to a soothing flute accompaniment.

As he speaks, a cartoon seaplane swoops down through computerized clouds to scuff the ocean waves, before rising over a CGI island shaped like a game preserve on the Serengeti. Each island represents a different country and features a range of enticing attractions, from computer-generated golf courses and castles to futuristic hotels that the cartoon guests inside seem to be enjoying enormously. It sure does look like a glamorous, carefree place to be, if you're a drawing.

"Architect your surroundings," the narrator continues, misusing a noun. "Customize the way you live with beautifully designed interiors that reflect your individual style." According to Hamza, the blobs of land on offer vary in price between $9 million and a very reasonable $45 million, "inviting a select few to build the ultimate escape."

As well as corporations, it's hoped that the select few will include a smattering of high-profile celebs, envisioning a halcyon day not so far off when Donald Trump will open the curtains of the castle on his island one morning to find Oprah next door on her island grouting her patio; a time when Barbara Walters, perhaps having trouble starting the motor on her Jet Ski, will call Rupert Murdoch and the Olsen twins, who'll rush over immediately with tools to help her; when Dakota Fanning, piloting her helicopter to her home on Fanning Island, will wave to Reese Witherspoon playing volleyball down below, gamely taking on Ang Lee, Reba McEntire, and Celine Dion's husband, René Angélil; and as, elsewhere, 50 Cent rubs sunblock on three of the four Baldwin brothers, and members of the band Korn mischievously drain Tom Cruise's pool under cover of darkness, while Jerry Seinfeld and Marvin Hamlisch stand by, acting as lookouts.

That's how it's going to be on The World. Fun, peaceful, harmonious. Everybody pulling together and getting along. The exact opposite of the real thing, basically.

Unfortunately, the bigger The World development grows, the less it seems to resemble the model. To my eyes, at least. Not to jump the gun here, because these are early days, but I've seen an aerial photograph of it and to me it looks like an X-ray of somebody's gallstones. The continents aren't as I remember them at all. They've become distorted and twisted out of shape, as though the builders couldn't quite remember where everything went, so they just stuck islands in wherever there was a space and hoped for the best. Things may yet turn out fine, of course. Sheikh Mo doesn't settle for second best. Though at the time of writing, instead of mirroring the layout of the earth's most prominent landmasses, The World resembles two grown-up yaks and a baby yak, grazing.

Doesn't matter, though. By some commercial miracle I don't understand, the moment villas or condos or islands go on sale in any of these ocean developments, they're snapped up without a second thought by foreign investors. Why is that?

"*Because* we're selling you a piece of Dubai," Hamza explains, showing me a scale model, which is so beautiful and intricately made that I'd be happy just to live in that! "Many people want to be here," he says, and goes on to list the reasons: "*Number one,* it's tax free. You don't pay any taxes. We don't know how to spell 'tax' here."

Really? "It's only three letters," I reply, stopping short of actually elbowing him in the ribs. "You'd think you'd be able to manage that."

Grinning, but patently unamused, he continues. "*Number two*: Good weather. It doesn't rain. *Number three:* It's safe . . ."

Ah, yes, safety. I've been meaning to ask someone about that.

But *why* is it safe, Hamza, hm? In a dangerous part of the world such as this, one that's never far from the brink of war, where innocent people are being blown to bits by rebel insurgents on all other fronts, what's the deal here? How come Dubai gets off scot-free? Riddle me that.

Even as I'm figuring out how to couch this key question in less inflammatory terms that won't have him calling for armed guards, I sense a certain frisson ripple through the crew. Can almost hear them muttering under their breath, "*Please,* no, don't say it." Tasha in particular. "Please!!!"

But is it right for me to hold back?

God knows, I'm no journalist. Quite the reverse. My take on a story is not only highly subjective, but also—and this is what makes me unique as a reporter, I think—it rarely coincides with anyone else's. It's not that I lie, exactly; there'd be no point. I just think my memory's shaky, that's all. Less of a storage system and more of a garbage chute: facts disappear into it and they're never seen again. Whenever I've worked in newsrooms in the past—CNN being a good example (I lasted just one day before I was canned)—I've made a point of telling my boss right at the start, "Please, *please* don't regard me as one of your journalists. Indeed, if you're looking for hard news, I'd go to the Brothers Grimm before I'd ever come to me." For these reasons and more, I don't seek out facts. I don't investigate. I don't ask the tough questions. Not as a rule.

However, maybe this needs to be the exception. Obviously, if the rumor Nick heard is true and a deal has at some point been made with Al Qaeda, and especially if I could get this man to admit to such a thing on-camera, I mean—jeez, this interview would be TV Gold. And not the fake sort of TV Gold either, the sort you get on a basic cable adventure show whose host eats cabbage lasagna with soil and pubic hairs in it and wins an Emmy. No, the sort that makes news bulletins worldwide. On real TV.

"Oh, for goodness' sake, just ask him!" I tell myself. "Go on. What harm can it do?"

And I have my mouth open, ready to take the plunge, when at the last minute I glimpse Jay and Nick standing off-camera. Jay's staring at me sternly, while Nick—well, he gives a little flinch. And it's that, the flinch, that kills it. Because if I step out of line, there's only one person who'll suffer. Not us—we'll just be expelled from the country. It's Nick and his company that'll bear the brunt. And I'm sorry, but I can't do that. He's such a great guy. I want him and his wife to be happy and free, safe and prosperous. In other words, I want them to move to New York as soon as possible.

So, despite an overwhelming urge to ask *the* question, the only one that really matters, I'm forced reluctantly to let it go, and allow the PR dice to fall where they may.

"*Number four,*" Hamza continues, unaware of my internal debate, "it's affordable. And *number five,* you get the best standard of living in the world. So you get everything you want in a safe environment . . ."

And so on, and so on, and so on.

Disappointed? You have no idea.

13

First Hint of a Problem

"So—*did you hear?"*

It was one of Fat Kid's ditzier hobbit underlings on the phone, squeaking like a chew toy.

"Hear what?"

"*About the* New York Times."

These were exhilarating days at the office. In my absence, things had been going particularly well. The place was grinding out shows like a well-maintained turbine, everyone was happy with them, audiences were starting to find us and watch regularly, and our viewing numbers were up. The Thumb was on top of the world; he couldn't have been happier. Basically, everything was sunny and wonderful. Which, as you know, is usually when life hits you with a curveball and knocks you right off your feet.

"What about the *New York Times*?"

Quite unexpectedly, a review of the show had appeared in the TV column.

"I'll fax it to you right away."

"Sure, take your time, there's no rush," I said, trying to sound cool, like I had a thousand things I'd rather do than read an article about myself in the number one newspaper in the country. I was in bed at the time, catching up on three months' lost sleep, but leaped out from under the sheets and flung myself down the stairs three at a time to stand by the fax machine. Gimme gimme gimme.

"Mr. Peters's series, . . ."

I read while it was still peeling out of the paper-feeder,

> which began in June, is described as a series of visits to unusual destinations where he is deposited with no money and no resources and is forced to fend for himself. It's a perfectly pleasant little show. . . .

A-ha!

> . . . as long as you accept immediately that it has nothing to do with its own premise.

Wha???

I reread the article several times, struggling to squeeze at least some goodwill out of it. But all I could find was: "A perfectly pleasant little show." Hmm. That's *sort* of complimentary, isn't it? If you isolate it and take great care not to read the rest.

The critic had given over much of her allotted column inches to one of our early episodes, where I was in Romania looking for the castle of Vlad the Impaler, the fifteenth-century warlord on whom Bram Stoker later based his Dracula character. I thought it was a really good show, actually. One of our better ones. And so did everyone at the office. Evidently, we were all wrong.

Mind you, as I said earlier, this had been my biggest fear. Ever since Vanuatu, in fact. To succeed, the show needed to fly under the radar, by attracting mainly the Dimwit Demographic (incorporating ADD sufferers and the easily pleased), not—I stress, *not*—intelligent, analytical, and cultured people like the TV critic for the *New York Times,* who were bound to start asking difficult questions and pulling the premise apart.

One of my close friends is a professor of medieval studies. She'd watched the show and enjoyed it, she told me, before going on to nitpick at the concept the way only an academic can. "It's just not believable," she kept saying. "If you have a camera crew with you, you're not marooned, are you?"

"Well, no, not strictly, but . . ."

"Of *course* people are going to give you food and a bed—they're being filmed."

"Not necessarily. Some of them say no to me. In Greece, for example, the lesbians wouldn't let me stay in their hotel room, so I ended up sleeping on a bench."

"But did you really sleep on the bench, or was it just for the cameras?"

"Er . . ."

"Precisely. It's. Just. Not. Believable." This is how she speaks when she's stressing a point, in one-word sentences.

"But we're not making a survival show," I pleaded for the fifty-thousandth time. "It's entertainment."

"I don't care," my friend insisted. "You're claiming you're all washed up in these places, but you're not. You. Need. To. Change. The premise. Or the title. Or *some*thing."

Damn.

And that wasn't all. It was about now that I started receiving e-mails from curious viewers.

Hi,

I was wondering, how long does it take to film one of the shows?

You're supposedly in the location for a day and a half, correct?

But how long do you really stay there?

And those people that you meet on the streets . . . do you really meet them and they show you around and let you stay in their homes? Or are they picked out beforehand by someone else that works for the show?

—MARGARET

Mr. Peters,

I watch your show with interest.

One thing I would like to know. When you sleep in people's homes . . . do you stay there for the whole night or do you leave when the cameras leave?

—Lisa, Connecticut

You see?? There you go, Lisa, *thinking* too much! Asking too many questions.

Does nobody take anything on trust any more?

These initial grunts of incredulity didn't die down, either; they grew louder and wouldn't stop, signaling that our balance sheet of credibility on this show had slipped into the red, as viewers, not content to still their minds and just enjoy the series for what it was, continued to employ a near-forensic dedication to detail, analyzing my every move. The more they saw the Bewilderbeest stumble across the breadth of whole islands on foot in a single day; or, though he didn't speak the native language, run quite accidentally into a translator who did; or walk up to a total stranger and conveniently be offered food or free lodging for the night with the bare minimum of discussion or negotiation, the more they began scratching their heads, thinking, "Hang on a minute. That can't be right, can it?" And nobody more so, evidently, than the critic of the *New York Times*, who in her review went on to apply the unerring scalpel of her wit to the "reality" aspect of our reality show, suggesting that everywhere the host went on location, everything he did, and everyone he met, seemed to be set up.

> When Mr. Peters visited Deadwood, South Dakota, the episode felt like a promotional film from the local board of tourism. He had no problem getting free food and drinks from people who, in return, had their faces and their establishments on camera.

Oh Lord.

Hadn't I been saying this all along? I *said* this very thing a thousand times. I did.

"A better title for the series," she concluded in the final paragraph of her review, raising her feisty scorpion tail for one last fatal jab, "might be Cash Peters: Comped."

Ouch.

Turbulence

14

Mutiny

G*abble gabble gabble gabble . . .*

I've got my ear pressed to the door, listening to a commotion in the corridor.

Must be about fifty tourists out there, bantering loudly in a language I don't understand. Hauling trunks and squeaky cases on wheels along the passageway, their little feet scurry in and out of rooms, not in orderly fashion, but frenziedly, like geese being shot at, as the jackhammer bang of each door reverberates through the walls, rattling the light fixtures.

Gabble gabble gabble gabble gabble.

Bang bang bang bang bang bang.

Gabble gabble.

Bang bang bang bang.

I haven't unpacked my bags yet, but to be honest, this hellish din has convinced me there's no point. I vote we call time on this crap hole right away.

Usually, the crew leads the charge on the issue of hotels.

Director Mark especially. Hailing from solid middle-class stock, he's used to a high level of comfort, one that won't be compromised without a fight. However, on this occasion he's not with us, so it falls to me to get the ball rolling.

"It's a *horrible* hotel," I grumble to Tasha in the lobby. "So run-down."

Apparently, it was a Sheraton at one time. If so, I can see why they sold it. Probably in a hurry, too, fearing it might collapse at any moment.

"But it's going to be such a hassle moving all our gear out," Jay groans, adjusting his sciatic leg and wincing. Poor guy's still in agony. How he continues on I don't know. I'd have quit weeks ago. "Plus," he throws in for luck, "I'm not sure if I have the authorization to take us someplace better, that's the problem."

"But we can't stay in a dump. We need rest, we need good facilities."

He doesn't disagree.

"Of course . . ." After a moment's consideration, his eyes turn to hot coals of mischief. ". . . if the host insists that he can't possibly stay in this environment, then we'd *have* to do something about it."

"We would?"

Oh my God, we *would*!

I keep forgetting: it's *my* show. I have the power to kick up a stink and make outrageous demands, a privilege I've been ridiculously slow to abuse thus far.

"Great. Then it's a done deal." And I issue a "clap, clap, make it so" of my own. Remarkably, it seems to work miracles, not only in Dubai, but in any place where people enjoy being ordered around by tyrants, because Tasha runs off to make arrangements.

"Where's Willy? Willy!"

Willy's our fixer here in Morocco. A shifty, grotesque little fat man with thick wet lips and a brutish swagger, who's as wide as he is tall. While Tasha's hammering out the accommodation problem with him in a corner, he shrugs several times and drags a chunky hand down across his round face.

"The host can't *possibly* stay here," Tasha's insisting.

At this, Willy scowls. "Oh? And this host you speak of," he says, "it is who?"

She points, and a pair of wounded eyes swivels in my direction. Eyes that could tear the still-beating heart from a man's chest.

"Hi," I say, and give a weak little wave, the sort that gets you raped in prison. "I'm Cash."

"He-lllll-oooo, Cash."

Who would believe there could possibly be a malevolent way of pronouncing those two simple words?

"Don't worry," he sighs in a thickly accented tone, far from happy, "I'll see to it."

We have more assistants working with us today than on any show so far. It's Willy's doing. As part of some complicated back-scratching exercise, he's invited along a posse of thuggish friends—four big, hefty guys, at least three and possibly all four of whom are completely unnecessary—and allotted them roles in the production. Spoiled for choice, we have one carry Kevin's tripod and camera bag; another walks behind the first guy, making sure he doesn't drop anything; the third is there to drive the extra vehicle we now need because we have too many crew members; and the fourth has been given the all-important task of smoking continuously while the rest of us work. If you ask me, we should put our communal foot down and dismiss three of these hangers-on outright, get it over with. But . . . well, things are never that easy with Willy, I discover. Somewhere along the line, he's done deals and made promises he can't renege on. Additionally, he's already annoyed about the hotel problem; one more complaint at this stage could push him right over the edge.

Our first location for this episode, the place where I'm supposed to be all washed up with no clue where I am, is in the Ourika Valley, an hour's drive south from Marrakech in the glorious High Atlas Mountains, which slice through this country west to east.

Although Morocco is close to Europe (extremely close: Spain's about seven miles away, across the Strait of Gibraltar; with the wind at your back you could probably jump it), it has thus far managed to withstand most major European influences and stay true to its Middle Eastern roots. Which seems laudable, even miraculous, especially when you learn that it's not in the Middle East at all, it's in North Africa.

In the early days, this region, known as the Maghreb, was populated mainly by Berbers: hardy, nomadic shepherd types (the word "barbarian" comes from them) who'd drifted this way from Egypt to set up small tribal encampments across the coastal plain and into the hills, where, for many years, they continued to live their quiet, pastoral, barbaric existence uninterrupted.

Unfortunately, this is History we're talking about. And in History nobody gets to live a quiet, pastoral existence forever. That's just not how things go. As we've learned, there's always some brutal dictator or scheming madman and his army lying in wait, ready to strip the shirts from the backs of others. And that's what happened here too.

Eventually, the skies darkened and a bunch of other cultures came bulldozing through the Maghreb. The Greeks, the Phoenicians, the Romans—all tried their hand at overthrowing the local tribespeople, taking their land and crushing them into lifelong servitude. What they didn't count on was the iron will and defiance of these humble peasant farmers, forged over centuries of hardship. Berbers: they're a tough, feisty bunch, man. They know how to put up a fight. They're also surprisingly choosy about who enslaves them. Instead of caving at the first sign of foreign aggression, the way the Lesbians usually did, for example, they stood their ground for years, battling relentlessly to maintain their indigenous culture and independence.

That is, until the seventh century A.D., when an enterprising Arab army from the Seven Large Patches of Sand to the east swept into the Maghreb, not to conquer it, but with the sole aim of opening up trade routes across the desert. Rather than launch a hostile takeover bid, the Arabs experimented with a different approach altogether: bribery. They bribed the Berbers with gifts of ivory and gold. They also introduced them to a fabulous new religion called Islam that came with all kinds of bells and whistles, both for this life and the next, and which, they said, had everyone captivated back home.

Well, how could the peasant farmers resist? Finally they quit struggling and submitted to outside influence.

The Berbers' past, in short, is a blood-soaked cardigan of rebellion, knitted steadfastly over ten thousand or more tumultuous years. And I guess that's the reason we've been sent here now. How fascinating and insightful it would be, the office must have thought, if the host of the show were to be all washed up in one of the most remote rural villages in the snow-capped sleeve that is the Atlas Mountains, and experience firsthand what it's like to live and work as a nomadic shepherd on the frayed hem of civilization.

Inspired idea. Love it.

Only one problem.

Realistically, to do justice to the subject matter in a documentary and capture the complex hues of what is obviously a unique culture would take about six months to a year. And that's at the very least, I'd say. Whereas we have—hang on, let me check and see how long we're scheduled to be here—ah, yes . . . *two hours.*

"Okay—everyone who's not in this scene please—*please* get out of shot."

Jay limps up and down the road, trying a spot of crowd control.

Over to our right, old men with worn-out gargoyle faces line the grass verge, watching our preparations. It's colder than a butcher's fridge out here today. Sensibly, they're wearing heavy white ankle-length overcoats called *djellabas,* hoods pulled up around their ears. The crew too is wrapped up cozy in sweatshirts and padded jackets.

"Willy!" Jay waves one last time. "For Christ's sake, *move*!"

"Who, me?" Hands plowed deep in his overcoat pockets, our fixer is standing beside an uncomfortable-looking tethered camel piled high with brightly colored blankets, gossiping conspiratorially in Arabic with its owner and three of the thugs. With a perfunctory "Ah. Sure," he moves, and continues his dark plotting behind a wall.

The morning air nips like tiny pincers at my flesh, fed by December snows from the mountaintops all around us. Farther along the valley, stone chimneys jutting from heavily wooded slopes puff out lazy blue trails, blending into a dawn mist that's long overstayed its welcome.

"Cash—are you ready?" Jay yells.

Not really. I'm f-f-freezing.

Our daffy wardrobe lady has done it again. After hearing me complain in the past about being overdressed in hot climates, this time she must have thought, "Morocco: that's a desert, yeah?" and immediately went out and bought me a gossamer-thin lemony long-sleeved shirt to wear, without ever bothering to check what winter in this part of the world might be like. Consequently, my entire body is gored to the bone with cold. My teeth are chattering the way they do in cartoons, and I can hardly speak coherently for shivering. Yet again, if this were reality and not merely a reality *show,* I'd be dead by now.

Between takes, Tasha runs over with Diet Coke—the equivalent of my daily fifth of gin; used to get me going each morning and give my flagging spirits a fillip—and also a thick wool-lined jacket, which she drapes about my shoulders. "Th-th-thanks."

"You're welcome."

"Okay—action!"

On Jay's cue, the jacket is snatched away, Tasha scarpers out of shot, and I launch myself onto a bridge over a little stream and across what looks to be someone's vegetable patch, programming myself into character as I go, forcing my imagination to make believe that I really am stranded, alone and helpless, in one of the most inaccessible spots in the world. It's a tough act, especially when there's a crew of at least ten people standing not twelve feet away. And sixty feet beyond them is a roadside souvenir stand.

Word spread fast that a TV crew would be in the area today to capture the authentic look of a Berber village. Eager to turn this opportunity to profit, the highly enterprising locals sprang from their beds extra early to line the streets with fancy merchandise. Fancy and cheap, I should add. Rugs, baskets, beaded hats, bowls—the kind of gaudy knickknacks that only tourists would buy, and which doubtless go from here to their hotel, to their suitcase, to their home, to the back of a cupboard, and from there straight to the Salvation Army, without ever being looked at again.

"Exc-cuse me? W-w-where am I?"

Jay has steered me toward a crude stone hut beside the stream. Quaking violently with cold, I hurl myself inside, where a short, dark-haired man in a brown *djellaba* stands staring at me. I'm used to the drill by now. Another handsome stooge planted by the local tourist office.

"You're in the Ourika Valley," he says, giving a little bow. His diction is wonderful, and that's what lets him down: he's much too sincere and coherent to be mistaken for a nomadic shepherd. Also, he has jeans and white sneakers poking out from underneath his *djellaba*! "Which is near Marrakech, which is a big city."

"And how f-f-far is th-that?"

"Fifty kilometers from here."

The guy introduces himself as Mohammed, although I believe his authentic Berber name is Tony. At least, that's what I heard people calling him off-camera. As I walk in, he's in the throes of doing something indigenous—another dead giveaway that this is a setup, which will no doubt thrill the *New York Times* TV critic and her many cynical readers. "Once again," I imagine her writing, "Peters just happens to hit upon a hut in which someone who speaks good English is, at the very moment he arrives, engaged in an extremely interesting photogenic pursuit." In this case, the man's grinding corn to a fine yellow powder to make bread, using two large rotating stones that he operates manually, the way his family has done for centuries. Or at least when they're being filmed they do. The rest of the time they probably buy it at Costco like everybody else.

"How l-l-long does it t-take?"

"Three and a half hours," he says.

Per loaf??? My God.

"And you d-do this every d-day?"

"Yes."

Of course you do. You're a miller and you stand in this perishingly cold hut every morning grinding corn. Sure.

"All the people in the village," he adds, "bring their packs of grain and they grind it here. And after, they pay for the milling with 10 percent of the grain."

Bullshit.

You know what this reminds me of? One of those Civil War reenactment villages you see in America, where retired women kitted out in elaborate period-style bonnets and crinolines address tourists in olde Englishe phrases they picked up from an audiobook of *Twelfth Night:* "Oooooh, *verily,* Sir Toby, nay! Avert thine devilish cuckold gaze, sire, lest my maidenly furnigrations grumpled ne'er can be," while they churn butter, shoe horses, and pump with gusto at the treadle of a spinning jenny, before knocking off at 6:00 and rushing home with a Whopper and a six-pack to catch *Entertainment Tonight.*

Playing along, I allow "Mohammed" to show me the fundamentals of Berber bread-making: how the corn pours from a four-cornered basket dangling from the ceiling through a hole in a piece of wood, and then onto the revolving stones to be ground into flour. The process is powered somehow by the fast-flowing stream beneath the mill.

"Could you not just get donkeys to turn the stones?" I propose, thinking that one word in the right place could propel this culture forward by up to a thousand years. Into the fifteenth century. "Or a man on a bike peddling very fast round and round?"

He looks confused. Evidently, nothing quite so wildly futuristic has ever crossed his mind. I mean, why would it, really? "For other types of mill we use donkeys." He steps over my suggestion. "Making olive oil, for example. For this we use water—"

"Look." I have to interrupt. Not only am I bored with his shtick, but I'm also mere minutes away from dying of exposure. "Do you have anything I c-could wear? I love the flour thing, it's f-fascinating, but I've got to g-get warm."

"Yes," he says, seeming a little disheartened. "No problem. My house is nearby. I'll let you have something, and a cup of tea."

Excellent.

"Aaaaaand . . . cut," Jay shouts. "Let's move on."

From the bread-making setup we shift along the road a little, ignoring a steadily expanding crowd of spectators, to Phase II of the Berber theme park: the family farmstead. If accurate, it's quite a shocker. Built to replicate the hardships of rural life around the time the Romans came knocking in 100 B.C., it's a series of crude stone buildings enclosing a muddy courtyard. Windows are just bare holes in the walls. There's no electricity, therefore no lights. The only warmth in those days came, as it does in this mock-up, from an open fire crackling away in the hearth of an outbuilding. As a nice touch to round things off, several extras have been bused in this morning for set decoration—a couple of children, a good-looking woman who's here to represent the Berber wife, and some toothless old bag draped in rags crouching in the doorway, playing somebody's mother. There's even a ginger tom sprawled across the ground, along with a chicken. A lowly, dispiriting scene of poverty and desperation if ever there was one, and I'm impressed at how beautifully rendered it is. Humbled too that all these wonderful people climbed out of their warm beds this cold morning to do our little show. They've really pulled out all the stops. Thanks, Morocco Tourism. Good job.

While I hog the fire, thawing out my hands, "Mohammed" dives into the house, reappearing moments later with a spare *djellaba*. "Here, try this on."

Normally I'd refuse. There might be things living in it. But since it's a prop, I'm safe. And when I slip it on over my head, it's instantly snug and warming. "Oh, I love this." Additionally, I'm sure it makes me look rather cute—though that's a secondary factor. All the same, I may buy one later to take home.

Pulling up a little stool, "Mohammed" hands me a homemade round of pita bread and invites me to tear off a chunk. Of course, you just know at this point that a dozen grubby fingers have touched it prior to now. The chicken pecked at it maybe, the cat licked the edges or even curled up and fell asleep on it for a while. These are the mountains, life is meant to be tough here, and this piece of living art is uncompromising in its portrayal of people from Ancient Historical Times and their hardships. So to hell with it, I stuff the bread in my mouth anyway, swilling it down with a glass of delicious hot green tea laced with peppermint, which begins a slow journey through my system, heating me up as it goes.

Once I'm done eating and drinking, and I've conducted a short interview about this ancient lifestyle, I see Jay checking the clock he carries around with him everywhere. Our two hours are almost up. Time to head back to town. "Ask him how you get back into Marrakech from here," he whispers in my ear.

So I do. "If I want to go to Marrakech, how would I get there?"

"I have friends," "Mohammed" replies. "Somebody will help you. I can find someone to bring you to Marrakech."

Of course, he adds, I might have to barter with the "driver," give him something in return. I pull at the sleeve of my *djellaba.* There's always this lovely coat I've just acquired.

"That's good," he smiles haplessly, pretending he's attached to the *djellaba* and that to lose it would perpetuate his hardship still further, which is just silly. There must be dozens of them in the souvenir shop.

And yet . . .

Alerted by a certain concern in his eyes, something occurs to me. A faint, distant, thoroughly implausible possibility . . .

No, surely not. It can't be.

. . . that "Mohammed," nicknamed Tony, is not *actually* a stooge from the Tourist Office at all. He's not in character, playing the role of a Berber farmer; *he really is a Berber farmer.* A Berber farmer called Mohammed. And he *does* mill corn flour for a living and this is *actually* his farmstead, with its glassless windows and no electricity. And the children, the wife, the toothless old bag, the cat, the chicken . . .

Holy crap. What an idiot I am.

The whole thing's for real, isn't it?

"This is honestly how these people live?" I whisper to Jay, praying for a denial.

Busy sampling the wonderful mint tea for himself, he looks up and smiles.

Oh God.

Good news. After an hour on his cell, Willy's struck a deal with a hotel on the outskirts of town. "I don't know if you'll like it," he mumbles apologetically. "It's slightly better than the other place. But hey, if you hate it, I'll try again."

He's still explaining this as the van we're in pulls through a set of wooden gates, past a sentry in a tall hat, standing to attention, and glides to a rest between two ornamental pools filled with floating red rose petals, the centerpiece of a courtyard leading to a magnificent, secluded, five-star villa.

"As I said," Willy grins wickedly, "if you hate it . . ."

Yeah, right.

Inside the main hallway, an Arabian Nights column-and-pool motif lends an air of understated mystique to one sunny room after another, each decorated tastefully with antiques and laced with an enduring stillness that somehow makes its sophistication effortless, the way good taste should be. To the rear of the main hall, a set of glass doors leads to a patio, and from there to a stunning landscaped garden bordering an exquisite diamond-shaped pool of still water, not because the pump broke and it's stagnant, which has been my experience with pools in the past, but because someone engineered it that way, to mirror the house's image back at itself, in case the old girl should need reminding from time to time how beautiful she is.

Built by a wealthy Moroccan family as their private home, it was recently turned into what is arguably Marrakech's finest out-of-the-way hotel, and stands in quite epic contrast to everything else I've seen in this struggling country so far.

"We have many big celebrity clients come to stay with us," the owner's son explains proudly. "When they do, they take over the whole house."

Dressed in a sharp suit, with rakish long brown hair down to his collar and an aristocratic French accent, he carries himself with an air of easy wealth, and none of that appallingly obnoxious swagger sported by the nouveau riche back in Hollywood.

Wait, did he say celebrities?

"Such as who?"

"Oh, well, P. Diddy flew three hundred and fifty of his friends out for a party . . ."

Impressive.

". . . and Will Smith brought his family here for a vacation last year."

Really?

And now *we're* here. It doesn't get any better than that.

Even as we're wiring our jaws back together, a gaggle of porters runs to grab our bags and take them to our suites—not rooms, note, but whole suites, one each—on the far side of the back lawn; a series of terraced bungalows as luxuriously decadent in their way as the rest of the villa, and filled with enough antiques and other classic touches to facilitate the fantasy that you too are connected enough or loaded enough to be invited to a celebrity's Moroccan hideaway, where the Cristal is flowing, Jada Pinkett Smith is sunning herself on the patio, Diddy's rapping freestyle in the cabana, and a couple of his homeys are in the suite next door getting their groove on with some bitches—or whatever the current degrading slang for "broads" is.

However, we're not celebrities, and we're certainly not loaded. This is only basic cable. Slightly worried, I ask Tasha, "Can we really afford to stay here?"

She bites her bottom lip. "Willy told me he's done a deal. He says he got this for the same price as the other place."

"But how? How is that possible?"

It's a mystery. As is almost everything Willy has a hand in. I know the guy is our fixer, and fixers are meant to fix things, but something about his expression, the permanent sneer, the leeriness in his eyes, his nudge-wink street-kid mannerisms, tells me that his whole life is probably lived under the table. Exactly why would this ultraluxurious hotel, which clearly has larger, wealthier fish it could be frying, allow a group like us, who obviously don't fit its target clientele, to stay here? Best guess is that maybe business is slow right now, and cable TV money is better than no money at all. But I don't think so. Something else is going on. Willy has sweetened the deal in some way; I can feel it. And deals have consequences. Whatever he's up to, his little maneuver may be fine now, but it's bound to backfire on us sooner or later. Bet you anything.

Once again, the issue of flights, and why we don't have better ones, has returned to dominate mealtime conversations, as it did in Dubai—as it does regularly on these trips, in fact. The needlessly roundabout journey back to L.A. in a few days' time is an ordeal the crew members are bracing themselves for with bleak fortitude. Especially Jay, who can barely walk any more without clenching his teeth and clutching his lower back, the way pregnant women do. If he moves too quickly, sharp bolts of lightning crackle up and down his outer thigh, a condition that won't be helped by switching carriers repeatedly, hopping from airport to airport, gate to gate, plane to plane, and being jammed into a variety of cramped Coach seats for the best part of twenty-four hours with no room to stretch his legs.

"Things are going to be even worse in Alaska," Mike says, causing everyone to freeze. "Oh shit!" Realizing what he's just blurted out, he rushes to cover his mouth. "Did you know, Cash?"

I didn't.

Future destinations are meant to be kept a secret from me. But hey, I know now.

"Sorry, buddy." He laughs.

"It's okay."

And we all pretend nothing just happened. We do that fairly often.

For dinner tonight, Willy has brought us to a place in the heart of the medina, the old town. He knows the restaurant owner, he says, and can get us a special deal, which, to be fair, he does, including a table on the second-floor balcony directly overlooking one of the greatest human spectacles on earth: the Djemaa el-Fna. Despite the millions of more easily pronounced alternatives, this is what Marrakech decided to call its central square.

Say the word "Morocco" to people and three main things usually come to mind. The Djemaa el-Fna is one of them.

Combining the mayhem and momentum of a medieval battlefield, everything below us, from here to the mud bricks of the city's twelfth-century fortress walls, is chaos; a frenetic thousand-decibel madhouse riot—flutes wailing, car horns blaring, mopeds buzzing, children crying, donkeys clip-clopping by, drums beating—that sets this place apart from all others, not only in Morocco, but anywhere, and which heats up still further by late afternoon, when thousands of people clock off work and stroll through Marrakech's narrow stone streets to join the thousands already here, mingling with tattoo artists, fortune-tellers turning cards, small banjo bands, chained monkeys performing tricks too cruel and gruesome for any human being with any conscience to watch, and therefore drawing massive crowds; and finally, large teams of trained acrobats, somersaulting, leaping onto seesaws, and assembling themselves into incredible human pyramids, a feat of balance that earns massive applause from the spectators but for which there is otherwise limited call these days, I should think, unless you're repairing gutters or need to deliver pizza to a third-floor apartment.

They also have real snake charmers! With *real cobras*—they're not sock puppets, like you might expect. To coax them out of their basket, a couple of grizzled old-timers squat on blankets on the ground, each blowing into a small metal trumpet-shaped flute-type thing, producing The Most Nerve-Jarring Sound in the World, a strangulated *neeeyaaa-yeeeeeaaaaaaaaaaaaaayeeeeeeeeeaaaaaeeeeeeeeeeeeaaaaaaa-*

yeeeeeeeyeeeeeeeeeyaaaayaaaaaaaayeeeeeeeeyaaaaaaayeeeeeee-ing noise, not quite music, not quite a persistent strident racket, but certainly more than is required to pierce the average eardrum, I should think.

"Allahu akbar . . . ashnadu an la Ilah ila Allah . . ."

Once in a while, however, the snake charmers find themselves outwailed by: (*a*) the Muslim call to prayer crackling from loudspeakers high in the central Koutoubia Mosque, which most people seem to ignore; and just as often by: (*b*) vendors from the myriad stalls that extend west from the mosque almost to the other side of the concourse, who yell for your business as you saunter by.

"Try my oranges."

"No thanks."

"Fresh oranges?"

"No thanks."

"Sir, sir, try my fresh oranges."

"I said no thanks. Really."

"ORANGES!!"

"NO!"

"Why you not try my oranges?? What is wrong with my oranges?"

"Jeez, he's going to throw them at us. Run."

If it's not oranges, then it's fresh cake, or mint tea, or succulent dates, or a hundred other treats. So many choices that you don't know where to start. You're just sure it won't be with the oranges.

"HEY! WHAT DO YOU HAVE AGAINST MY ORANGES? SIR! SIR?"

Of course, such a dizzying blizzard of hyperactivity is irresistible to Kevin's restless cinematic eye. One look at the confusion, the ghostly corona of smoke circling the hurricane lamps that hang from stalls frying chilies and shrimp; the men with orange lampshades on their heads dispensing fresh water from an urn for pennies; the entertainers; the bums; the pickpockets; and he's inspired to shoot a time-lapse from the restaurant balcony, capturing the multitude, and, beyond them, a panoramic backdrop of finger-thin towers that skewer the clouds like kabobs. As the sun, a shimmering dollop of honey, slithers down behind them and twilight creeps stealthily into night, these towers, along with the entire horizon extending as far as the hills, magically fade to black against a hot curried sky.

The shot will take an hour to play out. Once it's set up, Kevin is free to relax, joining us for a delicious meal of roasted chicken, couscous, bastillas, and lamb.

The Moroccans, same as the Greeks, same as almost everyone else in the world, it seems, enjoy food cooked, basted, fried, tossed, bathed, or drizzled in oil, which again makes it hard to find anything I can eat. In the end I settle for a small salad and a chicken drumstick. Though that's only after I've fussily scraped the glistening marinade off it with the back of my knife, a move that draws a brief but obvious Crew Look.

Their mood tonight is noticeably downbeat, and in obvious diametric contrast to our frenzied surroundings. Off to one side, Mike sits alone with his phone, locked in another of his long-drawn-out negotiations with an airline booking agent, trying to wangle a favor. A less punishing route home maybe? Bulkhead seats? Better yet, an upgrade. But as smoothly seductive as his efforts are, for once they come to naught, and he hangs up, stymied and miserable.

"Dude, this is freakin' nuts. It's the holidays. Everything's booked up. I don't know what else to do."

The others fall into restless contemplation.

Tasha has zoned out, and remains quiet for the longest time before making a confession. "I can't do this any more," she says solemnly, letting the words slip out unobtrusively between mouthfuls of couscous. "There's too much hassle."

I know how she feels. Even the best of road warriors grows weary of battle sometimes.

"It'll be okay," I reassure her. "Everybody's tired. We'll be home soon."

"Sure. But . . . still . . ." Another mouthful of couscous.

Still?

I guess my disappointment is etched into my facial expression, because, having dropped this terrible bombshell, she immediately rushes to lessen its impact—"I'm sorry. I mean, don't get me wrong"—or at least to head off accusations of desertion. "I've had an amazing time making the series, I love everybody, and it's been great . . ."

"Okay."

". . . but I . . ." Her lips are smiling, her eyes are not. She can't hide anything. "I want my life back."

Well, who doesn't?

Truthfully, Tasha has better reason than most to jump ship. Got engaged not long ago to an Emmy-winning TV editor and misses him like crazy; says so regularly, sometimes with tears in her eyes. There's also her upcoming wedding in Florida to plan. Hard to do on the road from Morocco or New Zealand or Alaska. So the writing was on the wall all along. As hard as it is to accept, one of our gang has reached breaking point and is about to dianaross our supremes.

Nothing personal, of course. I know that. She's not angry at me, or with anything I've done or said. It just feels that way.

My show, my crew, my friends, my fault if they leave.

She's right about one thing: this schedule, it's eating us alive. If we're not dog tired, we're annoyed and snapping at each other; if we're not annoyed we're in pain; if we're not in pain we're homesick; and if we're not homesick, but especially if we are, we're threatening to quit. We all have full personal lives apart from our work. Kevin's got a wife and kids waiting for him in Malibu; Jay is happily married to a lovely woman who is herself in the running to cohost a morning show on network TV; Mike is single and free. When he's not traveling extensively for his job, he travels extensively for his own pleasure and enlightenment. And of course I'm as good as married these days: great home, solid circle of friends, a relaxed, harmonious life in Hollywood, one that, as far as I'm concerned, could be made better in only one way: by my actually being there to enjoy it—as opposed to being here, in yet another foreign land, eating in another foreign restaurant, putting stuff in my mouth that is speculatively classified as food but which more than likely will, by this time tomorrow, have turned my complexion to bubble wrap.

"Sorry," Tasha mumbles again, big brown eyes fixing me with an unwavering stare. "I'm going to miss you." And she gives my arm a little squeeze.

"Er . . . excuse me, guys."

It's Willy. Spotting a moment of tenderness that needs disrupting, he shuffles over to our table, looking . . . well, shifty, what else?

"About the tickets," he says, "I think I may be able to help you." His cocky tone would be perfect for selling fake Rolexes, I've decided. Or condos in Dubai. "I have contacts at the airlines. If you like, I will talk to them, see what I can do."

Everyone cheers up instantly.

Mike's elated. "Hey, great. Thanks, dude."

"Give me your tickets; I'll go to the airport first thing tomorrow, okay?"

Ah.

Our initial flush of enthusiasm gives way to the same

grumbling concern that accompanies any dealings we have with this odd little man. There's a trust issue. Not to mention a simply-not-liking-him issue. Me, I don't want to be giving any stranger my ticket. Without it, I won't be able to get home—obviously. However, the others seem inclined to take a chance, and their childlike innocence wins me over. As one, we gather up our airline tickets into a single stack and pass them to him, even as my intuition is telling me that this is the equivalent of opening the nearest Dumpster and tossing them inside.

When I wake up next morning, with the fevered clatter and bang of the Djemaa el-Fna still ringing in my ears, I'm alarmed to find my stomach acting up.

Remember, I said there were three things you think of when you hear the word "Morocco"? Well, this is the second: food poisoning. I don't think I've met anyone who's been here and not at some point fallen ill.

Has to be the chicken I ate in the restaurant last night. Who's to say what happened to that poor little drumstick on its journey from farmyard to plate? How many unwashed fingers manhandled it en route; how many rusty radiators it accidentally fell behind; how many hours it lay in the hot sun on a window ledge crawling with flies before being breaded and marinated in delicious Arabian spices; how many dogs ran off with it and had to have it torn from their jowls before the chef could wipe the saliva off with a dishrag and finally sling it in a pan and slow-cook it to perfection?

But we're here to make TV. I can't let mere nausea drag me down. A whole team of people is depending on me. So I scramble out of bed, swallow a couple of charcoal tablets with my tea at breakfast to put the frighteners on the bacteria, and continue on with the day as normal.

While our fixer is at the airport sorting out the tickets—probably—one of the Thugs drives us to the medina again, this time for a tour of the souks, a sprawling labyrinthine tangle of ancient alleyways and dead ends threading like spider veins across a wide area to the east of the Djemaa el-Fna, and jam-crammed with tiny shops, some little more than alcoves, no wider than the shoulders of the traders running them, selling a wide range of goods: jewelry, fresh produce, spices, baskets, rotary phones, severed goat heads, pointy shoes, hats, musical instruments, and, of course, oil lamps—the ones that regularly pop up in fairy tales. To my surprise, the souks are awash with them. And it stands to reason they can't all have genies in them; it's not statistically possible.

My companion today is a local man with an intimate knowledge of Marrakech.

"Hi, good morning."

"Hello," he replies distantly, not really paying attention.

He's tall, middle-aged, balding, and wearing a functional blue anorak to ward off the morning chill. Haj is a taxi driver in Marrakech. He's been enlisted by Willy to walk me around the medina. I stumble across him, inasmuch as I stumble across anyone in these shows now, studiously picking through a jumble of artifacts outside an antique store, searching for something called a Hand of Fatimah. It's a gift for his sister's birthday.

"We hang it in the house or on the door. The Hand of Fatimah," he explains, digging into a stack of them, "protects you from 'bad eyes.'" To illustrate, he makes his own eyes bulge out of their sockets in a scary thyroid way. "We put them on the door to protect us from bad-looking."

Fatimah was the only daughter of the prophet Mohammed. Those Moroccans who are superstitious—in other words, all of them—like to keep a talisman in the shape of her hand, and sometimes several, around their house to ward off hexes, jinxes, evil spirits, and Satan, when in most instances a simple dried octopus would be quite sufficient.

"But why would I want protection?"

"Oh, Gawwwwwd," Haj groans in his thick Arabic accent.

When you're groundlessly superstitious, a question like this is considered so silly and obvious that it doesn't warrant an answer.

He then goes back to selecting a hand, evaluating two in particular. Which one, he's calculating, is more likely to frighten Satan: a plain tin one etched with curlicues, or a plain tin one etched with curlicues *and* with a raised bejeweled eye at the center of the palm?

After much inner wrestling, he opts for the hand without the jewel.

"How much is this?" he asks the shop owner.

"Two hundred dirham," he replies.

"Awwww, come on!"

We don't realize how lucky we are sometimes to live in a Western economy, where purchasing something from a store is such a simple process: we choose what we want, we pay for it, and we leave. That's it. It's a great little system.

Alas, not so in Morocco. You can't simply buy stuff you need here. That would be considered eccentric.

"We have to bargain," Haj tells me sternly. "You must bargain for everything."

And the bargaining is super-complicated. It comes in a three-phase protocol.

In Phase I, you dispute the quoted price with a look of utter dismay, even horror if you're up to it, not only refusing to pay, but going full out to berate the shopkeeper for his lack of business sense in charging something so laughable in the first place. Shame on him. *Shame and damnation!* Once that's done, and the store owner is staring at you, going, "What the hell are you talking about, you son of a camel? That's cheap!" it's time to embark on Phase II. Here, you play complicated mind games, acting out a bell curve of emotions, by turns outraged, insulted, hurt, chagrined—if that's even a word—and desolate, in any order you like; walking out of the shop, coming back in again; shouting, pacing up and down, waving your hands, in a fine-tuned choreography of offers, counteroffers, and histrionics designed to leave the customer exhausted and drive the store owner to slit his wrists.

And all for a 5 percent discount!!!

Finally, in Phase III of the protocol, things calm down a little. You and the store owner arrive at a price for the item that's mutually agreeable, and all too often the exact same price it started out at.

So, the Hand of Fatimah Haj has chosen—a cutout metal shape with a hook to hang it up with, which might come in useful for breaking into cars perhaps, but doesn't look like it's capable of protecting anyone from anything—carries a price tag of two hundred dirham (roughly twenty-two dollars).

Naturally, Haj is disgusted and throws in a counteroffer. "One fifty."

"No, two hundred," the store owner insists, waving his arms. "Two hundred. Good price. Very good price."

"One hundred sixty," Haj tries again.

"Two hundred."

"No, no. One sixty, or I don't want it. How much is your lowest price?"

"Two hundred is my lowest price."

"I give you one hundred eighty."

"Oh, no, my friend. Two hundred dirham. If you don't want it, leave it."

And so it goes on. The convoluted dance of deception escalates from light banter at the start to a staccato outburst of taunts, jibes, and insults—or "a discussion," as Haj calls it—until the poor, bludgeoned store owner, fearing one of them is about to have a heart attack, agrees (though with much eye-rolling), to let the Hand go at the price Haj originally offered for it—150 dirham.

Yay! Tradition has been honored. A bargain has been struck. It's over!

But wait a second. Something's wrong.

Haj is far from happy.

"No." With the capricious whim of a lunatic, he runs a large hand over his bald head and gives the trinket back, sighing, "Never mind."

"But . . ."

As a casual observer to this drama, I'm aghast. And if I'm aghast, then the store owner must be apoplectic. He's left clutching his cheap, mass-produced tin hand, not knowing quite what to do next.

"*You don't want it?* After all of that?"

"Nah." Haj turns up his nose. "I go somewhere else."

And he walks out.

I feel sick. The stomachache I woke up with is growing worse. The longer I hold out, the more nauseous I become. Sweaty, woozy, unsure how I'm going to make it through the rest of the day without throwing up.

"You have the . . . ?" Haj inquires, and he mimes a bad tummy. "Mm?"

I nod: "I'm sure it was the chicken last night."

"Ah." And he adds, mysteriously: "Come, there is a place. Follow."

It's not on the schedule, but Jay decides to let the situation run. For once, something real and spontaneous is happening. Imagine that!

So, with the crew following closely, we dive into the souks along a dark intestinal conduit of pointy-shoe shops, *djellaba* stores, and stalls displaying entire hillsides of dried fruit—figs, dates, apricots—as well as large drums of saffron, coriander, and other herbs and spices in an array of startling colors, each one fashioned invitingly into a cone shape, like torpedoes. The foot traffic is hectic, threading past us in tangled, free-flowing lines. A man carrying two live chickens by the feet, flapping upside-down at his side, dodges into an archway, just as a teenager on a moped, then two more, spewing copious exhaust, rip rallycross style into the banks of shoppers, evidently not much caring if they hit anyone. Used to it, Haj steps aside calmly just in time, and I do too, but it's a near miss, and leaves me coughing fitfully in a rolling cloud of fumes.

The atmosphere is claustrophobic down here, dark and menacing. Spears of dust-speckled ochre sunlight, bursting through broken slats in the roof, hack the polluted air into slices, guiding our feet to a crossroads. Here, the path forks and we take a sharp right, emerging into daylight, and journey's end.

Merchandise in this part of the souks contrasts distinctly with everything else I've seen so far. There are cages hanging on hooks, with *things* shifting inside them. One store has a six-pack of salamanders on a rope—I guess you never know when you're going to run out—plus dead snakes, rows of empty tortoise shells arranged on shelves and easily mistaken for WWI military helmets, and an iguana on a stick. In another, a display of fresh fruit and vegetables is topped off attractively with the severed head of an antelope. Severed recently, too, I'm guessing, because it looks very surprised.

A few more yards and we step out of the flow of human traffic into a corner shop. A small space, it's jammed with the inventory of an infinitely bigger one: mainly glass containers filled with powders, herbs, and some small pebble-like objects I can't even put a name to, stacked as high as the ceiling. While I stand to one side, clutching my stomach, Haj, with the studious intensity of a taxi driver pretending he's a doctor, pores over the merchandise. While he does so, the owner tries to interest me in some not-to-be-missed bargains, including a jar of live scorpions . . .

"For the black magic," he intones mystically.

"Aaaagh! Get that away from me. Get it away!"

. . . followed by today's special offer: a live chameleon, which sits on Haj's sleeve for the longest while, staring up at him, its eyes swiveling independently of each other, blinking.

"It has seven colors of change," the store owner insists.

But though we indulge it for several minutes, the creature refuses to turn blue to match Haj's anorak. Faulty, obviously.

"No, we want something," Haj explains to the man, handing it back, "that will stop the gas in the stomach." In ways that, say, swallowing a live chameleon wouldn't.

"Gas?" the storekeeper says.

"In my stomach. I'm feeling sick."

To clarify—BLEEEEEECCCCHHHHH—I belch obligingly.

"Ah." Leaping to the shelves, he returns with a jar of brown powder. "This will be of help."

It's cumin. The stuff they put in curries. Considered the best natural cure for food poisoning, apparently. Haj buys four spoonfuls, which the shopkeeper measures out into a plastic bag. I'm then pulled into a back alley outside and made to swallow half of the powder, washing it down with bottled water. It's disgusting.

"Okay." I wipe my mouth across my shirtsleeve. "Now what?"

"We wait." And he smiles cryptically.

Old Dead Eyes is back. Willy joins us from his trip to the airport.

"So how did it go? Any luck?" Mike asks.

He shakes his head, saggy jowls wobbling. "I tried. But there are no direct flights," he says. "And other flights are full. I couldn't get you anything better."

"Upgrades?"

"Sorry."

Or maybe he just hung out in a bar all morning with his pals. I certainly wouldn't put it past him. It's definitely not the news we were hoping for anyway. This being Christmastime, we always knew it was going to be a long shot, so our expectations were never that high. All the same, it's a low blow and only depresses everyone further.

"So can we have our tickets back, then?" I ask as an afterthought.

For some reason I'm detecting hesitancy.

Without explaining further, because that would only complicate matters, Willy dismisses my request with a brusque "later," and walks over to speak to one of his thug henchmen.

For once I don't care. I'm shaking badly. Sweating. I have shooting pains across my abdomen, which feels like it's close to exploding. I could throw up at any minute.

At my side, Haj hovers nervously with the plastic bag, awaiting his cue.

"Not yet!" Jay shouts from across the street. "Not yet! Hold it."

"I can't, Jay."

"Hold it!!"

At the last second, Kevin appears, running, with Mike and Tasha behind him. They've been filming a monkey dancing on the end of a chain. Inhumane, but irresistible. In a great rush, he plants his tripod on the cobbles and adjusts the camera's focus.

"Okay—go."

About time! Ordered to vomit, I rush behind an open gate, crouch close to the ground, and in ten or so bursts hurl the entire contents of my stomach, everything I've eaten and drunk since yesterday lunchtime, into the plastic bag.

"You alright?" Haj asks when it's over, taking the bag and tying a knot in it.

"Alright, yes." I cough, wiping my mouth on my sleeve.

Concerned that I might not have grasped the finer technicalities of what just happened, he adds, "Cumin makes you throw up."

"Yes, I get that," I say, and thank him again.

Then, before he can give me the bag of vomit back, which he's welcome to keep as a souvenir of our fruitful and exciting time together, I shake his hand and leave in some haste.

Returning from a difficult day, we step into a scene straight from an Arabian harem, and feel instantly uplifted. While we were out, our hotel has gone through a 180-degree transformation. Dozens of lanterns have been placed around the indoor pools, scented candles shimmer dimly on tables, harassed by a light breeze from the patio, and the outdoor pool too is illuminated underwater, its barely moving surface reflecting the stars. With a few well-orchestrated touches, what was merely exotic and five-star this morning is elevated tonight into a magical grotto nourishing to the senses. The perfect backdrop for a mutiny.

Dinner is served in a dark corner of the main hallway. Despite the fact that there's no place set for him, Willy joins us anyway. The man has the table manners of a horse, shoveling ungodly amounts of bread and vegetables and rice and braised lamb into his mouth, not to mention all the wine he knocks back at our expense, his armor-plated ego impervious to the daggers of loathing being flung his way.

"Hey, guys," he says mid-forkful, head buried in his food, "do me a favor, will ya? Shoot a few scenes of the hotel and put them in the show." It's so casual, the way he does it. A throwaway line tossed out randomly, giving us the option to say no, while at the same time leaving us in no doubt that doing so would be a *very* bad idea. "Please? Just a couple—in the grounds, your rooms, and so on. It would really help."

Help? Help whom?

Then the penny drops.

The sly dog. I knew it!

This is the deal. The deal he's done with the hotel. That's how we got such a great rate, by using the leverage of free publicity. "They're from an American TV network," he must have told the owner's son, clearly spelling out the word "American": M-O-N-E-Y. I can see it all now. "Give them rooms and I guarantee you publicity in the show." When a little more research—say, by asking us—would have told him that we never put the hotel we're staying at in the show itself, as that would spoil the illusion; only the place where I spend the five hours we call night. So we couldn't do the sweaty, conniving creep a favor even if we wanted to.

By now, several pairs of "bad eyes" are trained on Willy, boring holes in his forehead. "Your home had better be stuffed to the rafters with Hands of Fatimah," I'm thinking.

"You're going to need all the bloody protection you can get tonight."

After a noncommittal "Hm, I'll see what I can do" from Kevin, to be nice, but which in TV terms is another way of saying "absolutely not," Mike hurriedly changes the subject. "Hey, buddy, d'you have our tickets with you?"

"Yeah," Willy says, guzzling a glass of Merlot. "They're in my coat."

"Well, could we have them?"

"Sure. But I mean . . ." Inconvenienced, he points his knife and fork at his food to show he's not finished. ". . . you know, first? Okay?"

"Okay. Just make sure you give me mine before you leave tonight," I say.

"I told you, I will," he snaps back, crossly. *"It's fine."*

Once he's labored over two helpings of dessert, devouring almost a third of a fruit pie, being sure to leave room for cookies, some of which he stuffs in his pocket, Willy slips away from the table, we assume to bring his coat, disappearing for several minutes. Then several minutes more. And, oddly, for several more minutes after that.

Having given him the benefit of the doubt for long enough, Tasha hurries to the window and lets out a gasp. "Hey!"

"What?"

"The sonofabitch! His car's gone!"

"NO!!!"

I run to the window too. I don't believe it. She's right. The clapped-out Skoda is no longer in the driveway. What the hell kinda game is this jackass playing?

Is it possible that he sold our tickets to someone else? Can that even be done? Aren't they nontransferable? And if not, does this mean that, instead of being upgraded to better flights and/or seats, we've actually been downgraded to having no flights at all and being stuck in Morocco over Christmas? Oh hell! My mind's doing cartwheels now. *Or,* is he merely holding them hostage to ensure we perform our side of a bargain we didn't even agree to?

As we're all mulling this over, the French owner's son emerges from the shadows, accompanied by a bronzed male friend with dusky features so flawless one can only assume that God himself personally signed off on them.

"Here," the owner's son says, handing out press packs and DVDs. "I've included an up-to-date price list and some stills. Use any material you like from the disc. If there's anything else you need, just let me know."

"We will," Tasha says, starting to bite her bottom lip.

All of us feel awkward, terrible. The poor sap's been duped, same as us. Much as we may want to, we won't be filming shots of his beautiful hotel for the show. There's no point. It'd be a waste of tape.

"Thank you for doing this," he adds, very sincerely. "We appreciate it."

"No problem."

Oh dear.

Once the pair of them have slunk back into the shadows again, going off to do whatever perfectly formed, beautiful, rich, important people do in Marrakech by night, Tasha slopes off to the other side of the room for a smoke and to file her daily report with the producers in L.A. Meanwhile, Kevin heads out onto the patio to take some still photos for his private collection, and Mike goes with him, leaving me alone with Jay.

"So how're you doing? How's the leg?"

Mere pleasantries. It's quite obvious how his leg is.

"I'm doing okay," he says.

The guy is such a bloody trouper. I couldn't be more impressed. The show is as good as it is mostly because of Jay's dedication and his attention to detail. And I admire his stamina enormously, the way he pushes on through the debilitating agony, sustained only by a steady diet of painkillers and the possibility that he'll be home very soon.

Problem is, painkillers will only get you so far; then you need something a little stronger. Such as a hospital.

"There are treatments I can have and I'm going to have them the moment I get back," he says. "I just need to rest."

"Of course you do. You must look after yourself. Luckily you have the whole of Christmas and New Year's to recuperate before we head off to Alaska in January."

Instead of agreeing with me, which is what I'm expecting, he goes quiet. "We'll see. Depends how I feel."

"I know."

"But to be honest . . ."

Oh no! Don't say it.

". . . I'm pretty sure I'm not going to be up to doing the Alaska shoot. And maybe not even the ones after that. I'll see how things go."

I mean . . . how can . . . what do . . . huh? You're *leaving* me?

I'm in shock. First Tasha, and now Jay!

"Sorry, Cash."

"No problem. Really."

Why don't you just take your butter knife and stab me through the heart with it?

With this hefty burden off his chest, he struggles to his feet, just as Kevin returns, camera in hand, looking anything but happy, apparently with his own announcement to make.

No, let me guess—you're quitting the show too.

"I've given this a lot of consideration," he says ominously, taking up a position at the end of the table from where he can address us all, ". . . and it's not something I do lightly, but . . ." He launches into a speech he must have been preparing in his head for days. It boils down to this: "I'm tired, man. And with the flights situation, and you know what's gone on these past few weeks . . . well, it's not the best situation, as you know. This job takes you away from home a lot. It's tough when you have kids. I need time to spend with my family. Take a vacation. Get to know them again. Which means . . ."

Bingo.

My eyes are pinballs, flicking from one face to the next—Jay, Kevin, Tasha—trying to feign calm, when I swear I'm due for an aneurysm any second.

". . . I won't be doing the Alaska shoot with you."

Oh my God. *Et tu,* Kev?

I don't know if anyone's keeping a tally at this point, but by my rough estimate I currently have no crew left, because where Kevin goes Mike goes too, we all know that, which makes the total—let me just double-check—yes, ZERO! The ship isn't even sinking, but the rats are leaving anyway. Actually, I mustn't call them rats, that's wrong of me, I take that back. I love these guys. I want whatever's best for them. Tasha's getting married, Jay's sick, and Kevin's right—of *course* he should spend time with his family.

We all should.

But I can guess the subtext. It's a protest vote, right? A tactical screw-you perhaps to the producers for all the inconvenience, the lousy flights, the excruciating layovers they've suffered these past few weeks.

"Sorry. Nothing personal," he tags on needlessly.

"I know."

Suddenly, I'm a goldfish in a tank. They're all staring at me, waiting for some kind of reaction. A bout of pathetic weeping perhaps? Luckily, by the good graces of Vishnu, creator of everything, I'm spared the inconvenience of a nervous breakdown when Mike reenters the room via a side door, beaming mischievously. He has an announcement too.

Yes, I know—you're leaving the show. Thanks. I'm way ahead of you, *buddy*.

But no. Well, yes, he *is* leaving the show, but that's not his announcement.

"If anyone's interested," he says, his smile shining a ray of light into a nightmare moment, "there will be a sampling of some prime Moroccan hash in room number six shortly . . ."

Ah, yes.

On the short list of the three things that Morocco is best known for, here's the third. I imagine he got the stuff in the souks this afternoon. If you can buy live scorpions, six-packs of iguanas, and as many dead, decaying owls as your home's decor will allow without going over the top, why not drugs?

In my case, I decline. The kava experience is still all too fresh in my mind. As relaxing and enlightening as it was, that's two hours I never wish to repeat.

Mike retires to his suite, taking everyone with him—to celebrate their freedom, I wonder?—leaving me hunched gloomily on the banquette alone, adjusting to the prospect of making future shows in unfamiliar places with entirely unfamiliar people around me: a new field producer, a new camera crew, and a new director. What a catastrophe.

Inevitably, when you spend as long as the five of us have together, you develop your own cosmology, with your own rules, your own shorthand and in-jokes and nicknames. Mine is Cashmatic 3000. Awarded because I guess I do so many jobs and I work so hard that I scarcely seem human to the others, more like a robot programmed never to rest. If that's the case, then "melancholy" must be my default setting, because it makes me very sad to think that these people will remember me this way, as aloof, overcommitted, mechanical. Another reason I could become utterly depressed if I allowed myself to. And yet I want to laugh out loud. I mean, how could anyone take this travesty seriously any more? We're talking a mass evacuation. I've spent my whole life as the outsider, playing it solo, refusing to be a team player. As a matter of policy, I don't join things or belong to things. I'm not a member of any clubs, don't subscribe to any causes or support any teams, generally refrain from all group activities, and, apart from a short period working for the government in Britain—which was a massive mistake; I think the government would be the first to admit that—I've never held down a steady job. Now, though, at long last, I finally break all of these traditions by joining a team, and the bloody thing falls apart.

"It'll be okay, you'll see." On her way to the door, Tasha gives me the biggest hug, head resting against my chest, smelling of Marlboro Lights. "I love you, Cashmatic. I'll miss you." With that, she drifts off to join the others, turning around at the last minute: "Oh, one other thing. I just spoke to the office."

"And? Any news?"

"Did Kevin tell you who'll be going to Alaska with you?"

"No he didn't . . ."

My God, that was fast! The walkout only just happened, but already they've replaced them. Such a cold, unsentimental business, this.

". . . who will it be? Do I know him?"

She's not smiling as she tells me. And when I hear the name, I could die.

"Noooooooooo!"

The next morning dawns colder than any so far. In fact, it's not even dawn when we arrive with our bags—and still no tickets—at the airline check-in desk.

"Morning, guys."

The terminal is empty except for a disheveled fat guy with the eyes of a recently bereaved corpse and a smug smile greasing his wet lips.

"Willy!"

As much as we hate this unctuous little worm, we've never been as overjoyed to see anyone in our lives. Especially when, at long last, he produces the tickets.

"Everything go okay with the hotel?" He smiles. "You got the shots you needed?"

"Sure, Willy, it's all good."

By this stage, I think we'd say anything, whatever it takes to get our travel documents back.

Taking us at our word, he says, "Well, guys, it's been a pleasure," finally handing over the tickets.

"Same here. Thanks for all your help."

Relieved, we shuffle from check-in to Passport Control.

Forty minutes later, as we begin taxiing out onto the runway, about to begin our long, difficult, around-the-houses trip home, I sink into my seat, consumed with relief.

This shoot, more than most, has taken a major toll on my spirits, to the point where I half-wish I could quit too. Though that's just the fatigue talking. Once I'm back in Los Angeles, relaxed, rejuvenated, hanging out with friends, enjoying Christmas and drinking in the New Year, that'll all change, I'm sure, and I'll look ahead to the Alaska trip and the whole crew situation with entirely new eyes. At least, that's what I'm hoping.

It's a hope that sustains me for several hours more, all the way to Gatwick Airport in England, and from there, on our most pointless layover ever, in a cab speeding across London to Heathrow, up to the check-in desk in Terminal 4, where a woman from British Airways flicks open my ticket to begin sorting through my papers, then stops abruptly, and with the professional coldness I've come to expect from my countrymen, born of centuries of bullying the rest of the world with impunity, hands them back, shaking her head. "Unfortunately, sir, you won't be flying today."

We're only two feet apart, but I'm thinking I must have misheard. Did she say I won't be flying?

"Correct. I can't let you board the plane."

And, picking up the phone beside her, she calls security.

15

Emma Thompson to the Rescue

"But—"

"Sir, there's nothing I can do."

"But—"

"Sorry. Now, please go back to your side of the desk."

"—But I'm on TV," I almost say, though of course that only works in America. And maybe not even there.

Without further argument, my bags are pulled off the conveyor and put back in my hands, along with my passport and ticket, though not my U.S. resident alien visa; but that's only because, imbecile that I am, I forgot to bring it with me! Left the damn thing in a drawer at home.

America's like an ATM. You can push the buttons on the machine as often as you care to, pound them with your fists, even jam a screwdriver into the slot, but unless you put your Visa card in, it doesn't work. Resident aliens in the United States are told, "Go overseas, by all means. Have a great time. Just make sure you carry your green card (which is actually white) with you, otherwise you're not coming back in again." That's final. There's no negotiation at all. And if the airline helps you out and lets you on board without it, they're slapped with a whopping fine.

"How . . . but . . . it's . . . I mean, what am I supposed to do now? I have nowhere to go."

The starched check-in woman, already on to the next customer, is becoming what's referred to in Britain as "annoyed." "Contact the American Embassy," she says, handing me a phone number. "Maybe they can issue temporary papers."

"And how long does that take?"

"A few days."

Oh. Okay. Not too bad, then. Although it is Christmas, so . . .

"You're right." She performs a quick recalculation in her head. "Two weeks."

Two weeks????

I'm starting to perspire. Barely holding it together. I don't have any physical money on me. Don't need to as a rule; the show pays for everything. I have credit cards, so I can get by. But London's pricey. Staying in a hotel for two weeks, what's that going to cost me at current exchange rates?

"Look, how about you let me get on the plane and I'll deal with this when I reach America? I'm legal. They have me on the computers over there."

But that doesn't wash because of the fines. And anyway, I'm too late. Security's arrived. A uniformed officer keeps maneuvering me away from the check-in desk until my fingernails are forced to let go. Giddy with shock, I retreat across the noisy terminal to dump my bags in a corner, out from under people's feet. And there are *thousands* of feet. The airport's busy as hell today, packed with travelers heading out for the holidays. Laughing, shouting. All with the right visas, too, I bet, damn them. Outside, a typical British winter rages, a driving rain lashing the windows. Not too dissimilar to a typical British summer, as a matter of fact. Each time the automatic doors slide open, a fresh batch of tourists is bustled by a force-ten gale onto the concourse, windswept and dripping. But at least they're dressed for it. Sweaters, raincoats, anoraks. Whereas all I have is my smart cocktail attire from Marrakech. Thin yellow shirt, slacks, not even a jacket. Oh, yeah, and *all my underwear is dirty*! Let's not forget that.

"Two weeks?"

This is Tasha. She's already on the plane. Luckily, she didn't turn off her phone.

"At least two. I'm completely stuck. What am I going to do?"

"Jeez, I don't know."

"What's happened?" asks a voice in the background. Jay, I think.

"Cashmatic forgot to bring his green card. He's stuck in the terminal."

And I swear I hear somebody giggle.

"Look, I have to go," is her parting comment. *"The plane's about to take off. Good luck."*

After a brief good-bye, the line goes dead. What the hell do I do now?

Suddenly I'm that six-year-old child abandoned in the department store all over again. Alone, lost, fearful, trampled by hundreds of strangers, and with nobody there to rescue him. Clueless where to turn, the Bewilderbeest slides down the wall and slumps on his case, the true extent of the trouble he's in only just beginning to hit home.

My next call is to the American Consulate, even though I already know it's a waste of time. Four P.M. on the Friday before Christmas, are you kidding me? The staff's probably been partying for three days already; if it's anything like the office I used to work in, there'll be sex in stationery cupboards by now and people photocopying one another's buttocks.

"You have reached the United States Consulate. Our offices are now closed . . ."

Told you.

There's one slim chance remaining. Mandy. My dear friend from my British radio days, the one who came to visit me at the Trump International during the New York upfronts. I can call her. She has a flat in London. She'll put me up.

"Hi. Sorry I'm not available to take your call . . ."

Oh, good grief!

". . . I'll be out of town over the weekend, returning Monday. But if you leave a message I'll get back to you as soon as I can. Thanks."

I'm tempted to hang up without a word. Instead, I stick a finger in one ear to muffle the din and mumble a few mournful grunts into her machine, ending with a glum, begrudging, "Merry Christmas anyway." Hey, spread a little cheer, why not?

And that's it. I'm right out of options.

Two bleak, empty weeks with no money, no clothes, no clean underwear, and no place I can stay without frittering away half my life's savings—that's what's ahead of me. I don't even have change to buy a train ticket into Central London.

Oh, and by the way, before you say it, I am totally aware of the deep irony of this situation, don't think I'm not, and how, if I had a TV camera trained on me right now and a crew standing close by, things would be very, very different.

If this were the show and not something as tedious and unwatchable as real life, then within minutes of being ejected from the British Airways desk, I'd be inundated by an army of helpers offering to give me food and take me on a whirlwind tour of the city on a big red bus, alighting at the Dorchester Hotel, where the duty manager would hail me with a "Hey, Cash, how *are* you?" before I'd even introduced myself. And straight away, for no discernible reason other than the fact that he doesn't want to look like a miser on television, he'd offer me his best suite for free, with full privileges. Oh, the time I'd have.

That's the world of reality television for you.

If nothing else, the dire situation I now find myself in has served a very important purpose, proving, in one single microcosmic real-world moment, how incredibly *stupid* the concept behind our show really is. My friends were right; the e-mailers were right; and, though it pains me to say it, *even* the bloody *New York Times* critic was right, bless her heart: when you don't have any money and you're not being filmed, then nothing is free, nobody comps you a goddamned thing, nobody feeds you or gives you a bed for the night, not even for five hours of one night, and total strangers are utter bastards. They won't lift a finger to help you. In short, you're totally screwed.

I'm still processing the absurdity of all this and questioning for about the fiftieth time why, why, *why* I allowed myself to get talked into doing a travel show in the first place, and how I'm going to manage on my own for the next two weeks, when my thoughts are interrupted by the muffled chirruping of my cell phone.

"Hello?"

"Cash?"

Never in my life have I been so grateful to hear from Oscar-winning writer and actress Emma Thompson. Or in this case someone whose voice is identical to Emma Thompson's. Same nasal diction, same upbeat theatrical twang.

"Hi! Where the devil are you?"

Mandy!!! Oh, thank God!

"Heathrow. Where are *you*?"

"Paris. Having Christmas lunch with the people from my housing association. I just called my machine to check messages and . . ."

But enough about her.

I pour out the whole story of my plight, laying it on thicker than a Victorian mattress, whatever it takes to induce her to cut short her long weekend in Paris and return home early. After all, what are friends for?

"Okay, okay, alright, I get it. Give me a couple of hours."

"You mean it? You'll come? I can stay?"

"Darling, of course you can stay."

If anybody ever asks, I love this woman to bits. Write that down and read it back to me. *I love this woman to bits.*

In fact, even as I'm scrambling to my feet, infused after experiencing my own little Christmas miracle with a fair dose of the Yuletide spirit, I'm so bursting with happiness that I resolve there and then to reward her for being such an incredibly loyal friend all these years. Yes, by way of a gift, I'm going to waive the hefty sum she owes me for the incidentals incurred in my hotel room at the Trump International, which she left without paying for.

Or some of it anyway.

Okay, half.

16

A Real Celebrity Calls

One of the most fascinating things about working in public radio—well, maybe "fascinating" is stretching it a bit, but one of the strangest certainly—is that, no matter how hard you try or how long you've been on air—years, or even, as in my case, decades—you nevertheless remain completely unknown to the population at large.

Don't ask me why this is, because our audience is in the millions, and the reach is coast to coast, so statistically, you'd think, there has to be someone somewhere who's heard of you. But no, that's not the case. For reasons nobody has yet been able to truly account for, the majority of public radio broadcasters tend to inhabit an alcove in the shadowy recess of some celebrity dungeon where the press refuse to take notice and the spotlight never shines. However, all that changed the instant the show began airing on TV. Within days, I noticed people staring at me in restaurants, actually to the point where I became convinced I had something on my face. Baristas at Starbucks, who'd never looked at me twice before, would scribble my name on the cup before I'd told them what it was. Weird shoppers in Whole Foods started taking uncommon interest in what brand of dried apricots I was buying. And now and then teenagers would circle me in the street, whispering into their cell phones, "I'm telling you, man, it's him—I swear. You know—*him,* that dude! He does that cool show where he flies around with no money. No, I don't know the name of it. Or him. But he's right here!"

And though none of this is in the same league, I admit, as hordes of paparazzi screeching down our street in SUVs every time one of our celebrity neighbors leaves his home to go to the supermarket, by public radio standards my popularity was stratospheric. Didn't matter where I went, someone would point at me or call out to me from an escalator, or walk up and shake hands, with a cry of "Oh my God, it's you! You're . . ." At this point they'd stop, hoping I'd fill in my name as if this were a DMV form, and when I didn't: "*. . . that guy!!!*"

That's right!

One day, I was walking along Westwood Boulevard on my way to the office when a young man eating breakfast in a diner came screaming out the door.

"Hey, Chris! HEY! HEEEEEEEEEEEEEEEEEEYYYY!!!! Chris, it's you! My wife and I, we're your biggest fans," he shouted, when he finally caught up with me three blocks later, because I run quite fast. "My wife—man, she never misses your show." He pulled out a disposable camera. "Would you mind?"

"Not at all."

I grabbed the camera, took a photo of him, handed it back, and walked on.

"No. Of us! Together. I'm telling you right now, Chris, she will not frickin' believe this."

These encounters are difficult enough as it is. But this one was made worse by the fact that I wasn't looking my best. Nine months of nonstop stress, long, tedious flights,[1] missed mealtimes, getting up in the middle of the night to take cars to the airport, and a schedule that would sap the strength of not one, but *five* gladiators, had left me emaciated, with protruding cheekbones and gray bags under my eyes the size of a Gucci purse. I was also, as it happened, newly discharged from hospital.

During our Newfoundland shoot, somebody gave me a battered cod's tongue to eat. It's a delicacy there (and *only* there, I should think), and very much what it sounds like: a fish's tongue with a jellied splodge of muscle like a giant booger at one end, where it was ripped from the poor creature's mouth, then deep-fried.

"Wanna try some?" a local fisherman had asked me, ordering a plate of them.

No thank you. Cod's tongues are deep-fried. I don't eat oil. It's on The List.

But hey, it's TV. And TV's about teamwork, apparently.

"Wow," I said, sinking my teeth into one, "these are fabulous."

Not *so* fabulous that I'd ever eat them again, mind you, but certainly as good as any piece of cod with a large deep-fried booger at one end could be.

---

1 I read somewhere that there's so much radiation on a commercial jet that every flight you take is equal to having one X-ray. Doing a quick tally, that meant I'd had around 153 X-rays in one year! Put in 1950s sci-fi terms, that's enough to turn a small blond-haired child into a knife-wielding monster that terrorizes a village.

Unfortunately, the fallout from this was calamitous. Not only did the batter bring me out in hives, forcing me to wear thick concealer for days afterwards, but it kick-started a series of events that almost killed me.

A panicked Tasha rushed into my room that night at the hotel to find me curled up on my bed in agony, belching—BLEEEEEECH!—clutching my stomach, and sobbing.

"It's your gall bladder," a doctor told me later. "It's gone into spasm. We may have to operate."

"But I'm shooting a TV show."

"I don't care. Once you have one gall bladder spasm, that's it—it's only a matter of time before you have another. I think you should let us operate."

"No," I spluttered, hysterical, "you *can't* operate. I'm a Christian Scientist."

Not strictly true, but Newfoundland's part of Canada, and I wasn't sure if Canadian doctors were up to speed on recent medical advances—anesthetic, for example. Unwilling to take the gamble, I instead accepted his kind gift of a large container of Demerol and checked myself out of the hospital next morning to continue making the show.

"Avoid oil and fat at all costs," the doctor said to me, last thing.

"But I already do."

"Well, obviously not!"

Bottom line: my gall bladder was now a ticking time bomb. One that could go off without warning at any moment, day or night. And there were still many more shows left to shoot.

Not that the guy in the street that day seemed to notice how bad I looked. Draping his arm around my shoulder, instantly incriminating me in a bank heist should he now commit one—"Here we are, me and Chris, just before the raid"—he got his picture and left.

I reached the office ten minutes later, first time I'd dropped in since my impromptu layover in London,[2] to find the entire production team teetering on the precipice of manic excitement.

"Did you hear, did you *hear*?" The usual junior hobbit rushed over.

"Huh?"

"You're—going—to—be—on TV!"

"But . . . I'm already *on* TV."

"Yes, but this is real TV. A major network. NBC. It's sooooo awesome," she gurgled, mouth open so wide I could see her tongue stud. "Conan O'Brien wants you on!"

Wow.

The timing couldn't have been more perfect. Lukewarm reviews in the *New York Times* and other places meant that the show's ratings were not as tip-top as they might have been (scheduled up against popular programs on other networks, we were placed roughly 45,000th in our time slot, I believe; lower even than *Celebrity Tools,* which broke my heart).

"But hey, that's okay," The Thumb assured me during one of our many off-the-record phone conversations. We both knew that a failure at this stage would have been catastrophic. He and I had conceived this baby together, and nobody wants to believe they've given birth to the ugliest kid on

---

[2] The ordeal lasted a mere six days instead of the projected two weeks. In the end, rather than wait for the Consulate staff to sober up and get their asses in gear, I had my partner FedEx my green card to me and was home in time for New Year's. My stay in London wasn't without its share of fun revelations, however. I discovered, for example, that every Christmas Day, Mandy invites all her friends over for mince pies and hot tea, after which they exchange gifts and crowd around the TV and watch *A Muppet Christmas Carol* in its entirety. It's a lovely way to waste a national holiday.

the block. "Anything new and innovative takes time to gain traction. That's just a fact. Give it a few weeks before you rush to judgment."

Still, what better way to fan the flames of public curiosity about our wonderful new series, and to raise my profile, than with an appearance on a major talk show?

Or, failing that, on Conan O'Brien's show?

Shortly after, a triumphant Fat Kid summoned me to his office to deliver the news personally.

"DID YOU HEAR? CONAN O'BRIEN'S PEOPLE HAVE BEEN ON. THEY WANT YOU TO FLY TO NEW YORK NEXT MONTH TO BE A GUEST." Behind the desk, he finished tapping out an e-mail, put a call on hold, took a swig from his water bottle, bit into an apple, checked an instant message on his PDA, then sprang to his feet, eyes on fire. "ISN'T THAT GREAT?"

"Yes, I know," I said quietly. "Someone already told me."

"Oh." And his fire fizzled right out.

I guess he was expecting backflips. Everyone in TV performs backflips. Hysteria is in their genes. But by this point I barely had the strength to unzip my own fly, much less jump about with excitement the way, say, someone who was well-fed, well-rested, unstressed, and not borderline suicidal with anxiety might.

"I may even come to New York with you!" he threw in, lowering the ante.

"You will?"

Once again, my resistance to leaping up and down had him nonplussed.

In fact, for one reason or another, Fat Kid was pretty nonplussed most of the time we worked together, I'd say. Nonplussed or pissed. I could never tell which.

One time he came bowling along the corridor toward me like I was the last pin in the lane. He'd just seen the final edit of our Moscow episode and loved it. LOVED IT! "Right there," he said, his little Hawaiian face beaming, eyes bulging wider than is medically advisable. "That's your Emmy, right there."

I'm sorry—what?

I felt the frozen fingers of delusion skitter up my back. What did he just say?

A man with no awards cabinet in his office—"You're telling me not a single episode of *Celebrity Tools* was nominated for a Golden Globe? Not even the one about Bill O'Reilly?"—but who, by the look on his face, was already mentally flicking through the IKEA catalogue in readiness, had dared utter the "E" word, the third most hallowed word in all of television, after Regis and Philbin.

Sadly, he was way off the mark. As entertaining and beautifully crafted as the Moscow show was, it was still only a "reality" show about a guy bumbling through Red Square making like he was lost, when both the critics and the audience had long since figured out that he wasn't really. We may as well face facts. No way would a "perfectly pleasant show" like that get as much as a nod, much less walk off with an actual award. Not, that is, unless a freak event happened, such as everyone else who was making reality programs in the same year accidentally dying. Short of that, we didn't stand a chance.

Of course, you don't want to crush a guy's dream or rob him of all hope. That would be cruel. But it doesn't pay to lie to him either.

So: "It's not going to win an Emmy," I put it to him soberly. "I'm sorry, it's just not." And watched guiltily as he slunk away, crushed and robbed of all hope.

That was a major turning point in our relationship, I think.

By this one simple, honest admission—that our show at

its very best probably wasn't good enough, not even in the eyes of its own host, to carry off a major award—I'd skewered Fat Kid's lingering fantasy, a fantasy every TV producer lives for, of standing up on that stage come Emmy night, tears in his eyes, and: *(a)* remarking on what a genius I was for thinking I could pull off a virtual carbon copy of *Survivor* and nobody would notice; and *(b)* offering his condolences to the families and loved ones of all those reality TV producers who'd died so tragically in the previous few months, but who by their sacrifice had made this very special moment possible.

Somehow things were never the same after that. A line had been crossed, his umbilical cord to almost-certain glory cut, causing him to seethe with disappointment.

"By the way," he threw out, the next time I passed his office, "has anybody told you who'll be going to Alaska with you?"

"Yes. Tasha did," I replied.

A bolt of frustration flickered across his face. "Oh, okay."

And, scowling, he went back to typing e-mails.

17

Aaaaaagh—Bears!

"WE'RE—ALMOST—READY!!"

The silhouetted figure in the North Face jacket yells at me through a megaphone of gloved hands, the words barely audible over the screeching of jet engines.

"WAIT TWO MINUTES. THEN WALK IN THROUGH THIS DOOR—THIS DOOR HERE!"—indicating to his left—"ALRIGHT?"

I'd reply, only my lips stopped working twenty minutes ago. Instead I signal back with a stiff wave. Two minutes. Walk. Through door. Got it.

With a thumbs-up, he trots away, but gingerly, across the frozen runway, past the "Welcome to Barrow" sign, and disappears indoors.

Behind me, airline workers unload boxes of tortilla chips from the belly of a 737, seemingly impervious to the minus-45-degree cold.

The wind, tearing at my clothes, creates towering eddies

of daggered ice particles that swirl and whip like minitornadoes around my head, then suddenly turn on me, slamming into my face with the force of an eighteen-wheeler.

On second thought, two minutes be damned!

I set off toward the hangar, using tiny steps on account of the fluid in my knees having seized up. By the time I reach the door, I'm a snowman.

"So," I mumble to the clerk on the Alaska Airlines desk, who's called Aroun. "What's going on in Barrow?"

"It's the top of the world," he explains. "The northernmost inhabited place in North America."

"Is there anything to do here?"

"Yes. It's a good adventure place. You can come up here, see the Northern Lights, polar bears. What do you *want* to do?"

I survey the full breadth of my options, then come to a decision. "Leave."

Barrow is 330 miles north of the Arctic Circle, cut off from the rest of Alaska by mountains called the Brooks Range, and so remote, so far from anywhere you've heard of, that it's almost impossible to reach by conventional means. I mean, you can try if you like. You could travel here: (*a*) on a barge, although that depends on the ocean melting, which it doesn't very often; or (*b*) on a dogsled, in which case we won't wait up for you; or (*c*) you could do what most rational people do: fly. That's how humorist Will Rogers got here in 1935. Sadly, he didn't quite get *all the way* here. His plane crashed into a lagoon seven miles outside of town, killing him and his pilot, Wiley Post. And I guess not much has happened since, because even today, eighty years later, this single acci-chievement seems to be what Barrow is most famous for.

Thankfully, Alaska Airlines has a much better track record vis-à-vis crashing into lagoons and has become the main carrier between Anchorage and Barrow. You've seen their planes—they're the ones with Bob Marley on the back. It's even rumored that they're sponsoring this episode of the show. I can't say for certain. Although I do seem to spend an inordinate length of time staring at their corporate logo on the wall, far more than I would in real life, while the crew films it and me from various angles.

By sheer luck, wink wink, Aroun happens to be coming to the end of his shift and says he'd be happy to drive me into town. From this I take it that he's a PR guy from the airline. I don't even bring up such things any more. It's a waste of my time and curiosity. But I do accept his kind offer.

As I step outside the Wiley Post–Will Rogers Memorial Airport[1] once again, a brutal, unfriendly cold lacerates my flesh, freezing the breath in my throat and leaving my hair and goatee crusty to the touch.

Barrow in midwinter clearly doesn't believe in making a good first impression, and risks being mistaken for a very dismal place indeed. On dark, desolate corners, signposts flap in the wind, their street names dusted with frost and barely legible. Plumes of steam pump from vents into the sky. Icicles dangle from a festoon of overhead cables like glass fangs. Cars lie buried in snow up to their windows—and when it's not cars it's abandoned snowmobiles—outside sturdy clapboard homes that lurk evilly by the roadside, lost in a postapocalyptic gloom that doesn't lift; it's merely

---

1 If somebody famous had crash-landed in a lagoon outside my town, I'd keep quiet about it. But not here. To be honest, naming an airport after two guys who died in a plane crash hardly inspires confidence, does it?

relieved here and there by fuzzy light from streetlamps folded deep into the mist.

"Close the door, Cash!"

I don't need to be told twice. Beneath an overcast sky the color of canned ham, Aroun throws his white Alaskan Airlines pickup into gear, ramps the heater up to full blast and eases forward, letting the tires roll into the icy troughs gouged out by previous vehicles before accelerating. There's no traffic to speak of today, nobody on the sidewalks. Now and then a Sno-Cat grinds by, spitting plumes of mush in its wake. Otherwise nothing. No people, no sounds. When our vehicle's engine stalls, it peters away into an all-enveloping silence. It might be dawn out here, but there's no dawn chorus. Because there are no birds. I mean, how would they survive? They wouldn't. They'd freeze to death on the twig. If there were twigs.

"So what's Barrow like after the snow clears?"

"Muddy," Aroun admits, slowing down from 13 mph to 9 mph to let a snowplow go ahead of us. He and the driver exchange waves.

"No trees?"

"No trees. Just mud. And moss. And water. It's not very attractive. There's nothing here. Everything we need, we have to bring in from the outside."

"But say we do a *Thelma and Louise,* and we just go, we keep driving. Would we ever get out of here?"

"No. It's like a circle," he says. "You can't get out of Barrow."

And on that cheery note, we accelerate to 14 mph and drive on.

A mile farther on, Aroun swings off the road and brings the truck to a stop.

"Come and see."

Night has lifted a fraction, giving way to a cheerless smudgy twilight so depressing it would make even Pollyanna suicidal. This is as bright as it will get all day.

"We're on the Arctic Ocean," Aroun shouts, a large blob of green padding stumbling ahead of me across the tundra, "and the Chukchi Sea."

In 1778 Captain Cook came through here on his ship HMS *Disoriented,* looking for places to rename, and also searching for the legendary Northwest Passage, a possible trade route that other explorers and merchants had spent centuries hunting down without success. In fact, soon after, rather than break with this tradition, Cook gave up, turned around, and went home, stopping a mere thirty miles before he would have found it.[2]

Slithering across sheet ice, I flounder like a blind man. A block-solid wall of white consumes my vision up, down, above, below, and sideways, *every* way, offering no horizon and therefore no depth of vision, no discernible distinction between water and cloud, earth and sky.

"Where does it begin, the ocean?"

Aroun etches a line in the snow with the heel of his boot, on what would normally be the beach, I guess—"The waves come up to here in the summertime."—evidenced by a tide of petrified breakers standing to attention, frozen in place before they could reach shore, and crisscrossed by a mosaic of hairline cracks.

It's a ghostly, incredible sight. Like walking into a piece of contemporary art in which the painter thought his feelings could best be expressed by leaving the canvas blank and

---

2 For further details, see my new book *Captain Clueless—Who Gave This Idiot a Ship?* Available soon.

going for lunch instead. If at one time I was the least bit concerned about global warming and the ice caps melting, after visiting Alaska I'm not so sure any more.

Venturing out farther. "Am I on the ocean right now, d'you think?"

"Yes, you are. There's water underneath us, so don't tread on the cracks."

"Why? Is it unlucky?"

"Unlucky for you if you do, yes."

Apparently, if you step on a crack, it may split open and swallow you, sucking you into the icy waters below.

"In the summer," he adds, "where you're standing right now, you'd be up to your shoulders in water—"

"I would?"

"—and maybe over your head."

Well, that's all I need to know. Since that psychic planted in my mind years ago that I'd someday die by drowning, I've not been able to shake off my profound fear of water, which these days sits very comfortably alongside all my other profound fears: heights, enclosed spaces, dogs, genitalia, spiders, and the rest. But that's not the only reason I decide to turn back. Apparently, there are roaming polar bears out here, too.

TV commercials and kids' picture books perpetuate the myth that a polar bear would make the perfect house pet: it's just a couch with a head after all, soft like chenille and super-cuddly to the touch. Now I discover from Aroun that this is nothing but clever PR. In truth they're ruthless, aggressive predatory carnivores, vicious as hell, who don't believe in snuggling. Try it, and they'll pounce on you, rip your arms and legs off, and use your lower intestines as a parasol. They do it to their own cubs sometimes, so why would they spare the likes of you?

Bears are a real menace in Barrow, particularly when

they wander into town and roam the streets scavenging for food. Their top preference is for ring seals. Those are favorites. The bears will lie in wait by holes out on the ice, then, when the seals pop out, they grab them by the head, crush and kill them. When seals are scarce, though, they'll eat just about anything—baby walruses, moose, pets, trash, you. They're not fussy.

I ask one of the local cops: given the choice of ways to die prematurely out here, which is better—falling through the ice or being attacked by a polar bear? He doesn't give it much thought. "I'd probably want to get eaten by the polar bear," he says.

"You would? Why?"

"It would be over quicker."

Gulp.

Continuing our ride into town, I'm startled by what a cadaver of a place this is, laid out on the slab of Alaska's North Slope, the *rigor mortis* of seemingly endless winter robbing it of all character, submerging anything that might be attractive about Barrow beneath sheets of snow and ice several feet thick.

"It's okay," Aroun assures me from behind the wheel, "it'll be light soon."

And by "soon" he means May. Just four months to go.

Up here, the sun sets in November (in their language, Inupiat, that's *nippivik tatqiq,* which translates as Moon of the Setting Sun) and doesn't rise again until the end of January (*siqinyasaq tatqiq,* or Moon of the Returning Sun), meaning it's night the whole time; then in May (*suvluravik tatqiq*, or Moon of the Flowing Rivers), after a few months of murky twilight, the sun eases back into view once more, bobbing a full 360 degrees around the horizon 'til August (*aqavirvik tatqiq,* or Moon When the Birds Molt), making it daylight the whole time. It's an awkward, extreme arrangement, forcing the locals to take drastic retaliatory measures to avoid a screwed-up body clock, from nailing thick black blankets (possibly made from the feathers of molting birds) over their windows during the long daytime months to help them fall asleep, to sometimes not bothering to sleep properly at all during the nighttime months. Instead, they'll nap for a while, then get up and do something else until they're tired again. It's a world unto itself. Time becomes irrelevant. If you like, you can play tennis at 3 A.M. or break for lunch at midnight. Nobody cares.

"You know what?" I say to Aroun, because a fabulous idea has just flashed into my mind and I can't keep it to myself. "I've thought of a slogan for your town."

"You have? What is it?"

"Barrow, Alaska—we put the 'ice' in isolated."

Isn't that great? They should have leaflets made.

Aroun doesn't appear to be as impressed with the idea as I am, though he smiles graciously anyway, bless him. Meanwhile I, at his side, am helpless—"My God, it's a winner! It's a *winner*!"—unraveling in giggles.

Seated behind me in the truck, Fat Kid,[3] Eric, and Chuck are helpless too, suppressing roars of laughter by stuffing fingers in their mouths to prevent them registering on the microphone.

"Sorry," Fat Kid says afterwards, which of course regis-

[3] Yes, he's here! My old nemesis. The mystery addition to our crew, the one Tasha taunted me with in Morocco. Our show runner, Chuck, has come along too. Chuck's a brilliant director and for this one episode is standing in for the recuperating Jay. Then there's Camera Mark and his sound guy, Todd. It's like a school reunion.

ters on the microphone. Then he bursts into laughter again, and so does that.

I must say, removed from his normal office environment he's an entirely different animal: lively, relaxed, pleasant, slightly juvenile, but heaps of fun with it. Gone is the loud, laddish masculinity of the superhero-with-something-to-prove persona he puts on in L.A., replaced here by a mellower clarkkentish side I've not seen before, making him altogether more approachable, both charming and disarming. Indeed, if I were a cynical man, which I'm not, but if I were, which I stress again I am not, but if I *were,*[4] then I might even wonder what could possibly have prompted such a sudden about-turn, and what he's really up to.

Hm.

At one point, he confides that there's a bottle of booze in the truck. We're going to use it to toast our success at the end of shooting what might be a grueling episode. Sounds great. At least to begin with. But really it's not the brightest of ideas.

As if a contemptible climate and months of perpetual darkness, all the way through from *nippivik tatqiq* to *siqinyasaq tatqiq,* don't make life tough enough already, the sale of booze is outlawed. Barrow is not "dry" exactly, more "damp." If you want alcohol, you have to import it yourself, and even then you'll probably need a permit.

There's a good reason for this. Not surprisingly, it dates back to one of the oddest eras ever, Historical Times.

In 1826, two explorers, Tom Elson and Bill Smythe, sailed across the Atlantic from Britain, thinking they'd drop in on

---

4 Which I'm not.

Alaska, see what was going down; maybe even map out a bit of the coastline if there was time.

When they arrived, they discovered a primitive settlement populated by the ancestors of today's Inupiat Eskimos, nomadic hunters from Siberia who'd lived here for four thousand years or more. Back then, the town was called Utquiagvik, an old Eskimo word meaning "out-of-the-way frozen hellhole." But since convention demanded that every place name be immediately changed by European explorers to something they liked better, and face it, nobody could pronounce Utquiagvik anyway, the settlement was quickly rechristened—though not in honor of the men who discovered it, as much as they may have wanted that ("How about Cape Elsmythe? Or even Smyleport? I LOVE Smyleport."), but after some aristocrat back home who'd funded their expedition: Sir John Barrow.

Within a few years, the people of Smyleport, as it was known right up until the "Welcome to Barrow" signs arrived from the supplier, were overrun with European merchants. They sailed in, bombed and harpooned whales, killed caribou for food and for the hides, and blithely shot wolves, polar bears, and arctic foxes for fur, then sailed away again to become very rich on the proceeds. Though it has to be said, this arrangement wasn't all one-sided. In the name of fairness, the Europeans did give the Eskimos many things in return, including a wacky new invention that had the exploring world abuzz at the time, called the gun; plus ammunition, ivory, and several lethal strains of influenza. The Inupiat were also introduced to alcohol. And that's when their problems really started.

Life in these remote outposts back then was dull and depressing. Even more than it is now, as hard as that is to imagine. There was so little to do half the time that people would resort to booze as an anesthetic to numb themselves against the reality of how wretchedly empty their wilderness existence was.

And I guess it's not changed much.

"If you don't do something here, the boredom, the seclusion will get to you," our gopher on this show, a sweet little Inupiat native called Morgan, confirms.

"How many days of night d'you get here?"

"Sixty days without sun."

"So you'd just go insane."

"You could. The endless dark, the endless cold, it tears a person apart mentally and physically. So you have to do something to override that."

And I guess the Eskimos chose alcohol. Trouble is, this led in some cases to domestic violence. Certain Inupiat men, when they got drunk, would go nuts and start beating their wives, forcing the government to step in and designate alcohol consumption a public safety issue, limiting its availability. The locals could import a certain quota of liquor from the outside if they wanted to, the authorities said, but the actual sale of alcohol in town would be banned.

Indeed, the rather stiff middle-aged couple running our hotel has even gone one step further than that. They hand us forms to sign when we check in, making us promise—on threat of expulsion—that nobody on the crew will drink alcohol on the premises and none of us is bringing any kind of alcoholic beverage into our room.

Faced with no choice—well, where else are we going to go?—we all sign it, including Fat Kid. Then, while the owner's wife is turning around to get our keys, he pulls open his bag. "Look," he hisses, nudging my arm.

Nestling at the bottom is a bottle of red wine.

"We can drink it in my room later."

And a devilish gleam crosses his eye, vanishing the instant the woman turns around again.

Needing someone to tell my inspired new Barrow slogan to, I come up with a great plan, and set off through the snow to the offices of KBRW, the town's best, and only, radio station. It has a ten-thousand-watt transmitter and a staggering reach across eighty-eight thousand square miles. So every square mile gets about nine watts each.

I barge into the studio during a live broadcast, which I assume is what everyone does, because it meets with no resistance at all, and throw myself down next to the startled host, Fran Tate, a tiny woman with blonde bangs, big glasses, and mustard stretch pants.

Fran's a bigwig in town. Came to Barrow from Anchorage in 1970. An electrical engineer by trade, she used to earn her living designing airstrips. Now, in what is a bit of a career leap, she hosts her own afternoon program, *Jazz Below Zero,* on KBRW—"Your source for news and entertainment across the North Slope." She also has a successful business selling septic tanks and owns Pepe's North of the Border, the best, and perhaps only, Mexican restaurant in town ("Please don't ask for a margarita"). Better still, she once got to appear on *The Tonight Show* and, by way of a gift, handed Johnny Carson the bone from a walrus's penis. Naturally, that made her quite the celebrity around here, and I'm a little in awe.

"I've got the *greatest* slogan for your town," I tell her off-air.

"What?"

"D'you want to hear it?"

She doesn't really, I can tell. She owns a septic tank business and once gave a penis to Johnny Carson; I'm nothing to her. But what the hell?

"Barrow, Alaska—we put the 'ice' in isolated." And I

laugh as much this time as I did the first. "Isn't that the best?"

"Yeah, that's really good." Fran chuckles.

"In fact," I say, "quit your show, let's go and have leaflets made. Come on."

But she can't. The current jazz track she's playing, a series of random notes apparently played in no particular order, is coming to an end.

If you ask me, jazz is a menace. It's as dangerous as alcohol and just as likely to drive a man to domestic violence. Basically, jazz is what's left of a song after you take the tune out. So why KBRW would devote an entire show to it I have no idea. It's just asking for trouble.

"You're listening to *Jazz Below Zero,* brought to you Saturdays at noon by a grant from Pepe's North of the Border."

Oh, really? Hm.

At the control desk, two frail white hands mess about with the faders, pushing one, dragging another, until another jangling jazz travesty begins. Then, Fran returns her attention to me.

"Basically, I've got no money," I tell her, laying out the format of our program, "and no place to stay. So what if I went on air during your lovely show—because nobody's interested in jazz—and asked if someone could put me up for the night?"

"Oh, that might work," she says.

Once the current CD track—a collection of odd musical phrases belted out by fourteen instruments at once for the benefit of people with a tin ear—herniates to a close, Fran adjusts the faders again and pulls the mic to her lips.

"We have an important announcement. We'd like people to help. This gentleman, Cash Peter"—almost right—"needs to find a place to stay for the night, or 'til whenever he can afford a ticket out of town. So could someone call in and offer him a home or an apartment or at least a cot to sleep on?"

"What I need," I interrupt, grabbing a microphone, because I know how people are; they need an incentive, "is someone to come forward, some Barrow person, and let me stay in their home. If you do, I'll tell you my new slogan for Barrow, which is great, isn't it, Fran?"

"Oh, it's wonderful," she coos, opening her mouth to say something else.

"No, don't tell them what it is!"

"Oh."

"If you come forward and let me stay in your home, I will give you this slogan."

"Yeah," Fran chips in, thrilled, *"and you can make pamphlets!"*

After this, and while yet another jazz tune is foisted upon the poor listeners—seriously, shouldn't this kind of abuse require a permit?—we sit back and wait for the switchboard in the other room to light up.

And we wait, and we wait.

But nothing happens.

Either their antenna's seized up on account of the ice and Fran's broadcasting to herself, or the zero in *Jazz Below Zero* refers to her audience figures, because out of a reach of eighty-eight thousand square miles my plea receives no response whatsoever. In fact, eventually she leaps in with an unprompted desperate plea of her own. "Come on, let's help this gentleman. We're known for our friendliness and togetherness and helping each other out during bad times. So please call in and offer him a room or a bed, someplace to sleep. Call in!"

But they don't.

Minutes go by, and still nothing.

"Come on, folks!" Her voice is shrill now: "This gentleman's going to sleep in the studio. We need to get him out of here."

When that flounders too, she finally gives up. "I'm sorry, Peter . . ."

But wait, Fran! What's that?

A solitary light is flashing on the board.

The proprietor of Pepe's North of the Border couldn't be more relieved. KBRW's antenna hasn't frozen up like everyone thought! Somebody out there from their key demographic, the human race, is listening. A man. Calling from the high school. If I'd care to meet him there in half an hour, he says, he'll find me somewhere to stay.

"Great!"

Sweet victory!

Thanking Fran for her participation, and doing her a big favor on the way out by suggesting to the station manager that her format be changed to Country, because everyone loves Country, I brave the gnawing cold once more, shuffling along empty, icebound streets to the intersection of Okpik and Takpuk (that's your actual Eskimo right there), thrusting my flashlight between houses and behind cars as I go, in case of polar bears, and into the snug bosom of Barrow's best, and only, high school.

In recent years, the school has become the focal point of the community. There's a body shop and a metal shop. People swim here, meet up here, train and lift weights here, practice Native wood carving here, and maybe, it being a school, even study here, who knows? Though not necessarily. In many parts of the American education system, you'd swear that the word "education" slipped in entirely by accident, since the students seem to emerge at the end as ignorant as when they went in.

Barrow High is also "The Home of the Whalers," according to a sign outside, though what the Whalers might be in this context I have no idea. And, oddly, no desire to find out.

In the lobby, I find a man waiting for me. Small, extremely cheerful, and clearly of Inupiat descent, bundled up in a thick woolen coat and hat. Spotting me, he steps up to shake my hand. "Welcome to Barrow," he says. "I'm Morgan."

"Yes, I know," I'm tempted to reply.

Because I'd recognize our gopher anywhere.

Of Barrow's population of 4,500, 65 percent are Native Inupiat Eskimo and descendants of the original settlers, a heritage they take very seriously indeed.

As Morgan leads me on a tour of the school, a group of colorful local musicians decked out in full traditional Inupiat gear just happens at that moment (wink wink) to be rehearsing in the gymnasium, hammering out a thunderous primal beat on large, flat tambourine-like drums to an accompaniment of plaintive howling cries.

"Yaaaaaaay-eeeeaaaa-aaaaay. HUH! Awww-eeee-aaaaaa-eeeee-awwwwww."

Meanwhile, a young man bedecked in feathers and jingle bells cavorts around like a wounded pelican, performing what they call the Welcome Dance, a vivacious display of shuddering spirals intermixed with spinning and kicking and the stomping of feet.

"Awww. HUH! Eeee-aaaaaaa-eeeee. HUH! Awwwww!"

As far as I can see, this is all it takes to make the perfect evening around here. Sing 'til you're hoarse, dance 'til you're pooped, then go home happy. I find it all quite captivating, and, if I'm honest, I'm left a wee bit jealous. Me, I could never settle for something this uncomplicated. My own needs are so much greater. I need external stimulation at all times. I need facilities, crowds, things going on. In short, I need Hollywood.

It's probably the wrong time to be thinking this, given that I'm supposed to be focused on making a TV show, but watching the Inupiat locals happily engaged in . . . well, whatever this is, finding boundless pleasure and joy in traditional family and social activities, it suddenly hits me—out of nowhere, bam! Just like that—how dreadfully homesick I am. And how wildly divorced I've become from the norms of everyday living, too. *And,* perhaps worst of all, how detached I'm starting to feel from all those people I meet on a daily basis who *don't* have their own travel shows. Which is basically everybody.

By the time this is over, this series, this gaping hole I've dug for myself, I'll have lived in the television cocoon for over twelve months. That's twelve months I can never get back. Twelve months of giant bugs, sunburn, thirteen-hour flights, punishing schedules, food I shouldn't eat, and cultures that, as strange and captivating as they might be, I could happily have lived without seeing. Of relentless, round-the-clock, all-consuming immersion in a single pursuit—making television; stuck on the road, or in planes, or in hotels, or in edit bays, or voiceover studios recording narration; forcing myself by means of chocolate-covered coffee beans to stay up 'til all hours of the night writing scripts to a deadline; having my bags searched at countless security checkpoints (especially my little red-and-blue backpack, which every trained sniffer dog from Tokyo to Guadalajara is convinced contains explosives); checking in to unfamiliar hotels that don't seem to want me there; arriving home in Los Angeles after my partner's gone to sleep, then getting up again before he's awake to find a limo already sitting outside in the darkened street, engine murmuring, the driver propped up against the hood, yawning between puffs on his first cigarette of the morning, waiting to take me to the airport all over again for yet another baggage search—"Please step aside, sir, there appear to be explosives in your bag!"—followed by another trip to an alien destination that's bound to be unbearably hot and uncomfortable or unforgivably cold and uncomfortable, it doesn't matter which. And all for the sake of a cable TV show that hardly anybody's going to see anyway. I'm sorry, but that's how I feel.

I realize I ought to be more grateful. Logic tells me I should be basking in the magic of such a glorious, rare opportunity. In fact, The Thumb said the same thing to me recently, suggesting that I'm whining a little too much these days and that other people who got to travel around the world at somebody else's expense, were paid substantial amounts of money for doing so, enjoyed the cosseted life of a TV celebrity with all its attendant glories, and were given free gift vouchers to a local spa for their birthday might be slightly more appreciative.

Oh yeah? Well, good for them. I don't care. Right now, I'm tired, I'm cold, my feet hurt, and I want to go home.

"HUH! Yaaaay-eeeeaaaa-aaaaay," the elders bray in unison as the man in the feathers continues to fling himself this way and that. "HUH! Awwwww-eeee-aaaaaaaaa-eeeee-awwwwww."

Would it be presumptuous of me to suggest that these are in fact the Wailers, and they just spelled their name wrong on the sign?

"HUH! HUH!! Yaaaaaaay-eeeeeaaaaa-aaaaay. Awwwww-eeee-aaaaaaaaa-eeeee-awwwwww. HUH!"

Heading back to the lobby, with Fat Kid and the crew in tow, Morgan introduces me to an imposing thickset man with long black hair almost down to his waist.

"This is my cousin," he says. "His name is Bunna."

"I run trips to Point Barrow every day to look for polar bears," Bunna says, his large round face curiously expressionless.

Really? How odd. "And why would you do that?"

This earns me a strange look. Seems not many people around here quibble over whether polar bears are interesting or not. They simply are and that's that.

According to Science, polar bears used to be raccoons. Don't ask me how, it's all very complicated and happened millions of years ago, before documentaries, but at some point in time the raccoons evolved into brown bears, and some of the brown bears then turned white. Or something. Honestly, I have no idea; that's what libraries are for.

Now, however, having lasted this long, the polar bears' very survival is teetering on the brink. There are, at current estimates, around sixteen thousand of them roaming the world, which still seems like more than we really need, but the number is getting smaller all the time, due in part to poachers illegally shooting them to sell their fur on the black market, but *mainly* because the polar ice cap is vanishing, slowly destroying the balance of the bears' maritime habitat. Less pack ice means less territory for hunting. Some bears even exhaust themselves while they're swimming around looking for seals to crush and eat, and simply drown. Result: Science predicts that polar bears will have completely disappeared from Alaska by the year 2050. Of course, from a conservation standpoint, that would be a catastrophe. Whereas for the rest of us it merely means there's less chance that something big, white, and hairy will come running out of the wild someday and eat our kids.

Anyway, Point Barrow is a clever decoy. Every year, the townsfolk haul a bunch of whale meat and bones out to this remote, snowy promontory and leave them there to keep the bears fed and preoccupied and away from their homes.

"I'm going out tomorrow to make a trail," Bunna says. "D'you want to come along?"

Goodness, no! Not a chance. I don't like Nature, I tell him, or anything to do with wild animals. Now, let's never mention it again.

Honestly, have we learned nothing in our short time together? Nature is not our friend. Fact. Surely, therefore, we would all be better served by leaving it well alone and minding our own business. That's my philosophy at least.

But apparently such an argument holds no water out here. Besides, viewers will be very disappointed if we come to the Arctic Circle and don't film at least one bear, Fat Kid reminds me. This excursion has been designed ahead of time to be the highlight of the episode. If I refuse, the show will have no climax.

So, against my better judgment, I change my mind and agree to go.

The windshield wipers flap lazily, flicking a confetti of frost into the morning air as the van plows deeper into the flat, featureless wilderness, following the line of a pure white highway barely distinguishable from the land around it or the sky above.

On the approach to Point Barrow, we start filming.

"Do the people here live in mortal terror of polar bears?" I ask Bunna.

"Not mortal terror." His face is expressionless as usual. "We're just aware of them."

"We're cautious," Morgan adds from the back seat. "People don't understand, these guys are filled with nothing but teeth and claws. They're not cuddly, they're not friendly, they're wild. Nature is unpredictable. Some days you can walk right by the bears. Other times you have to run away from them."

"Oh—look!" Bunna cries out, but quietly because bears startle easily. "I see one!"

Easing off the gas, he allows the van to putter to a stop, clearing condensation off the window with his sleeve. Now, finally, his eyes come alive. There's a current of electricity flowing through his body that wasn't there ten minutes ago. Tracking these bears is way more than a job to him, that much is obvious. He has an affinity for them, is fascinated by every aspect of them—their look, their gait, their habits and behavior—and treasures every second he can spend alone here at the Point, more so than ever right now, now that they're on the fast track to extinction.

"Oh, wow, that's a big one!"

"Where?" A quarter of a mile to our left is the Bone Pile, the bits of excess whale meat and bones that the Eskimos dump here to draw the bears away from the town.

"D'you see it?"

Squinting into the blinding white emptiness, I'm able to pick out an object the color of dog pee.

The longer we look, the more objects appear. Soon there are three. A female and two cubs. They saunter up to the bones and begin chomping, the female gazing around the whole time, looking very nervous.

"Why would they think they're in danger? They're in the middle of nowhere."

"A mother with cubs always thinks there's danger," Bunna drops his voice to a cautious whisper. "If she comes across a male, he'll first try to kill the cubs, then he'll impregnate her with his genes. It's survival of the fittest."

I understand. It's not very different from working in television, really.

"I've always maintained," I say, "that Nature is just things eating other things."

"Yeah." And he adds with a barely perceptible wry smile, "Hopefully it won't be us today."

Hopefully?

There are two facts about polar bears I didn't know. Actually, plenty of facts, but two really big ones that differentiate them from other animals, in particular raccoons.

First, as well as being one of the most vicious predators on the planet, polar bears happen to be particularly fast on their feet. If they spot you and see you as a threat, they'll quite probably charge after you. And when they move they can reach speeds of up to twenty-five miles per hour. Forty-five if they're on a moped!

Second, don't think you can escape by hiding in your truck. Their claws are can openers; they'll charge the vehicle, tear you a new sunroof, and pick you off one by one inside. You don't stand a chance.

These two facts together have me very nervous indeed. But that's okay, we're due to leave anyway. I've seen a polar bear now. Job done. No point hanging around.

"Okay, come on." Bunna makes a move. Only, instead of firing up the engine, he reaches behind his seat and produces a shotgun. "Get out of the van," he says, confusing me with MacGyver. "But *carefully*."

What???

Fat Kid leads the way, followed by Eric and the others. Mark, displaying not a scintilla of reservation or fear, tiptoes across the ice and sets up his tripod within clear view of the bears, which, more frighteningly, gives the bears a clear view of him.

The mother turns and sniffs the air. Oh no!

"Get on your knees," Bunna whispers in my ear.

A rush of adrenaline floods my system. I'm being maneuvered into the open, pushed to the front like bait, with the mother bear looking directly at me.

"Is this okay?" My voice has shot up an octave.

"Slowly, slowly, slowly."

"But Bunna, I'm totally exposed."

His rifle's raised just in case. "Slowly. Get down. Good."

I'm now closer to wild animals than I've ever been before. Close enough for them, with their extra-sensitive ears, to hear me crap my pants. Frankly, this is one phobia I never really wanted to conquer. But because it's on television and people are judging me, I'm driven to brave it out.

And you know what? I'm really glad I do.

Crouching as low as I can go beside the van, I get my first uninterrupted look at the bears, three distant blobs of urine-yellow fur mooching around the Bone Pile, gnawing on the whale carcass. Now that Bunna has his gun out, their urge to attack us seems to have worn off and we're able to relax and appreciate this moment of privilege for what it is: one of mankind's rare opportunities to observe polar bears in their natural habitat before mankind destroys that natural habitat altogether and every living creature in it. From now 'til then, every day's a battle, a slow, silent slaughter. Either they'll kill us or we'll kill them. And I think I know which one it'll be.

In the meantime, something as simple as watching a bunch of predators gnawing at bones on a windswept icy plain suddenly becomes a spectacle to savor, making every scrap of hardship we've experienced on this trip so far seem most worthwhile.

"Isn't this great?"

"It's amazing." Bunna sighs.

And I swear there are tears in his eyes.

Dinner is at the home of a guy called Massak, a cute, kindly munchkin of a man in a fur parka, who I think, if I were to probe a little deeper, I'd probably discover is Bunna's father and we're paying him.

The meal he serves up consists mostly of frozen whale meat. Eskimos are subsistence hunters, hunting, fishing, and trapping wildlife year-round. They're very much dependent on locally caught moose, caribou, duck, and seals to survive. But also bowhead whales.

"Why are you allowed to hunt whales? I thought there was a ban."

"Without them we wouldn't have food," Massak explains. "There's no work here in Barrow, so it's how we survive the winter. We can't go to the store and get what we want, because meat here is so expensive."

They hunt for whales twice a year, in April (*agaviksiuvik tatqiq,* or Moon When We Begin Whaling) and October (*nuliavik tatqiq,* Moon When the Caribou Rut). It's a cooperative effort. The whole community joins in, after which everyone takes home their quota of the spoils to live on throughout the winter. Nobody goes without, nobody starves. Such a contrast to Los Angeles, where, generally speaking, the guy with the most money would swoop in, grab every scrap of whale going, lavishly feed his own family and friends with it, and, without a second thought or losing a wink of sleep, leave everyone else in town to die.

Massak has arranged the chunks of meat on a tray of cardboard torn from a box.

"I think I'll have that." I select a small brown lump at random, thinking it might not look quite so unappetizing once it's been defrosted, then sautéed in a little lemon marinade with tarragon and some shallots, and maybe a splash or two of wine. If necessary, I can pitch in with the seasoning. "Yes, and perhaps a couple of those too." Pointing at two more brown chunks.

Only to find that there's no cooking involved at all. The whale meat is simply handed over as is, straight from its cardboard tray, for me to suck on frozen. I wouldn't even call it meat, really; it's more of a chewy, crystalline fatty substance—the Inupiat call it *muktuk*—hacked from just beneath the skin of the whale and either dipped in seal oil, for flavor, or pickled, which is probably the only time it stops tasting like very gritty tuna.

Seeing me struggle, his wife gives me directions. "It's better if you put all of it in your mouth," she says from the other end of the kitchen.

"Including this bit?" A flapping piece of skin that looks like a price tag is still sticking out from between my teeth.

"Yes. The flavor comes from both—the skin and the blubber together."

I'm sure she's right. Still, I feel terrible, because I hate to offend my wonderful hosts after they've extended to us such gracious hospitality. Even so, I'm sorry, guys. My body won't take the fat. Blubber wasn't on The List of Things I Mustn't Eat, but that was simply an administrative oversight. And dunking it in seal oil makes things worse on two counts: (*a*) it's oil (obviously); and (*b*) it lends the *muktuk* a rancid, paraffinny flavor that I wouldn't be able to get down my throat if I sat at this table from now until *nippivik tatqiq*. I mean, no offense.

During dinner, Massak introduces me to a marine biologist friend of his called Jeff. On the spur of the moment, he offers me a ride on his dogsled to see the aurora borealis.

"Oooh, yes please, I'd love to."

The northern lights are like movies to Alaskans. A cosmic Mardi Gras that regularly ignites the heavens over Barrow, filling them with flaring incandescent bullwhips of red and green. It's one of the few wonders of Nature that isn't waiting to ambush, wound, or kill us, so of course I'd like to go.

Just one caveat: they're only visible on clear nights. And tonight—wouldn't you know it?—there's a blanket of cloud cover. Regrettably, by the time we find this out, I've ridden across half the North Slope on Jeff's dogsled in minus-42-degree cold, from which I emerge a popsicle: wet, coated in ice particles, my nostrils plugged solid with snot, the blood vessels in my blue-tinged face as stiff as stair rods.

"Oh G-god, I'm-f-f-reez-z-z-in-g-g-g," I shiver as I stumble off the sled in search of some source of heat.

"Here! Wait." I hear a voice behind me.

Turning, I'm surprised to see Fat Kid rushing over. The guy's as chilled as I am, yet in a display of kindness entirely at odds with his usual tyrannical ways, he whips off his gloves, cups my frozen nose with his hands, then rubs my knuckles and fingers vigorously to work some feeling back into them.

"Oh, th-that's s-s-s-o g-g-good. Th-th-thank y-you."

"You're very welcome." He smiles through a drifting ectoplasm of breath.

I'm beginning to think I misjudged the man. Many of my former perceptions are slowly dissolving away. Torn from the pressures of office life, he's much more affable. Last night over dinner, we were even able to sit down together and calmly tackle the hot-button issue of flights and multiple carriers that caused Mike to lose his sound gear before Dubai and pissed the crew off repeatedly throughout the season. Well, not any more. Fat Kid was adamant. "That's over," he told me with an easy grin. "It will never happen again. I promise. You have my word on it."

What a refreshing about-turn. I almost like him now.

Still rubbing, he leans in close, whispering seductively out of the corner of his mouth, "Don't forget, we have red wine at the hotel."

Oooh! It'd completely slipped my mind.

At the risk of being expelled from our rooms, we're going to celebrate the success of the spectacular Alaskan shoot, and the fact that I tackled my fear of wild animals, by going nuts with half a plastic cup of alcohol each.

"Ohhhhh. Th-that s-s-ounds w-wonderful." A hint of sensation is creeping into my fingers. Finally, I'll be able to unbutton my own fly to pee. "In fact," I throw in by way of a light joke, because we're friends now and you can mess around with friends, "if you l-let me h-have s-s-some w-w-wine, I p-p-promise to do another s-s-season of the show with you."

Hahahahahahahahahahahaha.

Just kidding. Face it, I don't even know if the network wants another season, or, for that matter, if Sir would be physically, mentally, or psychologically up to the workload involved and the grind of traveling. Right now I'm thinking not.

"Deal," Fat Kid leaps in quickly, letting go of my hands. In that instant, a new mood takes over. His regular old mood, in fact. The eyes glint now with a dagger-blade intensity, the true self suddenly shining through once more, like sunlight after a storm. "Let's get together at 8:30 tonight." He grins. "And celebrate."

No—wait.

Oh my God, what have I done?

The game's been won. A game I didn't even know we were playing. Nobody told me. I took my eye off the ball for a second, and already it's over. Damn.

Television is about power. Power, politics, manipulation,

scoring points. I should be aware of that by now. To Fat Kid, who's a seasoned pro at this, the promise of a new series of non-award-winning shows means more money for his bosses and their production company, work for the staff, continued employment for the crews and for him. That's an important goal worth pulling out all the stops for. In the treacherous, volatile world of TV, every deal is crucial. You can't afford to give an inch.

Beneath the mound of clothes he's wearing over his super suit—the hat, the scarf, the fur hood—Fat Kid's olive cheeks are lanterns.

"Thanks, Cash," he says.

"Hey—no problem," I reply. And I smile warmly.

Sonofabitch.[5]

---

5 Don't worry. All wasn't lost. That evening at the hotel, I went into full damage limitation mode. The way I saw it, our verbal deal was only valid *if* I turned up and drank his wine—right? Exactly! So instead of celebrating with the rest of them, I stayed in my room the whole night. But then, damn it, around 9 P.M., the worst happened: a production assistant showed up at my door with a glass of merlot, courtesy of Fat Kid. Realizing that if I even sipped it, then, in my subconscious at least, I would have fulfilled my side of the bargain, I rushed to the bathroom, tipped the whole thing down the toilet, and flushed it away. Hah! Touché. *Your* move, buddy.

18

The Bomb Goes Off

I think today's Sunday. It's so easy to lose track. At any rate, it's the very last day of shooting the first, and with any luck, if the gods are with me and willing to let me off the hook, last season of the show. Last location. Eighteenth and very last episode. And I find myself uncharacteristically idle, left alone in a distant city in Northern Italy, with not much else to do but sit here telling you this.

The crew has gone back to Los Angeles. They left this morning after breakfast, with the usual cries of "Missing you already. See you soon!"

I'm less lucky. For reasons of flight availability, I leave tomorrow, armed with an itinerary that could only have been devised by opening up a map and letting a small blindfolded child scribble on it for ten minutes with a crayon. So much for "It'll never happen again."

"Bye, Cashmatic!!!"

"Have a safe trip."

"You're sure you'll be okay?"

"I'll be fine. Don't worry."

"Bye!"

The crew van, having been parked half on the curb blocking traffic, which is how they do things in Italy, swerves into the narrow ravine of a street, nearly hitting a pedestrian, which is also how they do things in Italy, and disappears from view, leaving in its wake . . . nothing.

Stillness. A vacuum.

We shot the ending of the show in a great hurry after breakfast in a sunny piazza close by our hotel. Took six takes to get it right. It's not a natural act, talking to a camera lens; even after eighteen shows, I'm still not used to, or good at, it. But finally:

"Cut—aaaaaaaaaaand it's a season one wrap!"

Veni video'd vici.

When Director Mark[1] barked these words, Eric threw up both arms into a victory salute, ready to receive the applause of a nonexistent crowd.

While the camera was being dismantled from its tripod, my microphone was removed from inside my shirt. A watershed moment of sorts, demoting me to civilian status once again. As of this minute, I'm a free man. Nothing to do, no scripts to write, no meetings to take, no plans to make, just an entire day to myself in which to embrace and admire one of Italy's most precious jewels: Turin.

Now all that remains is to figure out what I'm going to do with it.

---

[1] Yes, Mark was with us again. Once you find yourself on this particular merry-go-round, it's hard to get off.

I didn't realize this, but at one time Torino—the Italians have a sexier way of saying everything, don't they?—used to be the capital of Italy. Then the government had second thoughts and moved to Florence, and, when it tired of that, Rome. Finding itself stripped at a stroke of all political clout and at a loose end, Torino decided to reinvent itself, becoming a major industrial hub instead, famed especially as the home of Fiat cars and Pirelli tires. Also, some of the world's greatest wines are produced in the fertile soils of the Piedmont region around it. And perhaps most important, during the eighteenth century, it was in this city that hard chocolate was invented. "Hard" in the sense that it could be carried in your pocket. Before then, it was only available as hot drinking chocolate, which meant it was continually seeping through your pants.

However, what Torino is most high-profile for, bizarrely, is the very least of its achievements: the Turin Shroud, a strip of linen that Jesus was supposedly wrapped in after his crucifixion (circa Ancient Historical Times). They know this because it bears his image. Although, before you get carried away with excitement, be warned; according to Science, the image is not of Jesus at all, just some guy who looks like him (very possibly Hulk Hogan—the resemblance is uncanny). The herringbone fabric of the Shroud, scientists insist, was woven much later (circa Historical Times), and is therefore a complete sham.

Sadly, nobody's had the heart to tell the people of Turin yet.

Hm. Now, *there's* something I could do today.

Consulting the front desk of my hotel, I find to my delight that the Shroud is nearby, preserved in conditions of heightened security to prevent you trying it on, inside the royal chapel at the *duomo*, the Cathedral of Saint John the Baptist, which the receptionist assures me is within walking distance, but only if you enjoy walking for a very, very long time, which, it just so happens, I do.[2]

Accordingly, I set off, following my nose through a circuit-board of eighteenth-century streets, most of them little more than deep stone shafts that shrink the sky to a strip of blue floss above my head.

Torino looks like Paris. A *lot* like Paris, actually. In fact, if Paris ever gets destroyed, it's comforting to know we have a backup. Both cities share the same love of baroque grandeur and pretension and a similar clutter of side streets opening onto magical squares and arcades. Yet Torino manages to outparis Paris in certain key ways. Anyone can do tree-lined boulevards, cute patio restaurants, and cake shops, their windows piled high with extravagant tarts and fruit pies in storybook colors. That's architecture-by-numbers. It's the larger-scale spectacles—the blissfully photogenic mansions, bridges, and ornate bell towers, often dating back to the birth of the city in the 1500s—that elevate Torino from your average two-bit civic pageant into an all-singing, all-dancing parade.

Before getting down to tackle the serious subject of the Shroud, I decide to fortify myself with a spot of lunch, and, a couple of blocks farther on, come across a lovely sunny restaurant that is very clean and inviting. Nearly every table is taken, a sure sign that the food is good. Or that they didn't buy enough tables. Better still, the menu has convenient little photographs of each dish that you can point at to save time. This spares visiting American yokels the sheer inconvenience of learning such complicated exotic words as *lasagna* and *tiramisu*.

---

[2] I do!! But at my own pace, that's all. And preferably not through sweltering untamed jungle, across ice floes, or around the rims of erupting volcanoes.

Jabbing at the entrées, I decide to celebrate my liberation from the restrictive rigors of making a TV series by going completely nuts for once and choosing *pappardelle* doused in a robust Bolognese sauce, which arrives thirty minutes later, steaming fresh, heaped in a bowl the size of a cartwheel, and looking just like the one in the photo.

Afterwards, stuffed to bursting but highly satisfied, I set off once again.

Torino's city center was fashioned under the supervision of the House of Savoy family dynasty, who were part Italian, but also part French, which must explain the Parisian flourishes. Somehow the architects condensed it all down and packed it tight, with streets so deep and claustrophobic in places that sunlight has given up hope of ever penetrating the four- and five-story baroque facades, except maybe at a freak angle or reflected off high windows, leaving entire blocks untouched by warmth and with an almost haunted feel to them, enough to give you chills as you hurry along their shadowy rat runs en route to somewhere brighter and more welcoming.

Turning in to a spacious, cobbled yard, I hurry past an impressive church that, in any other city, you'd be tempted to explore and find out the name of. Not here. Here, among so many, you just go, "Pah, whatever!" and, pushing by a cluster of nuns—"Excuse me. Coming through."—move on to the next fascinating thing.

For a *duomo* dating back to the fifteenth century that may possibly house one of the most significant religious artifacts of our time, the Cattedrale di San Giovanni Battista's dull, gray-walled exterior is disappointing and reminds me in more ways than one of the Alamo. Indeed, if, someday in the future, interest in the Shroud should wane and the building had to be vacated, it would probably make an excellent storage warehouse. Or even a flagship Taco Bell. Given the overall drabness of what I'm looking at here, I doubt the conversion would arouse much protest.

As my eyes adjust to the interior, I pick out people wafting reverentially among the pews, generating the kind of noises you make when you're trying desperately to be quiet—muted coughing, whispers, the clack of fashionable high heels on marble floors, and occasionally, to someone's eternal shame, stifled laughter.

Hoax or not, there's something enthralling about the Shroud phenomenon. So what if Science happens to be right for once and it's not Christ's burial blanket as he was lifted down from the cross at Calvary, but rather a medieval forgery devised to dupe religious nuts? Who cares, frankly? To a total sucker like me, the mere remote possibility that the tobacco-yellow linen I'm about to look at, touch, and possibly throw over my shoulder and prance around in for photographs, could *conceivably* have come into contact with Jesus of Nazareth's body all those centuries ago, gives me goosebumps.

"I've come to see the Shroud," I hiss to a little bald man who works here.

"Okay, come," he hisses back, and leads me along a pillared walkway to a far corner, where, cocooned within the dark solemnity of a praying area, stands an aquarium-type structure, out of which they drained the water, I guess, and laid the casket. A casket, by the way, that's been dressed up like a Victorian Christmas hamper, wrapped in a red ribbon labeled *"Domine,"* and topped with a pleasing coil of twigs for decoration. Inside, it's temperature controlled, waterproof, lightproof, and bullet-proof.

"But where's the Shroud of Turin?" I ask, drawing close to the glass.

"This is the Shroud. There is a casket, in which there is another casket . . ."

"But I don't want to see caskets. I want to see the Shroud." I sound as if I was expecting it to be just hanging there on a peg.

Shaking his head: "Is not possible. The Shroud, she must remain in the dark, otherwise light can give less visibility to the image over time."

"But how do I know it's even in there?"

The man looks surprised. "Because I tell you that it is."

"Oh," I nod, "in that case it *must* be!"

With their customary flair for drama and overstatement, the Italians have hidden it inside *two* boxes filled with argon gas, and refuse to bring it out. "It is a very exceptional case in which the Shroud can be visible," he tells me, adding that the next one will be in the year 2025. And don't even waste your time storming up to one of the clerks and demanding a sneak preview sooner, because I tried that and they get quite snippy.

However, for anyone who's impatient, or if you have a plane to catch and can't wait, then just down the aisle from the aquarium stands a life-size rectangular photographic replica dating back to 1898.

At first glance—and I feel terrible saying this, because someone's bound to be offended—as is the case with the building it's in, the Shroud is a little unimpressive. Like a faded hearth rug. There are burn holes in it, and bits missing. In fact, if some jokester told you it was a length of dirty roller towel, the sort you see crumpled up on restroom floors when the dispenser breaks, you'd be inclined to believe him.

"Where does his head start?"

My little guide points out the features. "Head, chest, arms, legs . . ."

"Aah, yes."

What I'm looking at is the front and the back of the man they claim is Jesus Christ. And if it is him, then, believe me, he was quite a hunk, ladies! Muscular, bearded, about five foot nine, with long hair parted in the middle, exactly the way he appears in movies.

There are two photographs on display, one in normal black-and-white, and then a second with the colors reversed for contrast, like a negative. It's in the negative that the features truly come alive, dispelling once and for all to my mind the theory that it's Hulk Hogan asleep. Most persuasive are the bloodstains: some close by his wrist, another alongside his waist, then many more down his legs, with a speckle of pinprick wounds around the forehead from his crown of thorns. The instant I see this, I'm a convert, utterly convinced of the Shroud's authenticity. No further proof needed. I'm in.

If only everyone in the world were as gullible as I am.

Sadly, they're not. In 1988, Science, which hates mysteries, examined the Shroud and came to the conclusion that Christ's image had not been burned onto the cloth by his Divinity as much as it had probably been painted on with watercolors. And that includes the bloodstains too.

Well, these were fighting words. Straight away, critics of modern carbon dating techniques, who had a vested interest in keeping their Christian superstitions alive, claimed that the material was contaminated and the tests were wrong, wrong, wrong.

"The method with the carbon," the guide says, "has a lot of problems, connected with the fact that the object, the linen, can have on it microorganisms, and also carbon from the fire that destroyed part of the Shroud when it was at Chambéry."

Chambéry's in France, and was the former seat of the Savoy dynasty. In 1532 the chapel there fell victim to a terrible fire that scorched the linen sufficiently to throw off carbon-dating calculations by a thousand years or more.

Meanwhile, the Catholic Church, for its part, won't commit either way, stating that, if you want to believe that the Shroud was the burial cloth of Jesus, that's up to you, buddy. Which is exactly the stand I'd take, too, if I thought I might have a total dud on my hands but thousands of pilgrims kept descending on my *duomo* every year demanding to look at it.

I ask my little bald friend what percentage sure he is that the Shroud is the real deal. "Sixty percent sure? Seventy-five percent?"

Astonishingly, he says, "Ninety-nine. On it we can see all the characteristics of a very particular crucifixion. Exactly the same characteristics that were written in the Gospels about who Jesus was, and in particular . . ."

As he's talking, something extremely odd happens, diverting my attention.

I feel a sharp twinge. Underneath my rib cage on my right side. To begin with, I dismiss it as indigestion. The pappardelle repeating on me. But I've had indigestion before, and this—this seems fifty times worse. And in the wrong place. Also, indigestion subsides, doesn't it? Whereas what I'm talking about is a persistent grumbling ache that once in a while will ease off a little, enough to suggest it was just a spasm, getting me all riled up over nothing. Then, for no reason, it'll peak again with a searing twinge that has me digging a hand into my side for support.

"Ow! OW! Jesus!"

Too distracted for further Shroud talk, I'm forced to bid a hasty good-bye to my guide and rush down the steps of the cathedral.

"Blecccccccccccccccccccchhhhhhhhhhhhhhhhh!"

Oh no.

Along with the belching comes a dose of real pain. Kitchen-knife-between-the-ribs pain. A slicing, hacking, being-sawn-in-half sensation that won't let up.

"Bleccchhhhhhhhhh! Shit."

I throw up in a doorway. BLEEEECCCCCHHH. And again in an alleyway two streets down. Oh God. This is it, I realize. My time bomb, the one primed by a battered booger in Newfoundland, has begun its detonation sequence, and at the worst moment imaginable. I'm on my own in a foreign country with nobody to help me and no place to go until I get home tomorrow night.

Thanks to a handful of Motrin and some deep breathing, the persistent stabbing unlocks its grip for just long enough for me to stumble back to the hotel, where I rush to my room, vomit three more times, then, bent double, sink onto the bed in fetal position, and settle in for an extremely grim and sleepless fourteen hours of pain, shivering, and hugging my ribs.

"BLEEEEEEEEECCCCCCCCHHHHH!!"

Oh, yes, and belching. Lots of belching.

"Does it hurt if I press here?"

OW!

"How about here?"

OWWW!

"And here?"

OWWWWWWWWW! YESSSS!! EVERYWHERE! STOP THAT!

Having made it back to Los Angeles, with the help and sympathy of a couple of United Airlines flight attendants and lots more Motrin—thanks, drugs, I owe you one!—I'm rushed to Emergency. First time I've ever been inside an ER, and now I know why: it's so depressing. Everybody's ill.

"So?"

A chunky duty nurse walks in with a file. He has a fuzzy

ginger beard that looks like he fished a handful of cat hairs out from down the back of his sofa and glued them on.

"According to the scan," he says, though I can't see his lips move, "the doctor in Canada was right: it looks like you have gallstones. Your liver's congested too, so most likely one of the larger stones has become lodged in one of your tubes." He draws a diagram with a ballpoint. "See? Everything's backed up."

"Oh dear. And what's the solution?"

Blecccccccccchhhhhhhhh. Blecccccccccccchhhhhhhhhhhhhhhhh!

"We have to get you into an operating room this afternoon."

Whoa, hang on! Let's not rush into this.

"Okay, here's the deal."

And I launch into a nutshell explanation of why that's not possible; about the show I'm making; my anarchic schedule that would challenge the might of, not one, but five gladiators; the pressure I'm under to get all the loose ends tied up; and so on. As it is, I'm at the tail end of everything, I tell him. I have a single piece of voice-over narration left to record for the very last episode in the series, which is due to be broadcast in a week's time, and I must complete it. But *then* it's over. The narration is nothing. It'll take three hours, tops. I can do that first thing tomorrow morning and be back at the hospital by lunchtime, promise, at which point, "I'm yours. You can operate all you want. How does that sound?" In the circumstances, it's my best offer.

But Fuzzface is apparently in no mood for negotiation.

Wearily removing the glasses from his nose to the top of his head, he digs two sets of chubby knuckles deep into his eye sockets, lets loose a monster yawn that lasts ten seconds at least and ends with him making wet cham-cham-chamaaaaaaah noises with his lips. Then he slides the glasses back down again and fixes me with his now slightly red, puffy eyes.

"And here's *my* deal, Mr. Peters." He sighs. "I can't stop you walking out of here, okay? This is America. Go if you want to. All I can tell you is, you're in bad shape. *Real* bad shape. Right now, your system is shutting down—and I'm talking literally. Your liver's not working. Your body's backed up. I'd say you have about twelve hours."

"Twelve hours for what?"

Shocked that I'm not grasping the full gravity of what he's telling me, he tries again, making it simpler still. "If you don't let us operate within the next twelve hours . . ."

"Yes?"

". . . you're going to die."

Five hours later, I wake up in an uncomfortably hard bed with the smell of disinfectant in my nostrils, a sharp cramp in my gut, and a tube from an IV pole attached very painfully to a hole in my wrist.

I'm sharing a room with another patient. Youngish-sounding guy. I can't see his face owing to a plastic curtain drawn between us, but I eavesdropped on one of his phone calls earlier on my way to the bathroom and overheard him telling someone he'd come in for a routine biopsy after finding globs of blood in his urine. Yeuw.

Popular "dude," though. Very Hollywood. Sounds like one of those well-oiled business types you might encounter at the Hyatt Regency in Century City, the place I first met The Thumb, the kind who are always "on," always wheeling and dealing to stay afloat. Roses arrive for him by the truckload almost daily. Some are delivered, others brought personally by a steady chorus line of male friends, plus a few—usually male—associates from his office, who drop in with scripts for him to read or contracts to sign.

Throughout his stay, the man's BlackBerry rings almost nonstop with work-related matters, whereas mine rarely stirs, although I did receive a couple of supportive messages yesterday, including one from The Thumb, which was good of him.

Nothing from Fat Kid, I notice. No e-mails, no calls, no cards or flowers. Naturally, this leaves me troubled. The host of a major cable travel show nearly dies on your watch, and you don't even check in to see how he's doing? I mean, it's crazy. Then again . . .

There's a rule in television: it's never your fault, even when it is. Any display of interest or concern at this pivotal time might be interpreted as an admission of guilt, or that he contributed to the problem in some way, and nobody wants to place themselves in that position. Therefore silence is the best option for now, he's probably thinking. Stay quiet, keep his head down, and let the crisis pass. Which means, no get-well e-mails, no calls, no cards, no flowers.

Ho-hum.

It's very boring lying in hospital. The doctors won't discharge you immediately after a gall-bladder operation, in case something went wrong during surgery and your bowels have stopped working. Plus, in my case, they have to completely flush the *laplap,* oily sardines, cod's tongues, pappardelle, and God knows what else out of my liver and get it back up to speed. Result: I'm confined to bed with the IV tube jammed into my wrist for almost an entire week.

Friends and neighbors have been ordered not to come visit. My stomach hurts too much to talk. And the last thing I want right now is the Vice President of Overseas Sales

(Pacific Rim) sitting at my bedside with a broad told-you-so smirk on his face. Damn him.

But I'm not completely without company. My partner drops in twice to see how I'm doing, which helps break the monotony. And, once, I open my eyes to find a crowd of student doctors hunched in around my bed, smiling, as if I've just told the greatest joke *ever.* Subsequently, I find that half of them are fans of the show and wanted to come up to the ward to tell me that. One of them admits that he'd like to host a TV travel show of his own someday. ("You do? Well, great," I mumble, unimpressed. "You can have mine. I'm pretty much done with it. Television's not for me. I'm just not suited to it. Physically, emotionally, temperamentally.")

Otherwise, the days crawl by without incident.

Mind you, I'm not whining. At least I'll survive. Which is more than the guy in the bed next door has got going for him.

I heard the result of his biopsy this afternoon. The doctor stopped by after lunch and addressed him somberly, dropping his already-soft voice to a grave, guarded tone that had me craning my neck to hear.

"I'm afraid the news is not too good," I caught him saying. He went on to add that the cancer was far enough along to be inoperable, hinting too, without actually vocalizing it, that he may only have a few more months to live. Weeks even. It was hard to tell.

A barely suppressed gasp rang around the room.

That was me.

Cancer? I didn't even know the guy, but I was shocked.

An intense conversation followed, during which the doctor mapped out the road ahead, reeling off in a steady drone various facts about treatments, using the bleach of his authority to scrub away any last germ of hope the poor, confused man might have of survival. Once these ugly formalities were over and the doctor had left, I slid slowly back in between my sheets, watching Fox News with the sound down—it's the only way any of their arguments make sense, I find—and for the next hour, maybe more, listened to the man in the next bed sob uncontrollably into his pillow.

It was while all of that was going on that my BlackBerry went off.

Two e-mails arrived, one after the other. First, one of the show runners dropped me a line—aha!!—commenting, with tactical understatement, "Sorry to hear you're under the weather."

Under the weather??

Are you insane? I've just lost an organ. I almost *died,* pal.

But of course his hands are tied. It's never your fault, even when it is.

The second of the two e-mails arrived less than twenty minutes later, and was even more startling. This one from the head of the network, of all people. Lovely man. I met him a couple of times during the up-fronts and he was never anything less than polite and enthusiastic. Like The Thumb, he sent his best for a speedy recovery. How thoughtful.

It wasn't his good wishes, however, that really gripped my attention; it was a comment at the end, which I read once, then twice, then a third time in utter disbelief. The two-line message, doubtless intended to lift my spirits during a difficult time, instead struck me like a baseball bat to the face, plunging me deeper into depression.

"If it's any consolation," the e-mail said as I scrolled down, "I'm renewing the show for a second season. Congratulations."

Wha???

Aw, shit!!!

A Slow Descent

19

Twist of the Blade

I've been hot-air ballooning three times in my life. It's quite an experience, cruising fifteen hundred feet above the ground across open countryside, with no birdsong, traffic noise, voices, or anything else to disturb you, only your accelerating panic at being so high up, and the occasional deafening ZZZZZZZHHHHHHHHHHHHHTTTTTT from the propane tank as the pilot heats the air inside the envelope while flicking madly through a handbook looking for how to land the thing, because chances are he'll have to at some point. What goes up must come down, right? I believe it's one of the fifteen laws of aerodynamics.

Trouble is, you don't really "land" a balloon. It's tempting to think you do. That it's some kind of primitive elevator, with a button that you press—*G* for "Ground"—and, after a slight bump on impact, you casually step out of the basket, adjust your hair, and go about your day. But it's not like that, which is probably why it never caught on and people still prefer to take airplanes instead. In fact, each time I've been hot-air ballooning, the basket just dropped out of the sky, period, the way meteorites do, or derailed roller coasters, smacking into the ground with a terrible force, and then, as I and the other passengers were heaving a sigh of relief at still being alive, and just as we were adjusting our hair and getting ready to go about our day, the wind picked up suddenly and dragged us with a jolt for another ten minutes or so, through fields, ponds, and hedges, slithering, hopping, and tumbling, until it shuddered to a stop in a ditch and tossed us out like slops. I'm shocked nobody was killed.

Anyway, that's ballooning.

Now, why was I telling you this?

Oh, I know! Because it's exactly what making season two of the show felt like.

"Did you hear, did you hear what happened?" gasped the excitable hobbit on my first day back after my operation, her voice an unoiled hinge.

Unable to walk fast, or even fully breathe due to the hole between my ribs that was (according to Science) meant to be healing, I sank deep into one of the plush square armchairs in reception, wincing all the way down.

"For the new season, the network is moving the show forward by an hour, to Mondays at 8 P.M."

"No!"

A great pit opened up in my stomach. Just below the pit between my ribs.

To me, this was the worst possible news.

Time slots are crucial. They tell you everything about a show: 9 P.M. means "adult"; it hints at grown-up situations, intelligent humor; it's a warning to pack the kids off to bed and maybe put a paper bag over the head of any old folks and wheel them back into their "special cupboard," because something a little more challenging and racy may be on its way. Whereas 8 P.M.—that's what's called "family viewing." Ugh. My heart sinks every time I hear those words. Years ago, it used to be a good thing, but not any more, not since the word "family" was hijacked by the Christian Right and came to be synonymous with safe, mediocre, insipid, condescending, predictable, derivative programming from major networks feverishly pandering to the self-righteous sensibilities of the Dimwit Demographic. Nowadays, with few exceptions, 8 P.M. is the dumping ground for pap fare. Mass *blah* entertainment. Shows to shoot yourself by. A time when everyone watching TV pretty much knows they'll be treated as if they're five.

"Are you okay?" the hobbit asked, seeing my face turn even paler than it usually is.

"It's fine. I'm fine."

It wasn't, though. And I wasn't.

Predictably, when the new season of fourteen shows debuted, the time slot confused many viewers. Six weeks into the season, I was still getting e-mails from fans.

Hi,
Love your show, but I have not seen a new episode for a couple months. Do you have any insight?
—Tom.

Hey, are you taking a break? Haven't seen your show lately.
Later, Randy.

Of course, I did what I could. Wore my thumbs to stumps on my BlackBerry, updating them about our new time slot and how fabulous it was; so much better than our old time slot at 9 P.M. because . . . well . . . I have no idea what cockamamie excuse I gave; I just made something up, aware as I was writing that my efforts wouldn't make even a tiny dent in the number of mystified viewers who scanned the schedules every Monday and, not finding us where they expected us to be, gave up looking.

Shame, because, to my surprise, everyone went into season two feeling so much happier. Rifts had been patched up, apparently, and sources of crew annoyance addressed; Fat Kid even chose to speak more softly a lot of the time, which was a huge step forward. Additionally, having been forced over the previous few months into addressing the worst of my phobias—in particular speed, wild animals, heights, spiders, horses, and water[1]—I was feeling a lot more relaxed

---

[1] In particular, I broke the back of my fear of horses on one of the domestic trips. In Idaho's Salmon River Wilderness area I hooked up with a posse of cowboys (really just a bunch of students who happened to be staying in our hotel and liked the idea of being on TV) and was coaxed into the saddle. Turns out, there's really nothing to it. You sit on its back for as long as the horse allows you to, then get off before you're thrown off. Simple. A day later, I cracked my fear of water, too. Waving aside the doom-laden prophecy of that psychic I told you about, who predicted my death by drowning, I was persuaded by Mark onto a dinghy on the Salmon River with the words, "It's safe, I promise," then sent hurtling into one of the most dangerous rapids in the whole of North America. A ten-foot thrashing, pounding, churning monster renowned for capsizing boats, knocking the unwary unconscious on hidden rocks, and, the week after I was there, actually killing someone, I heard. In case of accident, a rescue boat was moored nearby and a helicopter primed to rush me to hospital, so clearly *someone* was worried for my safety. Yet, miraculously, while the two rafting experts alongside me emerged from the rapids drenched and gasping and thanking God for sparing their lives, I was almost *completely dry.* It was quite unusual. According to bystanders on the bank, the waters parted at the last second, the way they did for Moses, and not a single speck of water touched my body. Since then, I've not been scared of water at all. And am, coincidentally, far less likely to trust psychics.

about the adventures to come. But above all, the shows were simply better-produced, thanks in the main to Jay's superior story-telling skills, even if individual situations within those stories were so contrived that they could only have been devised by monkeys high on methamphetamine.

In each case, the resulting train of events was entirely believable, *but only if* you didn't stop for a second to think about what you were being told, or to ask awkward questions. Questions such as—off the top of my head—how is it possible for an ordinary man, on his first trip to Seattle, to be invited into Microsoft's headquarters, casually bypassing security measures that couldn't be breached by a crack team of Marines armed with F-16s and nerve gas, and run around playing freely with their new inventions? And maybe I'm naive, but what are the chances of a guy who's all washed up in Philadelphia taking shelter from a rainstorm in the doorway of a boathouse and, within half an hour, being recruited to row with the Vesper Boat Club's ladies' Olympic rowing team? Or, even more ludicrously, to be standing staring at the grandeur of Niagara Falls one minute, and the next find himself being best man at a complete stranger's wedding?

I mean, sure, any one of these things *could* happen. Possibly. At a stretch. Once in a lifetime. But in every episode?

In fact, while we're on the subject, what are the chances of someone wandering aimlessly in a hundred-degree heat through the bush in Amboseli, Eastern Kenya, for three days and not getting eaten by lions or hyenas? No, wait! That's one question I can answer. They're zero!

20

Aaaaaagh—Lions!

On the first day of our Kenya shoot I'm befriended by a group of Masai tribesmen.

Things like that are happening to me a lot these days.

I was picking my way across the scorched dusty plain outside their village, stepping over the thighbone of an impala that had been torn apart by wild predators then scattered over a wide area, followed by the bleached skull of a buffalo that fell and never got up, wondering how long it'd be before the same thing happened to me, when nineteen Masai warriors in full tribal gear walked out in a long line to say "hello." Or *jambo,* as it is in Swahili.

Two things strike me about them immediately. First, they have no trousers on. That always sets off alarm bells. Also, their lean, angular bodies are swathed in blankets dyed a threatening red, contrasting starkly with the lush greens and sandy yellows of the bushland around us. On their feet they wear homemade rubber sandals fabricated from motorcycle tires. Multicolored bracelets jangle at their wrists. Additionally, several of the men have their earlobes stretched into a hoop so large you could thread a hotel bath towel through it. Or hang lanterns.

As it turns out, their leader happens to speak excellent English—am I the luckiest guy in the world, or what?—and seems particularly well educated. Looks different from the others too. Healthier. Better fed. Suggesting that maybe he flew in specially to be on a TV show, though nobody's 'fessed up to that one yet, and after the disaster with "Mohammed" in Marrakech, I'm reluctant to jump to conclusions. Bald and cheerful, his name is Wilson.

"This," he says, leading me through the village, "is where we keep the animals at night for protection."

Known as a *manyatta,* it consists of a series of thorny acacia hedges and mud huts arranged in concentric circles like a large target, which as far as neighboring predators are concerned is exactly what it is. At the center stands a huddle of nervous livestock. Skinniest damned cows I've ever laid eyes on. And the goats are almost two-dimensional. Handy if you want to stack them in a cupboard, I suppose, but not if you're hungry. There's barely an ounce of meat on them anywhere.

Now it registers: protection. "To protect them from what?"

"Lions, cheetahs, and hyenas," Wilson replies.

"So if you didn't put your animals in here, they'd be eaten by lions?"

He nods solemnly. "Eaten by lions."

Okay. "And what's to stop the lions eating you?"

"We have warriors. The young generation. They walk around the village and protect the community."

You're telling me that the village's first line of defense against an attacking five-hundred-pound predator powerful enough to fell a buffalo and scatter an impala over a wide area is a gang of college-age boys?

A couple of these *morani,* as the Masai call them—or Breakfast and Lunch, as the lions and hyenas call them—acknowledge me with a polite *"jambo,"* then look away.

"How many people have the lions eaten?"

"Six people."

"The lions have eaten six people???"

"Yes."

"Recently?"

"Recently—sure."

OH MY GOD!!!!!

"So in the middle of the night, *every* night, the lions come and attack your village?"

Wilson smiles. "Right."

Jay's standing off to one side out of camera range, squinting at his clock. Looking up, he nods his answer to the silent question I'm asking in my head: "Yes, this is where you'll be spending the five hours we call night tonight."

In short, I'm as good as dead.

The Masai are pastoral gypsies. Sweeping down from the Sudan in North Africa hundreds of years ago into Kenya and Tanzania, they set about fearlessly rustling other people's cattle while looking for lush plains to graze their own. Mind you, that was in Historical Times, when you could get away with almost anything.

At one time Masailand was vast, covering eighty thousand square miles of territory, giving the tribes plenty of room to maneuver. But everything changed, and centuries of harmony were squashed to dust, once the usual roster of avaricious European colonialists arrived. Germans to begin with, followed in the 1890s by my British ancestors,[1] who took over large chunks of Kenya, enslaving the people, exploiting them, and revolutionizing their primitive society with rifles, railroads, and, most curiously of all . . . trousers, which, as an act of defiance, the Masai refused—and still refuse—to wear.

More critically, the British decided that the local wildlife population, the lions, leopards, hippos, hyenas, buffalo, etcetera, that were so profuse in this region, wouldn't be profuse for much longer if the tribespeople's cattle kept chewing up all the foliage. So, in 1899, as a way of protecting the wild animals, the authorities cordoned off an area 150 miles square on the Kenyan-Tanzanian border in the shadow of snowcapped Mount Kilimanjaro, declaring it a game reserve, an arrangement that stayed in place for over seven decades, until someone with a keen eye for detail pointed out that the phrase "protecting the wild animals" was being defined a little too broadly and seemed to include killing them in large numbers for sport, after which its title was quickly changed to Amboseli National Park and

---

[1] Oh, no! Not again. How many times am I going to have to apologize to foreigners for the imperialistic abuses of my forefathers? Whole nations may still despise the French, the Spanish, the Portuguese, and those rascally Dutch for the trouble they wrought in the past, but it was the British who, throughout Historical Times, were the real problem kids in the playground. Nobody else managed to upset the natural balances of a foreign culture, or cause quite the level of unnecessary disruption and mayhem founded on equal helpings of greed, selfishness, discrimination, and sheer supercilious, we-know-best bloody-mindedness, quite the way that the British did. And the Masai, like so many others, felt the full force of it.

all hunting banned. Good news for the wildlife; not so good for the Masai, who were banished entirely from the lush parkland, which was theirs in the first place, and confined to the dry bush plains beyond its perimeter, a move that caused outrage at the time. And believe me, they're still pretty cut up about it.

Today's a big day for Wilson. He's moving into a new house in the village. The structure reminds me of a freshly risen bun loaf: one story, short sides, large, bulbous, crusty roof, no windows. It's in a prime position, midway along a desirable avenue of similar mud huts, offering a broad, prestigious view over the livestock pen.

As we arrive to take a look, only the roof remains to be completed. No worries, Wilson assures me. We're leaving to visit a nearby water hole now; by the time we get back it'll be finished and he'll be able to move straight in.

"So you built this?" I ask, indicating the house.

My question generates the strangest of looks, part bemused, part aghast. "No," he says. "My wife built it."

"Have you ever built a house yourself?"

"No. This is the work of women."

Uh-oh. Something tells me we've been here before.

In fact, almost everything in this place is the work of women. The men put up the acacia fences, hone metal into sharp spears, and sit with penknives for hours, making sandals out of motorcycle tires; but all other jobs fall to their wives.

Lucy, Wilson's lovely better half, emerges from the low arched doorway, head bowed. She's petite, but with large, masculine upper arms from a lifetime working in construction. Her delicate looks are set off by the jewelry she uses to adorn herself: copious strings of beads, topping off a cotton dress that clings to her hips but freefalls elsewhere. In her hands she holds a dirty plastic keg, which she plans to carry to the water hole by strapping it to her head.

"Lucy is only one of my wifes," Wilson informs me with some pride. "We Masai, we are allowed polygamy, so we have more than one wife."

"And how many do you have?"

"Five."

Five wives? In some countries, that would be considered greedy.

Not here. In a Masai village like this one, a man's wealth is calculated by the number of cattle he owns, and a woman is considered to be worth three cows. So, let me see . . . that's five wives . . . divided by . . . three plus four . . . carry the one . . . that means Wilson is worth about *fifteen* head of cattle. My God, the man's a bullionaire!

"And what-number wife is Lucy?"

"She is number one." He smiles.

"Ah. So she gets all your favors?"

"Yes." And he smiles again, only broader this time.

Meanwhile, Lucy isn't smiling at all, I notice.

Water for the village comes from a local spring fed by melting snows from Mount Kilimanjaro, an imposing purple silhouette hogging the western horizon across the border in Tanzania, and permanently obscured by sheaths of foaming cloud. The spring is reached by making a quarter-mile trek across a broad treeless plain—you know, *the* plain, the one where the lions, cheetahs, and hyenas live?

Moments like this make me realize how very little I know about Nature. It's going to sound daft, but most of the information I've gleaned over the years about wild animals comes from cartoons I used to watch as a kid, and I'm learning a little too late that most of that information was pretty basic, if not full-blown inaccurate.

So in the same way that cuddling a polar bear can lead to traumatic head and neck injuries—who knew?—I now find that:

- Hyenas do not have a rollicking sense of humor that makes them endearing to other species. They're actually ruthless killers that enjoy disemboweling things. *You* would be a good example;

- Whales are only hollow up to a point; you certainly can't live in one or build a fire on its tongue while you wait to be rescued;

- Flamingos, turned upside down, cannot be used to play golf;

- Elephants, rather than being gentle, playful, and harmless (and in some cases aerodynamic), in reality *hate* and fear human beings and will trample you to death at the first opportunity, flying down from the tops of trees in great numbers to attack you if you stray too close;

- Individual ants are absolutely devoid of personality and humor;

- Coyotes don't have the wit to send off for packages in the mail nor to assemble machinery when it arrives;

- There is no stage during an emperor penguin's life cycle when it learns to sing and dance;

- A snake's eyes do not revolve hypnotically just before it kills something;

- A zebra is a whole new animal—it's not a poorly designed horse;

- Barnyard pigs and geese don't discuss the farmer behind his back; and

- Lions, while they may give off an air of intelligent, affable nobility in films, are not smart academically, nor are they trustworthy in any meaningful way; by and large they exist solely to sleep, breed more lions, and kill everything else on this list (with the possible exception of penguins).

As we stride boldly across the plain, Wilson assures me, hand on heart, that I'm in no danger from lions, not during the daytime, if we all stick together. But I'm not so sure.

A hundred or so feet out, it's all spookily quiet and still, and I'm already feeling a little exposed, even though we're quite a sizable group by now. Not only have Wilson's other wives, numbers two through four, come along for the jaunt, each with a plastic beer keg strapped to her head, but we also have the crew running around filming us, *plus* someone else: a shady background figure sporting a red beret and carrying a loaded rifle. Not a soldier, even though he dresses like one; more likely a game warden. The guy never speaks, never allows himself to be caught on-camera. Prefers instead to loiter a few yards away from the group, staring vacantly off in another direction, distant but always with us, his presence underscoring my point for the umpteenth time, that if this weren't a TV show and I was actually stranded out here in the wilds on my own, I'd be a goner.

"Oh, look!" Wilson cries, bending down to scoop something off the ground. Enthusiastically, he sticks a small brown pellet under my nose.

"What is it?"

"Donkey dung!"

Oh my God. "Get it away from me! Get it away!"

"This is from a donkey."

"Yes, great. Now, put it down!"

He tosses it away, not quite understanding what the problem is.

Turns out, this is his main area of expertise. There's nothing Wilson doesn't know about feces. And he has an infinite variety to choose from. In fact, what you don't realize when you see movies, and what documentaries never tell you about Kenya, I guess because it's not considered interesting, is that the whole place is ankle deep in shit. It's everywhere. The beautiful, sprawling savanna, the bushland, the lush wooded valleys, wherever you choose to set foot, it seems to be coated in a fine veneer of excrement from roaming animals. I don't think I'm exaggerating when I say that you can't walk five feet out here without stepping in something that squelches.

"Look at this big slab of poo here," I say, deciding to test his expert knowledge with a couple of dinner-plate-sized pats. "Which animal did that?"

"This is buffalo dung," Wilson declares with the lofty air of a man who's trodden in something similar on many memorable occasions. "It looks like cow dung but it's more solid." And he crouches to show me.

"No, don't pick it up!"

Three feet farther on, I come across a whole cluster of cue-ball-sized droppings covered in flies.

"What's this one?"

"This one?" The poofessor peers closely at it.

"And *don't* pick it up!"

"This is donkey dung."

Again? Strange, because I've seen not a single donkey since we arrived. Giraffes, yes, buffalo, yes, even an elephant or two that wandered close to the perimeter fence of our hotel yesterday, but no donkeys. Yet their feces are like wall-to-wall carpeting.

Bored already, I walk on in search of new thrills. "What else is there?"

"Zebra?"

Oooh.

"Where's zebra dung?" Rushing to his side, I'm disappointed to find a bunch of brown golfballs, same as before. "That looks like donkey dung again."

"Yes, but it's bigger."

"And what's this one?" At my feet is a zigzag of chalky-looking hemorrhoids.

"This is hyena dung."

"Why is it white?"

Wilson grabs a handful and crumbles it into the wind.

"It's white because the hyena eats a lot of ashes."

And a lot of people, he omits to say.

To my relief, the watering hole is finally in view. Sadly, in my haste to reach it, I plant my foot squarely in a heap of grassy turds the size of grapefruit.

YEEEEUUUWW!

Behind me, his five wives start giggling.

"This is elephant dung," Wilson explains with great exuberance.

"Really? Elepha— stop, *don't pick it up!!*"

Too late. "Elephant dung we use for making fire."

They do. Like the Tanna islanders, the Masai, being uncorrupted by corporate greed, are earth-friendly, recycling every natural resource they can for reuse in the village. Nothing goes to waste. Their carbon footprint is the size of a doll's.

The spring, when we reach it, is a pool of dark water behind some rocks, surrounded by a crescent of mud that's been churned up by the paws and hooves of a dozen other, not altogether friendly, species. It takes just a few minutes for the women to fill their plastic bottles to the brim. Instantly, each one becomes a dead weight that they must strap to their head and carry home.

"What happens," I ask squeamishly, because, like Jay, I slipped a disc once and can't look at these women staggering laden across the plain without remembering the horrific pain I was in for six months or more, "if you're out here and you get a back injury?"

Wilson doesn't miss a beat. "That's why we marry more than one wife," he replies cheerily.

"You mean, you just dump her and get another one?"

"Yes."

As predicted, by the time we reach the village again, Wilson's new house is well on its way to completion. A team of women swarms busily all over it, threading twigs together to bolster up the roof, then slapping on handfuls of a bright brown squishy substance to seal it. This primitive cement dries extra quickly in the noonday sun, forming a solid crust that, while it may crack and blister, is well up to code, strong enough to withstand heavy storms during the rainy season and keep the interior dry.

Just one thing: that stuff they're slapping on, which I assumed at first glance to be mud—it's not mud.

"This is a house of cow dung," Wilson announces with the same pride he uses for telling people that his "wifes" do all the work. "Drawn from a cow, today. You see, it's quite wet."

I see only too well. The women's arms and legs are plastered in it.

"So how long does it take a cow to poo a house?" I ask.

"One day."

"One day??? That's all?"

"Yes."

No wonder the cattle are so thin. They're practically hollow.

One of the most remarkable things about the tribespeople, I notice, is how relaxed they are in front of the cameras. While the crew and I squeeze ourselves uncomfortably into their dangerous world, balking at the prospect of being eaten and refusing point-blank to hold a handful of wet feces up to our noses, Wilson seems incredibly at ease in ours. He takes direction like a professional, delivering information on cue, standing patiently on his mark during technical discussions, and if necessary—if the microphone misses a word, say, or there's a problem with the background that needs sorting out—going back to the beginning and repeating everything he's just said with the studied skill of someone who's appeared in way too many documentaries over the years to be fazed by retakes, cutaways, or the dozens of other minutiae that go into making pictures move.

Whenever the camera's off, the rest of the Masai relax even more, becoming a little less last-century about everything, less "tribey," and even letting us hug them—something they're obviously not used to; happily posing for photographs with the crew, especially the kids, who gather around in a large group, laughing and roughhousing, craving attention the way kids do everywhere.

After a while, possibly because they're tired of being hugged, Lunch and Breakfast and some of the other warriors parade to a meadow, where they start to dance.

Actually, it's less of a dance, more a raucous display of yelping and leaping up and down on the spot, but quite mesmerizing. I can't take my eyes off it.

Despite all of their achievements over the years—staying alive being the main one, evidently—this is what the *morani* have come to be best known for: their dancing.

Visitors and wildlife film crews puzzle endlessly about how these warriors manage to be so athletic and leap so high, sometimes three or four feet at a time; whereas to me, quite honestly, it's hardly a puzzle at all. I mean, am I really the only person over all these decades to figure out that it's because the dancers are wearing rubber sandals made from motorcycle tires? Come on, it's no secret!

According to a man I met at our hotel, a major sneaker company once recruited tribesmen like these for one of its national TV ad campaigns. A film crew came to Africa, gave the warriors special promotional sneakers to wear, and asked them to perform their usual leaping routine for the camera, while chanting in a local dialect called Maa. You may even have seen the ad; I'm told it ran in America for a while. Then again, maybe you didn't see it, because it was yanked off our screens rather quickly, after Maa-speaking viewers[2] noticed that what the tribesmen were actually singing was something along the lines of "These shoes are too small, these shoes are too small; we hate them."

There's no vouching for the accuracy of this story, by the

---

2 Seriously, what were the chances? Who among us speaks Maa any more? Personally, I forgot most of it years ago. The only words I know now are *yes, no, tank yu*, and *banana*.

way. But the man at the hotel swore it was true, and he was wearing a sports jacket, so I have no reason to doubt his word. Nor do I doubt that the Masai would do something like that. They have a wicked sense of humor. At one point, I ask Wilson what the Swahili word for "European visitor" is, thinking I can use it during my commentary for the show. He tells me it's *msengo.* Accordingly, throughout the Kenya episode, that's how I refer to myself: as a *msengo.* Only months later, after the episode has been rerun several times, not only in the United States but across the world, do I find out that *msengo* is Swahili for "homosexual."

Well, as you can imagine, I am outraged.

"Oh, dear Lord, he's doing *what*??"

"Preparing a dinner in your honor."

"Well, tell him to stop."

With night closing in and the bushland's broader definitions dissolving into twilight, and as the last few leafless trees turn to black skeletal fists against a pink-and-orange sky, the time is approaching to film me going to sleep in the village, which it's decided will happen inside Wilson's new, and still slightly wet, cow-dung house.

Before that, though, we have to eat, and word right now is that Wilson has gone off somewhere to murder one of his goats.

"You should come and watch the ceremony," Eric urges. He wants to film it.

"Not a bloody chance! I am *not* standing by while a poor little animal gets slaughtered on my account. It's barbaric. Tell Wilson I don't want it. I'm not hungry."

But the deed is already done and within an hour the two-dimensional goat, which didn't have much going for it in the first place, is in pieces. And any hope I might have of quickly reassembling it is reduced further still when I find part of its rib cage roasting over a crackling fire.

"Sit—please," Wilson says, indicating a log.

Call me paranoid, but I'm acutely aware the whole time, as I settle down to eat under the stars, that hordes of scheming, ravenous eyes are trained on me from afar. Not in a *Scooby-Doo* way; I don't see pairs of white dots out in the blackness, but I definitely sense something.

Now and then, dogs—the Masai's alarm system—growl, then bark crazily at the thornbush fence. Never a good sign. Something's out there, circling. There's also an indefinable sporadic chatter too, possibly from hyenas casing the joint.

"Thank you very much for showing me around," I say, chewing on a goat rib. One hundred percent gristle, I was right! "But from everything you've said, it's clear that if I go outside the village now I'll get mauled and eaten."

According to Jay's plan, this is Wilson's cue to invite me to stay in his lovely new dung hut tonight. And sure enough, the man plays his role like a pro.

"Then you'll have to stay with us," he volunteers.

Stay overnight? Me? Here? Oh, gosh.

Once again, glancing to one side, I catch the twinkle in Jay's eye.

I have to say, the design of these bun-loaf houses is cleverer than it looks. The doorway isn't just a doorway; it's a mini maze, a tight, low-ceilinged corridor that winds around and back on itself like a paper clip before finally emerging into the room beyond, in the hope that, should the lions make it past the *morani* and leap the acacia fences into the housing compound, they'll become so utterly baffled by the intricate entrance mechanism to each home, which works on the same principle as a roach motel, that they'll withdraw and revert to Plan A: chasing Lunch and Breakfast.

On the inside, the hut has the feel of a subterranean cavern to it, all narrow and muddy, with a low ceiling that barely lets me stand up straight. There are three sections, each one partitioned by curtains: a small central living room, including a space where Wilson's wide-screen TV will go someday if Sony ever invents one that can be powered by excrement. Then, on either end, two bedrooms. Sole illumination is from a fire burning in a crude stone hearth, emitting a steady plume of smoke that fills the house with a thick, gaseous haze, clogging my throat and making my eyes sting. The Masai do this to kill mosquitoes and other bugs. How it doesn't kill the occupants too is beyond me.

On the plus side, the house doesn't smell anywhere near as awful as I thought it was going to. More earthy than dungy. The bed I'll be sleeping on is yet another large slab of dried dung raised about six inches off the ground, compacted down, and covered with a blanket to hide—well, that it's a load of crap.

While the camera is being set up to shoot all of this and Kevin's lighting the space,[3] Jay takes me back outside, away from prying eyes. "So what are you going to do?" he asks, fixing me with his most earnest hangdog look.

"What d'you mean?"

"Will you be staying?"

---

[3] It's so cramped inside that Kevin has to resort to a novel way of lighting it. I don't want to get too technical or give away professional secrets, but basically what he does is wait 'til Wilson is looking the other way, then punch a hole in the wall with his fist and place the light outside the hole, shining in. Not to worry, they can fix it next time their cow takes a dump!

I didn't know I had a choice. But now that push has come to shove and lions have come to eat me, it seems I do.

"I've been told that under no circumstances must I put the host in serious danger," he continues, "and this could be a *very* dangerous situation. You heard the man: people get eaten. You'd be totally justified if you decided not to stay. If you want to come back to the hotel in the van with us, nobody's going to say anything."

"But what about the 'sleeping for five hours' thing?"

After all we've been through, in Vanuatu particularly, and all the multifarious ways the integrity of the show has been nibbled at since, I realize I must come across as strangely obtuse to be defending this policy right now.

"Cash," he says in mild disbelief, "it's a frickin' TV show. You're not expected to risk your life for it. I mean, I'm not telling you what to do, but if you come back with us in the van, nobody's going to blame you or say anything. I'll personally tell the office how dangerous this was. They'll understand. On the other hand . . ." Fidgeting, he stares into the middle distance, to where the hyenas are prowling. ". . . if you decide to stay, we'll do our best to protect you, but—that's your decision."

In other words, put up or shut up.

It's a major dilemma. When I started out on this yearlong adventure, an issue as basic as "Do I want to sleep in a village under siege from ravenous lions?" wouldn't have troubled me for even a split second. I'd have fled. "I am *not* MacGyver," I'd have said haughtily. "I am *not* a type A maniac like the rest of you and I don't give a damn about being on your stupid team. I did not sign up for this show to go and put my life on the line for other people's entertainment. I don't bungee jump; I don't walk across ten-thousand-foot-high icy mountains in cheap boots with no grips on them; I *may* climb erupting, windblown volcanoes, but *only* if someone hangs onto me the whole time and I get to complain about it all the way up and all the way back down again. And, as the natives of Yakel Village will happily testify, I don't like Nature or the wild and I don't sleep on muddy, bug-ridden floors in the middle of nowhere. That's just not me. Sorry."

My God, what a pompous ass I must have seemed back then. No wonder there were so many Crew Looks. And no wonder everyone expressed such grizzled exasperation as they frantically tried to figure out last-minute solutions to problems that would never have existed if celebrity lawyer Star Jones had been the host, or that guy with the anger-management problem from *The Partridge Family.*

But that's how much I've changed. Reflecting on the "me" that began filming this show a year ago is like looking at my graduation photo from the 1970s, in which I'm wearing an ill-fitting suit, a boring shirt with a supersized collar, and I have big Bee Gees hair. Frankly, I don't even recognize that guy any more. Hard to say what's changed. Whether it's the constant debilitating pressure I've been under all these months that's throwing my judgment off axis, or a side effect of the dragging fatigue that hounds me everywhere I go and never seems to lift, or just the numbness to fear that inevitably follows after you've crammed ten full lifetimes of worldly experience into a single, tumultuous twelve-month period, or the fact that I came close to dying a few weeks ago and was half a day away from never being able to complain about climbing an erupting volcano or standing on an icy mountain, or anything else for that matter, ever again . . . I honestly can't give you a specific reason why my MacGyver switch got flicked to *on,* whether it was facing the lethal rapids in Idaho or the polar bears in Alaska or drinking emulsion paint spat from a boy's mouth in Vanuatu, but, compared to all of these things, for some reason the prospect of sleeping in a house made from fresh cow dung, surrounded by preying lions and hyenas, scarcely makes me blink.

In short, of *course* I'll be staying in Wilson's home overnight. Now, turn on the tuck-in cam, somebody shout "Action!" and let's get on with it.

"Okay, then." Jay shrugs wearily. "If that's what you want."

He looks worried, and is obviously hoping I'll change my mind, though my willingness to sacrifice myself so readily in the name of cheap cable programming secretly quite impresses him, I think.

Minutes later I catch the bang of doors, the roar of an engine, and the squeak of suspension, steadily diminishing, as the van bounces away across the plain into the night, leaving the host of the show, or possibly the former host if things don't go well, lying all alone, smelling of dung, on a pile of dung, in a dark, claustrophobic cow-dung hut.

Not that you're ever really alone in a cow-dung hut, because the house, I now discover, is full of bugs, most of them entering via the hole Kevin punched in the wall. Every last airborne insect in eastern Kenya seems to have been notified that I'm here and decided to drop in on 24 Shithouse Lane to see what's cooking, because within minutes I'm being eaten alive. And in the quiet blackness of my bed, as unidentified legs crawl up my neck and I feel the brush of fluttering wings against my eyelids and lips, and as the hyenas howl outside and the lions scout the perimeter fence in search of Dinner—my new Masai tribal name—I suddenly start to feel rather proud of myself. For the first time in my entire life, I showed a modicum of bravery here tonight. I stood up to my instincts to back down and run in terror, making a decision that withstood the gravitational pull of convenience and good living, and chose to embrace discomfort instead. And I did it, not just for me, but for the show. For the good of the team. Another first. Furthermore, having made that decision, I stuck to it, rather than merely saying the words simply for effect, then changing my mind again almost immediately, which is what I usually do. In most situations, cowardice is my natural fallback. It comes very easily to me, I find.

But not tonight.

Tonight I was actually brave. And no one's more shocked than I am.

Of course, such heady foolishness can get a guy into trouble if he's not careful. For instance, it can lead to him lying in a dung hut in the middle of Kenya, being attacked and bitten by a swarm of bugs.

But for once, odd as it may seem, I don't care.

"I did it" is the only thought in my head right now. I did something brave that I didn't think I could do. I took a stand and didn't retreat from it. That's an achievement. One I should be very proud of. Doubtless, "I did it!" was the last triumphant thought that ran through the mind of my skydiving buddy Adrian, too, shortly before he hit the ground after his parachute didn't open, and it will probably be the very last thing on my mind as the lions are eating me alive, a just reward, some might be inclined to say, for being so bloody reckless. Still, I did it.

I DID IT!!!

And with that, I turn my back on the dung, the mosquitoes, the insects, the barking of the dogs at the thorn fence, the braying squeal of the hyenas outside the thorn fence, the smoldering fire choking my lungs, and, against overwhelming odds, drift into an easy, happy, smoke-filled sleep.

21

Scar Tissue

One day I was sitting in one of the edit bays merrily tinkering with the Alaska show, which had turned out great, by the way—*better* than great. TV Gold. Maybe even Emmy worthy; who knows?—when Fat Kid came charging down the corridor, dressed in his usual supersuit of tight V-neck sweater and taken-in pants, black hair slicked back into an almost-ponytail, now wearing a pair of bifocals to further hide his true identity.

As he sat down, a shadow of dark concern fell across his face.

"Something wrong? Is it Conan O'Brien? Did he cancel my appearance?"

His lips tweaked themselves into a grimace. "No, it's not that," he said in a low voice. Low for him anyway. "The network's moving the show to Wednesdays."

They're moving us *again*??

"But first they're taking us off altogether."

"Oh—my—God. How long for?"

"No idea. Maybe a month. During the winter Olympics."

In general terms, networks only resort to such desperate tactics just before the axe falls. In essence, they're raising a red flag, telling you you're officially on life support. It's tactical; there's nothing personal about it. A show gets jerked around erratically from night to night, slot to slot, playing whack-a-mole with viewers' loyalty and patience, in the hope of somehow garnering new fans, even if in the process it means losing the old ones. Above all, though, a slot change tells you that your balloon's started to lose altitude.

"The wind isn't behind us any more," I confessed grimly. "We're a 9 P.M. show, an adult show, not an 8 P.M. show. That's the problem. That's what's dragging us down."

Those "family" viewers at 8 P.M., they can be an ugly crowd, I discovered. Whoever gave these people computers and e-mail accounts and access to the network's message boards has a lot to answer for.

This show would be great if it wasn't for the host. My seven-year-old said that she thought he was very rude and annoying.
—Karl, Kentucky.

I think [Cash's] next trip should be a week in Abu Ghraib, or drop his white butt off in Iran wearing flip-flops, American flag shorts, and a "Who farted?" tank top. Am I the only person who can't stand this dildo?
—Bill W., Miami.

Apparently not, Bill. Look—here's someone else:

Sir,
I find you to be an imperialistic, uneducated cultural elitist. The things that come out of your mouth are abominable and I cannot bear to watch you make fun of cultures that are not your own. I only watch your show to see how far you will go . . .

Oh, so you do watch it, then.

. . . and each time you disgust me further. You are NO Basil Davidson.

Now, hang on! That's quite enough. And *please* don't bring Basil Davidson into this, unless you're also going to explain who he is.[1]

You suck, basically, is all I'm saying . . .

Wow.

Looking depressingly mortal for once, Fat Kid reached deep into his reserves of American gung-ho spirit and gave my leg a pat. "Hey, you know what? It's not over yet. We have a great show. It'll find its audience."

"You think?"

I only wished I was half as sure as he was pretending to be.

To add to the general level of despondency, a couple other series with remarkably similar concepts to ours had

---

[1] Note: Davidson, Basil: award-winning historian. Prior to the Carnation Revolution, he was considered one of the world's top experts on Portuguese Africa. Further note: Revolution, Carnation: coup d'etat ushering in democracy in Portugal in 1974. In light of this, I guess the guy's right—I am definitely no Basil Davidson.

sprouted up on other networks. I'm not one to point fingers, but in the same way that I'd taken the theme of *Survivor* and made it my own without first checking with CBS if that was okay, these other shows seemed to have taken my theme—guy dumped in the middle of nowhere, having to survive with nothing—given it a jazzy new title, and waltzed off with my viewers. More annoying still, audiences were flocking to watch them. Both shows had become ratings sensations in no time at all. It was very dispiriting.

On my way out the door that night, my mind swimming, I bumped into one of the editors, who said the same thing Fat Kid had said, more or less, all the while beaming a one-hundred-percent-confident smile that caused my floundering spirits to soar again.

"Dude, this shit is groundbreaking," he said. "It's the best goddamned series the network has. They'd be idiots to shut us down. They're testing the waters, that's all. Remember, NBC almost canceled *Seinfeld* after two seasons. The original *Jeopardy!* was canceled. The *Police Squad* series—that was canceled after only one season. Hell, even *Star Trek* was canceled after only three seasons."

"But it *was* canceled—right?"

"Er . . . my point is, that won't happen to us. These things take time to grow, and a network knows that. They're smart people. Someone there will have the vision and the courage to keep us going. It'll be fine, you'll see."

Ironically, on the morning the decisive call came through, I was busy preparing a talk. A favor for a professor friend of mine. She'd asked me to give a short address to her art students at Woodbury University in Los Angeles. The subject: "What I Learned from Having My Own Travel Show on TV."

I'd marked the date on my imaginary calendar six

months previously, then completely forgotten about it until the week before it was due to happen, when I was at my laptop, deleting requests for money I routinely receive from Nigerian dignitaries, and found an e-mail.

"All systems are go for Wednesday," my friend had written, adding that flyers had been posted all over campus with my face on them, so she was expecting a big turnout. "See U then. ☺!"

Damn.

"P.S. There'll be cheese and crackers."

Oooh.

Which explains why, on that particular Wednesday morning in May, having just returned from our final trip, to Barbados, and with work on season two all but wrapped up, I found myself sitting in the kitchen at home with a notepad, trying to figure out what on earth a guy of my years could reveal to a bunch of ADD-eenagers on the subject of "What I Learned from Having My Own Travel Show on TV" that might help them launch a career in the creative arts, and, you never know, maybe someday take them one step closer to ripping off a CBS reality show of their own and appearing in it.

My first thought was simply to amuse them by plucking a few travel stories from some of the locations we'd visited over the course of thirty-two shows, because there had been some incredible ones: Tokyo; Cambodia; Kenya; New Zealand; Romania; the Australian Outback; Savannah, Georgia—places I would return to in a heartbeat given half a chance, and, more important, if someone else was footing the bill. Then there were a few more I didn't warm to quite so much: Niagara Falls (a bit dreary), Seattle (it rained nonstop), and Philadelphia (see Seattle; also, when I asked for free food in the spirit of the show, street vendors in Philly actually yelled at me and chased me away!). While a couple of places fell squarely into the "hell will freeze over before I'd go back" category. I won't name them here; that would be unkind. All I'll say is that I'd rather drink formaldehyde straight from the bottle than ever again step into a town where half the population is called Bent, Ulle, or Bjorn. Let's leave it at that. Diabetic indeed!

So travel anecdotes was one way to go. The predictable way.

OR, and this was more intriguing, I could tell the students something else.

Given carte blanche to say whatever I wanted to, I was feeling more than a little rebellious that day and in the mood to spread unrest, which is never a bad thing in college, is it? Fired up by this, I began jotting down ideas.[2] Not conventional ideas—stuff they might be expecting to hear—but, rather, stuff I thought they *should* hear. Life lessons. The kind of stuff that can only be taught from the perspective of someone who's circumnavigated the globe on someone else's dime, experiencing close-up and firsthand a wide variety of foreign cultures, and almost died doing it.

Delivered in no real order—although I find numerical works just fine—they came to me, as these lists often do, all at once in a rush, and went as follows:

#1: The news networks are wrong: it's not a hostile world. The vast majority of people out there are good, kind, and friendly. Go visit them, see for yourself.

#2: An excellent way to repel mosquitoes is to stick a sheet of Bounce fabric softener inside each of your socks. Bounce is kryptonite to mosquitoes.

---

[2] I'd had a similar epiphany some time earlier, as a matter of fact, following a short trip to Harvard University. Those particular lessons are featured in my previous book, *Gullible's Travels: The Adventures of a Bad Taste Tourist.*

#3: Courage is a valve. Turn it on, even a little bit, and the knob gets stuck.

#4: Most people stick with what they know—traditions, beliefs, boring studies, depressing jobs, stifling marriages—not because it's good for them or even because they like it, but because they fear what might replace it if they let it go.

#5: Strangely, what replaces it if you let it go is usually a thousand times better than what you had. Belief first, proof later, always.

#6: Nature is not our friend. (A concept most adults are entirely familiar with, but I figure it's never too early to begin indoctrinating the young with our fiercest prejudices.)

#7: The people who start wars are seldom the people who die fighting them. Ask your average Cambodian.

#8: Just because you believe something, doesn't make it so. For every principle you'd stake your life and reputation on, there are millions of people around the world who fervently disagree with you and think you're nuts. And very probably you are.

#9: There's no limit to the extent of human gullibility when it comes to believing what they're told. And the more far-fetched or ludicrous an idea is, the more people are likely to buy into it.

#10: Women are oppressed the world over. In fact, I'd venture to say that, except perhaps for where *you* live, feminism barely has a foothold. And don't even get me started on homosexuality.

#11: Hard work is good for you, but working too hard and stressing out will stop your liver from functioning and apparently can kill you.

#12: Most people in the world totally *freak out* if you try to hug them.

#13:

Sadly, I didn't make it as far as twenty. I'd just scrawled "#13" on my pad when the phone rang. *"Hi—Cash?"* It was The Thumb. A TV person calling to talk to another TV person. Happens all the time. *"How's it going?"*

"Great." Flopping down on the mat by the kitchen door, I felt my scrotum start to tingle. Uh-oh. "So is this it? Is this the call?"

"Yes . . ."

Ohmygodohmygodohmygod.

I couldn't bear the tension. It was like waiting for the results of an AIDS test. "And . . . ?"

". . . and . . ."

The balloon I'd been soaring in for the past year took one massive lunge into the air, buoyed up by the propane of hope . . .

ZZZZZZZZZZZZZZZZZHHHHHHHHHHHHHHHHHHTTTTTTTTTTT!

". . . I'm sorry . . ."

. . . and nosedived into a hedge.

"I know how hard you worked on this and how much it means to you, but we won't be . . ."

Noooooo!!!

Come on. You're kidding around. It can't be.

Did my scrotum deceive me?

". . . picking up the show for season three."

Well, apparently, yes it did.

The show was canceled. Things had come full circle, *All Washed Up* being not only the original title, but now, coincidentally, my new career status.

The main reason for the cancelation wasn't a secret: it was the viewers. More specifically, there weren't any. At least, not enough to set the ratings on fire, and *certainly* not enough to make a very expensive series like ours worth the financial outlay.

Networks live or die by "the numbers"; they'll all tell you that, and our numbers must have kept dwindling, I guess, killed either by the move from Mondays at 9 P.M. to Mondays at 8 P.M., or by the move from Mondays to Wednesdays, or perhaps by being taken off the schedules for three weeks to allow for a major sporting event; or even by being subsequently moved again, this time from Wednesdays to Fridays, and then from Fridays to Saturdays. All in the space of fourteen episodes! It's hard to figure out the logic behind this. Maybe the guys at the network were embarrassed by the show. It's possible. And especially by their new, renegade host who—confound him!—kept giving his honest opinion about places he didn't like, rather than sugarcoating it in the usual bland PR blurb. *Maybe* they simply had to keep the series out of the public gaze, like a loud and difficult uncle who gets drunk at weddings and starts telling dirty jokes to children, then cancel it ASAP, or risk never being able to shoot future travel shows in the places he'd criticized ever again. Honestly, I have no real idea what went on; it's a mystery to me. All I know is, there's a simple equation that executives are taught at television-making school: No Audience = No Advertisers = No TV Show.

That's the hay and rags of it.

Yet, though I understood the reasoning behind the decision—and I did; it was all very logical, simple mathematics, nothing personal—it still felt for all the world like someone had just ripped my newborn baby's head off and was using it to play volleyball.

I continued sitting on the floor, hugging my knees, dazed, stymied, giving my Mystified Look one final surprise airing, only this time it was for real.

"Pah, that's okay, never mind," I bounced back, evincing exemplary calm in the circumstances. "I'm always very *philophosical* about such things."

Philophosical?

The fact that I stumbled over the word betrayed the true depth of my distress. Truth is, I wasn't *philophosical* about any of this. Nothing like. I was *seething* mad.

"But I did it for *you,*" I wanted to scream down the phone. "I gave up a year of my life—and one of my organs, let's not forget that—for you. And now what? You betray me? What the hell is that about? You Judas! It's a *perfectly—pleasant—little—show.* No less a person than the TV critic of the *New York Times* said so. How can you give up on us now? Oh, and another thing," I ranted silently in my head, "if what you say is true, and you care so much about the numbers, how come I never appeared on *Conan O'Brien*?"

Then I realized that this last bit wasn't in my head, I'd said it out loud. Oops.

I don't know for certain how many viewers Conan has, but let's say fifty. (He's on late at night.) Surely, if all the people who caught me on there were tantalized enough to tell their friends and they all tuned in to our show to see what the fuss was about, wouldn't that have boosted our meager audience significantly? I bet it would.

The Thumb agreed. It probably would have helped, yes,

but . . . well, it just hadn't worked out. He couldn't explain why. Clearly, somebody had dropped the ball. Sorry.

From here, we turned our attention to the future. I let him know that I was thinking of writing a book about all of this: about my year in the wilderness. Or as he would call it: television.

For some reason this led to a surprisingly awkward moment. I could imagine his eyes rolling to the ceiling in paranoid exasperation. Oh, God, please no, not a book!

"You *will* be kind about me, won't you?" he jumped in, anxiously.

About you? Kind?

Er . . . honest answer? I'm very upset right now. You've just ripped my newborn's head off and you're playing volleyball with it. So . . . probably not.

"Of *course* I'll be kind," I told him.[3] "I'm always kind, you know that."

"Yeah," he said, not entirely believing me. Then, in a sardonic tone of voice sharp enough to slit my throat from ear to ear, he issued one last, and very conclusive, *"Bye, Cash."*

And the line went dead.

It was over.

All of it.

---

[3] Ooh, that could be my #13. It's something I've picked up from television people over the years, both in Britain and the United States. In the world of TV, where scruples are often rarer than unicorns, bosses and colleagues seldom say what they truly mean in case it incriminates them somehow in the future. So they'll say something tangential and unfathomable instead. That way nobody can call them on it later, because it never made sense in the first place. A devilish trick that destroys trust and corrodes the foundation of any earnest endeavor—but hey, trust is grossly overrated anyway, right?

There's really no disguising the level of disappointment I felt after I hung up the phone that day. I'd be lying if I told you otherwise. The best I could manage was a minicollapse behind the door, where I stayed for an hour or more, deflated and chagrined (if that's even a word), 'til my ass grew roots. Couldn't think straight, couldn't stand up, couldn't even muster the energy to drag the corpse that was my confidence off the mat and onto a chair. There's a peculiar gray area between grief and relief at times like this, I find. One I've only experienced once before, and that's after my mother died: another catastrophic and badly timed ending to something rather worthwhile, but also a source of major relief, knowing that the months of excruciating pain had finally loosened their grip and she'd been granted release at last. Well, same goes for the show. Along with the abject misery of defeat came that same sense of release, an undeniable rush of thankgoditsoverness that was profound and, quite honestly, uplifting.

"You're going to cry, aren't you?"

"Certainly not," I told myself defiantly. There'll be no crying, no self-pity. It's only TV; it doesn't matter. (#14, this, maybe![4]) Although I was very touched, I confess, by the hundreds of messages that came flooding in from fans once word leaked out.

> *I just wanted to express how upset I am that your show was canceled and how badly treated it was at the end. It almost seems like a seek & destroy mission.*
> *—Ted.*

---

[4] By the way, there's synchronicity, then there's coincidence, then there are events that are simply too whacko to be true. *No word of a lie*—I swear on the life of my now-headless child—the date my professor friend and I fixed months previously for my talk at her college, a random Wednesday in May,

Well, I see the network finally got what they wanted. I'm SO sorry to hear about the show being canceled. I'm PISSED. I wrote to them to let them know how much they sucked.
—Jacqueline.

I can't say I'm shocked your show was canceled. Every time I find a show that rises above the general crud on cable TV, it's like my brain sends a signal to the executives whose job it is to keep intelligent and original content from being broadcast. I should have known that my loyal patronage would be your show's demise.
—Brian.

You should be proud! The show was unique, creative, and different. You had a strong vision and stayed true to it every step of the way. Please don't diminish what was a great creative outlet for you.

This last one wasn't from a viewer. It's how one of our show runners summed it up later that day.

And I *was* proud of the series. No doubt about that. If you discount Fat Kid's input, as well as that of The Thumb, Eric, Jay, Tasha, the camera crews we used, and all the planners, editors, producers, and technicians back at the office, then I'd *single-handedly* made thirty-two travel shows in just over a year, and done it without dying. That's an incredible achievement.

---

was *the exact same Wednesday* the TV travel show I'd be talking about was canceled. Surely, only something as mean and uncaring as Reality—with a capital R, not the fake TV kind—could perpetrate a deed as cruel as that and get away with it.

Now, at the very least, I could look the Vice President of Sales (Pacific Rim) in the eye and say, with the humility of a man who'd been beaten by the odds more than once, but survived, "You were wrong, pal. See how wrong you were? Here I am, I'm still alive, I didn't get addicted to coke, and my relationship is still intact.

"Oh, sure, I was hospitalized three times, twisted my knee badly at one point, threw up on- and off-camera, visited Madrid on four separate occasions for no reason at all, got stoned, bitten by giant fleas, stripped naked and whipped, run over with an Infiniti SUV, fell down several hillsides, lost an organ, sustained permanent damage to the hearing in my left ear (from too many takeoffs and landings in one day), and aged ten years in the space of one, but really, isn't that a small price to pay to be where I am today?"

And after a pause for thought, he'd no doubt look at me and go: "You mean unemployed?" because he can be sassy that way; he's got a bit of a mouth on him.

Once again, though, that's where he'd be wrong.

I wouldn't be unemployed, would I? Not at all. Having the show axed prematurely was a drag, there's no denying that, but it wasn't the end of the world. Quite the opposite: essentially, the cancelation freed me up to (and if I was going to cry, this would be the point, I think) resume my career in public radio, which, now I come to think of it, is not unlike being unemployed. For me, it carries exactly the same sense of hopelessness, despair, and underachievement. The only difference is that someone pays you to feel that way.

Though that's not what I told him, actually.

The next time we met, it was on a crisp spring morning about two weeks later, at the end of our respective driveways at the base of the Hollywood Hills. The Vice President of Sales (Pacific Rim) was on his way to work, as usual, and I was . . . well, I was watching him go.

"So what's next for you?" he asked, climbing into his executive car.

"Next?" I said, surprised.

What was *actually* up next, although I didn't know it yet, was six months of physical therapy, plus a further two years of psychological counseling. Beyond that . . .

"Oh, rest. Take a few months off. Write a book about my travels."

"Great. And then?"

Er . . . no idea.

Genuinely, I had no clue. After the hobbits at the office had assured me that the network would not make the mistake of canceling the show, I'd been foolish enough to buy into their optimism and therefore had lined nothing up. But you can't leave a fellow hanging like that, or tell him you're doing something utterly lame like heading back to radio with your tail between your legs. At least I can't. So, on a wild impulse I came up with something a lot more interesting.

"Movies," I said, boldly. "I'm going to be in movies."

And before he could respond, or ask me any further tricky questions, such as "Huh?" or *"You?"* or "Are you out of your mind?" I ran back up the driveway and closed the gate behind me.

www.cashpeters.com